Acknowl<

MW01528896

Deborah, you are the only person in my life who has been with me from the beginning to the present. Thank you for being there for every moment of my life, for the big events and the small ones. Thank you for all the phone calls, visits, and experiences we have shared. I will always be grateful to you and Josh that we could give our children the experiences of cousins we always wanted! I know we are bonded in this life and the next.

Christopher Taylor, you are the foundation of my world. Thank you for dreaming big with me, encouraging me, and staying by my side through it all. Thank you for the last year of cooking most of the meals, doing most of the laundry, and always making sure I had time to write. Our dreams are growing bigger, and I can't wait to live them out with you.

Stephan and Liam Taylor, you are the reason I had the courage to fight, and I will always fight for you. I hope I can be the parent for you that I needed growing up. Thank you for teaching me how to be a mom and growing with me as we work through the complications of life together. I can't wait to see what adventures life has in store for you guys, and I want to be there for all of them.

Vandy, you have supported me on my writing journey, starting with the angry journaling letters through the completion of the book. You talked with me through each chapter as I gathered my thoughts. I am so grateful you were the first one to read my book cover to cover. Thank you for stepping in and guiding us through life's changes.

Mica Murdock and Isa, you were the first ones to make me believe in the success of this book, and you both gave me the energy I needed to keep writing, even when it got tough. Thank you for giving Chris and me a fresh path to believe in after walking away from the religion that had torn us down. You both have changed the direction of our lives with your love and guidance.

Beverly Sanders, I can never thank you enough for all the help you have given me. You have contributed the most to editing the pages of this book, going over it multiple times for months on end. You gave me someone to be accountable to, as I was excited to hear what you had to say about each chapter. Your motivational words kept me going. Thank you for your belief in me and in this book. You helped make it happen.

Prologue

The summer of 2012 was a hard year. It was the year I lost my family.

Since then, the words in this book have been vibrating around my head with nowhere to go. I wrote them down, and for a time, it was enough. I felt compelled to work a regular job because of our finances, but the words were always in the back of my mind, insisting on being brought into the world.

The loss I experienced would not allow me to sleep. When I showered, there was no peace, as the raging words took over. When I cooked dinner, the words swirled, trying to express the hurt and pain from the past. I wrote letters to my father expressing the emotions I kept quiet for years. There was so much rage, so much hate in those letters. The words poured out of me in cathartic amounts, as if my very soul depended on them. There was no relaxing until the words had their way. They needed to be out, and it was my job to bring them into this world.

The raw, raging, anger laid out on the pages covered up the underlying emotions I was yet to process such as the fear and panic from living in an abusive home, confusion as I wrestled with my faith, and grief when the relationship with my parents shattered. I needed the time to process, understand, and then heal. It took about ten years to turn those writings into this book.

During that time, I did not know how my book would turn out. Was I writing just for myself? Would it turn into something I could pass on to my parents? As I wrote each memory, the story started to shine through, and I could see this wasn't just for me. I was writing for the thousands and thousands of people who had been where I have been, for those who have felt the fear and pain that comes from abuse, for those who felt the betrayals and confusion of a high-demand religion.

Each of us has our own stories of trials, trauma, enlightenment, and joy. We have our own learned truths, and those words need to be spoken. By sharing my story, I hope you are encouraged to share yours.

I am sure each person in my story has their own view of how things happened, and it will differ from mine. Truth can be a subjective thing, slippery with how we perceive things. I have done my best to keep the story as honest as possible, only changing names, towns, and a few details to protect identity as needed. My parents will have a different view than me. The Mormon religion will not agree with my perception of them. This book has been about my thoughts, my processing, and my emotions.

The story is from my viewpoint and does not represent the thoughts and beliefs of the characters in my story, or the Church of Jesus Christ of Latter-day Saints, aka, the Mormon church.

What is the truth?
That depends on your perception.
This book is my truth.

Chapter One
Save me?

I was seven years old, lying in the green silky sheets of the queen-size waterbed I shared with my ten-year-old sister. The light from our glow-in-the-dark stars had long faded out, leaving the room completely dark except for the sliver of light from under the door. The hair on my arms was raised, warning me of the danger. I listened to my heartbeat pick up speed, beating louder every second. I tried to calm myself by focusing on my breathing. My hand rested on my stomach to feel the consistent motion of my long, slow, breaths like I was sleeping. I had to stay calm, stay quiet.

I wish I really had been sleeping, then maybe I could have woken up from the nightmare. I heard my father in the hallway as he walked up to my bedroom and stopped. I knew he was listening for mom's snoring. He was checking to make sure he would not be caught. His heavy breathing came through my door, like the winds of a hurricane right before it destroys everything in its path. He stood there for a moment, resting his hand on the doorknob. Each second stretched into infinity as I prayed he would just go away.

Take a breath, I reminded myself as I scooted to the edge of the waterbed and pushed myself down between the mattress and wooden frame. The pressure from both sides compressed my body, comforting me. I scooted down until I could feel the hard plywood bottom, careful not to make the bed wiggle too much. It had to look like I was asleep when he came in; it was all I could do to keep myself safe. I pulled the covers over my head, leaving a small space so I could still see the doorframe. My heart beat even faster as the fear took over. I sank into my space a little further as the door opened. It didn't matter how well I tried to hide. He always found me.

Light poured into our room, illuminating his black silhouette that filled the doorway. He slipped in and quietly closed the door behind him. I squeezed my eyes shut and did my best to block out everything around me. My sister was lying on the other half of the bed, asleep, as far as I knew. She had been still a long time.

Deborah was my calm in the chaos of our world. Every night we talked about what happened during the day until the words were gone and sleep washed over us. She always had my back and was there when I needed her. She rarely got mad at me, even though I stole the quarters from her piggy bank and my side of the room was a mess. Deborah looked for ways to make peace with those around her and to raise their spirit.

I felt the sloshing waves of water as he climbed into Deborah's side of the bed. I was too scared to open my eyes. I tried to imagine he was just cuddling with her. *You would never hurt her, would you, dad?* I thought to myself. *She is too good, too pure, to hurt her as you hurt me, right, dad?* I ask him silently. *She is everything you are not,* I silently screamed as my anger rose. He had been over there a long time. I knew I should open my eyes, cry out, or yell for help, but I was paralyzed by the fear. If he knew I was awake, he would get me next. If I yelled, there would be repercussions. Besides, he was just cuddling her, telling her goodnight. I repeated it to myself so often I believed it.

After a while, he slid over to my side of the bed, and I felt my blanket being taken away. His large, sweaty, meaty hands grabbed my exposed arm and leg, pulling me out of my safe spot. I tried to protect myself by repeating the words frantically in my mind: *act like you're asleep, act like you're asleep, act like you're asleep.* Maybe if I just closed my eyes a little tighter, he would go away. If I didn't make any noise, he wouldn't know I was here. If I could just hide better, make myself smaller, he wouldn't see me. The screaming voice in my head disappeared, replaced by the blackness that keeps me safe.

Time had little meaning when he was in our room because every second felt like an hour and every hour an eternity. Every moment is spent in paralyzing fear, every muscle tensed just looking for a way to escape. He pulled my underwear off and dragged my feet up to his shoulders. I wanted to scream or run, find a way to save myself somehow, but I couldn't move. Besides, he had already made it clear if I screamed, if I made a noise, if I told anyone, I would lose my family and be sent away to foster care. The family would be destroyed, and it would be my fault. How is a seven-year-old supposed to shoulder such an enormous burden?

*HOW COULD YOU DO THIS? DON'T YOU LOVE US?
JUST GO AWAY! GO AWAY GO AWAY GO AWAY!* I
screamed the words internally as loud as I could to make them
drown out his movements on my body. The words eventually faded
into a whimpered, silent plea as my life and innocence were drawn
out. *Won't you please just go away.* I never said it out loud. It wouldn't
have done me any good. All my father cared about was his own
licentious desires.

Where is mom right now? Probably in her bedroom, sleeping. *Mom,
dad has been in here a long-time, aren't you wondering where he is?* I silently
ask her. *Why are you not here? Don't you know what he is doing to us? Why
are you not saving us? Is there a reason?* The thoughts are racing faster
than my mind can process, trying to ignore the reality of what is
happening to me. Maybe she doesn't really know what is going on.
Maybe she fell asleep and didn't realize how long he has been gone.
Because if she knew, she would save us. *You would save us, right, mom?*

He is STILL here mom, are you going to help? Are you going to save us?

Mom?

*MOM, SAVE US, I scream so loud in my mind I just know she can hear
me even when I didnt't make a sound.*

Please, mom!

Mom...

∞

The next morning, I laid on the floor in the living room with a
pillow propped up under my chest and watched my favorite movie
for the second time that day while pretending to do my schoolwork.
Today it was social studies, but it didn't really matter because all I
did was copy the answers from the back of the book. I'm sure I
would get in trouble if mom and dad knew I was just copying the
answers, but if it looked like I did my work, no one really cared.

I sat up and grabbed some cushions off the couch and dragged
them to our oversized bay window, creating a soft spot to sit. The
bay window had a long wooden bench surrounded by several large

window panels, each separated into its own dark, worn-out wooden frame. Looking outside, I could see both ends of the street while I sat in the corner waiting for the yellow school bus. The movie ended and two more episodes of cartoons came and went before I finally saw my old school bus pull onto our street, dropping off my friends. I watched them walk down to their houses, talking to each other and laughing. I desperately wished I could ride the bus and walk with them again.

I jumped down from the window and ran through the living room, kitchen, and then down the stairs to ask mom if I could play outside. She was hidden behind her computer desk filled with massive amounts of unsorted mail, old flyers, and other paperwork. I knew she was probably playing solitaire again; she would play for hours without moving. Her office space was up against the wall with her desk turned to face the stairs. On the right side of the room was a door to the backyard and a table where all the unknown things went to live. The table was piled high with half-finished projects, including a few model cars and rockets. Under the table was a six-foot-long rabbit cage where Thumper lived. I petted him while waiting for mom to answer me. His cage was covered in a thick layer of rabbit poop spilling over from his litter box. My brother had received the rabbit a few years earlier as a gift. I wondered how the people would care about his current living arrangements.

"Mom, can I go play?" I asked again.

"Sure, be back before dad gets home," she answered apathetically from behind her screen. I went to the garage to grab my bike.

The garage was filled with old storage boxes, Christmas decorations, and photos. Near the garage doors, our bikes had been thrown onto each other in a pile left there from the last time we played. I jumped on my pink bike. The tassels had fallen off a few years ago. Our driveway was too steep to go straight down, so I peddled diagonally across the yard, pushing myself in a constant race to be faster, to be better. The grass and weeds were so high they chaffed my shins. I wished our grass looked neat and trim like the other houses in the neighborhood.

I peddled my bike to the opposite end of the street from the bus stop and knocked on the door of my friend's house. Her house was covered in dark brown, wood paneling, with a bay window like ours. Her backyard was surrounded by towering pine trees and had a walking path with heavy, wooden, landscaping planks lining the

4

outside of the play area. Inside the play area, there was a turtle sandbox and a large swing set with a slide and tree house built in. Her mom brought out a plate of cookies to share while we played. We imagined her dolls were real, and we had to babysit them.

"Do you want to go ride bikes?" my friend asked after we ate the cookies.

"Let's race to the top of the hill!" I responded excitedly, running out of her back gate to my bike. We rode around the corner where the road sloped down and then curved back up to a steep hill. The best part of racing up the hill was being able to fly back down faster than we could ever peddle on our own. It was a moment of freedom, with the wind rushing past my face and feeling like I was flying. A few other neighborhood kids joined us as we raced from house to house until a mom said it was dinner time and we parted ways.

Mom was making us spaghetti tonight, which was my favorite meal. Dad would be home soon, and his mood would determine how the rest of the evening. If he was in a bad mood, then he would start screaming the minute he walked in the door. It could be because the chores were not finished, the house was too messy, or he just had a bad day at work. There didn't have to be a reason for his anger. When he was angry, that anger would spill onto us.

When he came home in a good mood, we could watch TV, or even relax if mom was home too. Sometimes dad would even joke around and play with us. We never knew what to anticipate, and I could feel the anxiety grip my heart as we waited for him to come home.

Dad walked in the door later than normal with his best friend David, holding a new toy called a Zube Tube. The toy was a colorful, long, cardboard tube, almost as tall as I was, with a spring in the middle that filled the room with loud thundering sounds when you shook it. Deborah got to shake it first. She was dad's favorite, and we all knew it. The ends had a cup you could talk into that expanded the sound and make it echo. "HELLO," she yelled into the tube. "HELLO, hello, ello," it echoed back at us.

"Me next, Me next!" I said, jumping up and down in excitement.

My older brother, Jason took his turn, shaking it as loud as he could. He made a loud fart noise into the cup, and we laughed as it echoed around the room.

"It's my turn now. Give it to me!" I said as I took it from him.

5

He tried to hold on to it a little longer before being chided by dad to let me have a turn. I held the tube above my head, jumping and shaking it as fast as I could, listening to the loud thundering sounds as they bounced off the walls.

The doorbell rang. "I got it!" Jason yelled as he ran to open the door.

The missionaries had been invited to eat dinner with us. Missionaries were mostly church youth who have been encouraged to sacrifice two years of their life after high school to convert people and give service to the members and community. One was from Utah and had been on his mission for almost a year, the other one was brand new from Texas. The missionaries stopped by our house often and we fed them about twice a month. They came in and played with us and the new toy.

"Dinner is ready, come and eat." mom called to us as she placed the pot of spaghetti on the table. I made a sandwich out of garlic toast and spaghetti while looking around the table. Dad sat on one end of the table, Deborah next to him and then me. On the other side of me was a seat often left empty by Rachael, my oldest sister. Mom was at the other end, then Jason, followed by the missionaries, and David, who sat on Dad's right side. With all these people here, the house was safe. I was safe. Dinner was filled with nonstop conversation and jokes. I loved that, in my family, the kids were usually a part of the conversation.

After dinner, the missionaries gave a short message about how our sins can be washed away through Jesus Christ's atonement, and then they said a prayer, blessing our family before leaving. I wanted to be just like them by talking about Christ and spreading his message of redemption. I wanted to visit with people, bring them joy, and help them. On Sundays, we sang about how God wanted us to be a missionary once we have grown a foot or two. I sang the song to myself as they walked out the door.

After the missionaries left, we drove to the movie theater as a family with David. Friday night movies are one of dad's favorite activities. Once inside the theater, dad bought the largest size popcorn and a Diet Coke. The employees filled up our bucket of popcorn. Halfway through the movie, dad asked to salt the popcorn. We all watched as he poured out a thick layer of salt, turning the popcorn orange. Dad handed the popcorn back so they could finish filling up the bucket, and then he added another thick layer of orange salt. The people behind the counter stared in shock, making comments about how much salt he used.

At the end of the night, we read scriptures before heading to bed. It was a good day, but now the night came, and the anxiety settled in. I tucked myself between the mattress and the wooden frame of our waterbed, making myself as small and safe as I could. I prayed dad would not come "tuck us in" tonight.

∞

I woke up the next morning relieved to see the sun shining through our bedroom window, knowing we had escaped my father's attention the night before. Dad spent the night hanging out with David, away from us. For now, the light of day meant I was safe, for a little while at least.

It was Saturday and that meant dad would be home all day and we would work on a family project. Sometimes it was gardening or a weekend trip to North Carolina. Today we were cleaning out the garage. Dad sat in a chair to supervise, barking out commands.

Gofers he called us: "go-for this, go-for that." Dad humor.

"Bring that box of kitchen supplies inside," he told Jason. Next, he looked at me, "Throw away all the trash on the ground." Then he looked at Deborah, "Pick up the bikes and line them up on the side of the garage." While we were going through all the junk, I found my parents' old picture box. There were very few pictures of us growing up, and I was fascinated by each of them. Snapshots of a happy family I wanted to believe in. But I knew differently. I could see the sadness in the picture of my oldest sister standing behind a plant, her smile not quite reaching her eyes. I knew the fears of the little girls smiling in their handmade matching dresses. I knew of the lies these pictures held hidden in their details.

The pictures were just thrown in the box. Many had water stains and were stuck together. Memories that had been tossed away in carelessness instead of lovingly placed into an album. As I dug deeper into the box, I found the layer of pictures with my brother Aaron, who died before I was born. I looked at the sweet face of my brother dressed in white, laying in his tiny coffin. I felt a connection with him, like I knew him without ever knowing him in this life. It felt like we were old friends, and we were supposed to be on this journey of life together. I felt he wanted to be here with us, but that

7

chance was taken from him. We rarely ever talked about him, and these few photos were all I really knew about him.

"Dad, in what year was Aaron born?" I asked.

"In January of 1982." He answered me as he continued to hand out more tasks to my siblings, who were still cleaning the garage.

"How did he die?" I asked.

My dad stopped to look at me before answering my questions. I knew he was wondering why I was asking this again. "He died because his heart wasn't strong enough. It had a small hole in it. A heart murmur," he answered before turning back to the other kids. It was all the information I could get.

There were a few pictures from when Aaron was born, the only child out of five who had been born at home. I continued to stare at his picture for a few more seconds, not wanting to let this connection with him disappear before I was told to get back to work.

∞

Sunday morning, we dressed in our best clothes to go to church. The church was a mixture of people: the kind and the unkind, the loving and the judgmental, the genuine and those who were just put up a facade. I was in a class with several other girls, one who had been my best friend for years. The other girls seem to delight in being mean to us. It didn't matter though; I had Amy, and she was the best kind of friend you could have.

We sat in our pew, just a typical family in a sea of typical families singing the opening hymn, "Nearer My God to Thee." We were waiting to take the bread and water. I watched the plate being passed from person to person, eagerly waiting for my turn. The bread and water finally came my way. I took my portion and went back to coloring. I know this ritual was supposed to mean more, but I just liked the idea of a small snack.

In some meetings, dad would take the bread and water, and sometimes he would skip. Today he skipped, then bowed his head in prayer. A few silent tears slipped down his face. This was not something I had seen before. I saw pain and anguish pass over his face, and it left me feeling confused. He tried to hide his face, to contain the small sniffles that had caught my attention. Was it regret?

After church, I begged to go to Amy's house. She was always up for an adventure and kept the secrets I told her. Her dad was stern but never unkind. Her mom would make sure we were well fed before running shooing us outside to play. There was a creek in the backyard with a rope swing that would take you from the safety of the backyard into the adventure of the unknown wilderness. We caught minnows, conquered yellow jackets, and sank to our knees in the squishy mud. We would talk about our families, church, and what we wanted to be when we grew up.

Her backyard was where I learned to swim, climb trees, and catch grasshoppers. It was a place of magic and adventure where toys came alive, and the creek was an ocean through our imagination. It was a place of normalcy and safety, my refuge away from the stress and anxiety at home. I always wanted to be there, and I never wanted to leave. Eventually, though, the sun would set, and it would be time for me to reluctantly go home.

Before bed, we sat together as a family piled onto our couches while dad read from the Book of Mormon. Mom said the family prayer where she asked for safety for the people in our lives. Afterward, my sister and I walked up the stairs to our bedroom. The fear settled into my muscles, making them tense. I wedged myself between the mattress and the frame trying to feel safe. Before falling asleep, I prayed, pleading with God to protect me from my father. I hoped the prayers worked this time.

∞

I woke up in the middle of the night to my father's black silhouette, framed by the light in the hallway. My heart sank. I closed my eyes as tight as I could, doing my best to pretend to be asleep, hoping this time he would leave me alone.

I block all the senses of the world out. I see nothing; I hear nothing; I'm in the blackness. I don't know how much time has passed. I focused on getting further and further away, disconnecting with my own body.

Where are you, mom? .

God, can you send her? Will she listen this time? Will she ever save me?

I'm so scared, mom. I don't want him in here. I can't breathe, it's too much.

I wanted to run away, but where would I go? He would find me, and I would lose my family. I would be the one in trouble. I would be the problem.

I wanted to scream so loud the neighbors could hear me and maybe save me, but I can't breathe, so I can't scream. I'm supposed to be asleep, pretend to be asleep, I repeat to myself. My muscles tightened, encroaching on the darkness to alert me of the danger as he walks over to my side of the bed. I silently scream louder and louder to block it all out. I was so scared my body was shaking, and I can't pretend I'm asleep if I'm shaking.

I wish I could just stop shaking.

Why can't I stop? Please God, help me stop shaking so I can pretend to sleep.

I'm pulled out of my safe spot by hands so much stronger than I could ever be.

STOP IT! I begged. It's impossible to hear the words that never leave my mouth. I could feel an escaped tear slide down my cheek. Maybe he won't notice it because sleeping people don't cry.

I hate this! I hate you! I hate mom for not saving me and I hate God for allowing this to happen! I hate myself for not being able to scream, I hate myself for not knowing how to make it stop. I hate myself.

MOM, WHERE ARE YOU??? SAVE ME. I remember nothing else, lost in the darkness that is my only refuge, my only escape. I don't have to feel anything when I'm in the darkness. There is no dad, no mom, no God, no fear, no anger, and no sadness. There is nothing.

I am awake, but I am dead.

I don't know how long he was there; I don't remember anything until the sun comes up the next day. He has taken what he wanted, and my sister and I are left to go about our day as if nothing happened. We are left to pretend to be that family who just hours earlier were sitting in the pew at church singing hymns of God. We had no words to describe the violations forced on us. There was no one I could talk to without destroying my family. There was no way to comprehend how the winds of that destructive hurricane would follow us throughout our lives.

Chapter Two
Milkshake

I lay in the waterbed enjoying the silence of morning as I watched the illuminated particles of dust as they danced in the beams of the morning sun. I took comfort in the soft snores of my sister, who was still sleeping next to me.

Mom came into the room to let us know she was taking us to the Discovery Museum today. An advantage of being homeschooled was that my parents bought season passes. My sister and I got out of bed and threw our clothes on excitedly before running downstairs to eat cereal. My brother came down a few minutes later to join us. Mom put two spoonfuls of sugar on our cheerios to make them extra yummy.

Our cats, Vega and Lil Bit, meowed incessantly to let us know they wanted to be fed. Mom threw down a can of cat food next to the empty ones from the last week that the ants were currently eating. As we ran outside, Jason yelled for the front seat while trying to trip me on the way to the car. I threw an elbow into his ribs to retaliate before jumping into the backseat. We had a sibling rivalry that left us both bruised and exhausted.

Once inside the Discovery Center, we ran to a space with a huge green wall on one side and a light that flashed on the other. Jason excitedly told us, "Jump into the air before the light flashes!" We counted to three together, and then all jumped in the air, leaving our shadows on the green wall for us to admire. Next, Deborah had an idea. "Let's do the YMCA!" We counted to three again, and all moved into position. The light flashed, and again our shadows showed up on the green screen as a temporary picture. We played in this spot, performing various funny poses for another twenty minutes before moving on.

The next room had a sloping checkered floor, several windows, and a television showing us what we were doing and how perception can change. It showed how each person could experience the same event, and yet their truth of the situation was different. On one end of the room, we looked super tiny, and on the other end, we looked like giants. We ran back and forth watching ourselves grow and shrink on a small TV, like Alice in Wonderland.

Other kids came into the space, so we took off for the jeep. It was a car in the middle of the room simulating drunk driving with delayed reflexes. We crashed the car a few times in the video and sprinted over to the next activity.

We spent all day there before going by Taco Bell for dinner and driving home. It was a movie kind of night. We all plopped on the couches until scriptures and bedtime. I was too exhausted to feel anxious, and I fell asleep as soon as my head hit the pillow.

The next morning was just like all the others. I woke up to sit in front of the TV pretending to do schoolwork, passing the hours away until my friends came home. I could feel the restlessness in my body grow impatient with the need to move.

Deborah, Jason, and I went into the backyard for a game of hide-and-seek. Right outside our back door were a couple of large bushes where Jason found a snake curled around a branch. He tried to pick it up with a stick. Mom, terrified of snakes, yelled at us to keep it outside. We watched the snake as it curled around the stick, unafraid of the kids watching him. The snake eventually dropped and crawled under the bush out of our reach.

We continued to play hide-and-seek on the paths we had stomped out in the pine needles that piled up from the many trees. We were always careful to avoid the scary tree with thorns at least three inches long, its branches reaching over the path. As we played, I heard the school bus down the street. I ran inside to ask mom if we could go out to play. Deborah and I had friends who were sisters, and we wanted to go over there together. "Go ahead," mom said as we ran back out the door again.

A few hours later, the streetlights came on, signaling it was time to go home. Dad was working late tonight, so mom asked us to clean up a bit before he came home. My chore was the upstairs bathroom and hallway, Deborah had to clean the kitchen, and Jason had to clean the living room. Jason threw the items from the living room upstairs into the hallway, which was my zone to clean. As soon as he would turn his back, I would throw it all back down the stairs back into his zone. He threw them back up, trying to aim at me as he did.

"MOOOOM, JASON is THROWING things at MEEE," I screamed in a loud indignant tone.

Jason tossed one more thing at me before mom came in the room.

"STOP!" she yelled at both of us, but Jason usually took the force of any punishment doled out because he was the oldest by five years.

"Go to your room!" she yelled at Jason as she turned to go back into the kitchen. He tried to trip me as he walked past. I threw a shoe at him once he was far enough away I could run if I needed to.

When Dad came home later, he stripped down to his underwear, as he often did. White briefs that had been worn so much they had turned yellowish-gray. Tidy whiteys we called them, even though there was no white left, and they had several holes worn in them showing more than any of us wanted.

"Will you please wear more clothes?" my mom asked him with a hint of frustration in her voice.

"No," he replied in an indignant tone. "I have to wear clothes all day at the office. I don't want to wear them in my own home." That was the end of any argument. He sat spread-eagled on the couch and watched TV During a commercial he got up, his bulging stomach folded over his underwear, and turned to go to the bathroom, revealing a few more holes in the back. It made all of us uncomfortable, but it never mattered to him. It was his house, and he was going to do as he pleased without regard to the other people who lived there.

As we climbed the stairs to our bedroom for bed, I heard mom and dad arguing more about how dad needed to wear his clothes around us, at least some shorts. Their arguing never ended well for us. Tonight, he didn't come into our room, though. I can only guess he was with my oldest sister, Rachael. I heard whispers of the things she must go through, but I was never brave enough to ask, or old enough to understand the things he did to her. Her pain had kept us safe, if only for that night.

The next morning, dad woke us up. "You girls need to get dressed. You're coming with me to work so you can get your schoolwork done." I knew my parents didn't really care about our schoolwork. I guessed mom just wanted a break from having us home all the time.

Dad worked forty-five minutes away at a computer software company. We stopped by McDonald's for breakfast and ate in the car while listening to Rush Limbaugh on the radio. I watched the traffic on highway 75 going from Marietta into the heart of Atlanta on their morning commute.

Dad had his own office, as did most employees there, with a few extra people left in cubicles. We sat on the floor in the corner of dad's office working on schoolwork most of the day, but also helping to make copies or whatever else was needed of us. It was a long and boring day.

We had to go with dad to the office many times after that morning. On one of these drives to work, I sat in the backseat eating my breakfast and thinking about all my friends who could go to school. I thought about how kindergarten was rough. I was always getting into trouble with the teacher. But after that year, I loved school! I loved the teachers, eating in the cafeteria, learning, and playing with friends. I remembered one teacher who taught fourth grade, two years past my second-grade year, who was incredibly kind to me. Every lunch period she would come over to me and offer me candy and encouraging words, a pack of Nerds and a compliment about my shirt. She stood out to me as one of the kindest people I had met her because she always gave to people but expected nothing in return. She just handed out these bits of love to the people who came across her path. I loved her for her kindness, even though I only saw her for a few minutes at lunch a few days a week. I wanted to go back just to see her. I wanted to go to fourth grade so she could be my teacher.

During one of my last days at Keheley Elementary at the end of the second grade, the second-grade classes were called to an assembly in the gym for a short film. We sat on the floor to watch a movie. It was an animated film about good touch and bad touch. I watched the surrounding kids, careful to mimic their reactions so they didn't know they were watching a film about me.

It was only a few days later that we were told we would not be in public school anymore. Maybe it was a coincidence, maybe not. We were told it was for our own good. My oldest sister had gotten into drugs, and our parents said it was the fault of the school system. My parents didn't want us exposed to such filth. The irony was missed by my young mind.

I remember being so excited about getting to stay home with my mom and siblings the first few days of third grade. But it quickly wore off, and I longed to go back to school. Now my days are spent in front of a TV or sitting in my dad's office. Rachael, the reason we were homeschooled, continued in public school.

I was brought back from my memories when dad switched lanes for the off-ramp. Rush Limbaugh was on the radio playing a clip from Paul Harvey's 'The Rest of the Story'. We pulled into the parking lot of his office building, a plain, one-level, brown brick building. Another day was spent counting the hours until we could go home.

∞

Wednesday night we had youth groups at church. Even though I wasn't old enough to go, mom would take me with her sometimes. She was the librarian, and while she worked and chatted as people passed through, I would run around the building playing with my friends while my siblings went to their classes. I begged mom to let me go tonight. Why would she even consider leaving me alone with him? She had to know what he did to me. It happened too much for her to not know.

When the adults didn't think we were listening, there were occasional whispers about how Dad had been caught and reported for abuse when my family lived in Utah in the early 80s. Mom HAD to know! But at the time, my need to believe in my mother, that she would protect me if she knew, took control of my thoughts. There is no way she could know, because if she did, she would save us. Was she really going to leave me alone with him? If she didn't know, then why did I feel so betrayed and angry as I watched her walk out the door with my brother and sister?

I pushed the confusion down as I turned around to face my nightmare. My father was sitting on the couch in just his underwear and a smile on his face that made my stomach clench. Dad spoke, "come over here and play a game of cards with me." He wanted to play war, a card game where each player flips a card over, and the highest card wins. We played a few rounds before he said, "let's make this more interesting." My heart stopped, and I held my breath listening as my dad continued. "The loser has to take off an item of clothes each time they lose." I looked around for a way to escape, but I was trapped in this house with no people to protect me.

What was I supposed to do when I was only eight years old, and my dad, this person who is supposed to be my protector, my pillar of strength, was my biggest source of fear? My father was 6'2," 300 pounds, and he was asking me to do something in a tone that implied it was not a question. I couldn't say no without consequences or a punishment. I was too frozen in my own fear to say no, too scared saying no would mean I would lose my family and be sent to foster care where the abuse was worse.

I knew I had to play his game. I tried delaying as long as possible. I flipped my cards as slowly as I could without getting into danger. I was grateful I still had my shoes on. When I lost the first time, I only took one shoe off. He was irritated, "the shoes should come off at the same time," he said. I held my ground on this little thing and he let me. The next turn I lost again, and I took my other shoe off. It seems like I was the one losing the whole time and I didn't know if I should feel grateful because at least I had clothes on to play his game. He was sitting there in his underwear, and I know the first time he loses, those were coming off. I lost again and took a sock off. I could see the irritation in his eyes as he tried to keep it light, like it was really a game I wanted to play. I lost again, and another sock came off. I lost again, and I had to take a shirt off. I had worn layers that day, and I still had one shirt on. I pried it off as slowly as possible without getting into trouble, pretending to get stuck in the shirt to take more time. Again, I lost. The safe clothing was off. I had nothing left that wouldn't expose me in some way. I sat there staring at him, looking for any slight chance he would relinquish this idea. My stomach lurched as he offered to buy me a milkshake tomorrow if I would just hurry.

There was no getting out of this. He was intent on his purpose. I took my skirt off sluggishly because I still had on my underwear. It was at least something to keep me sheltered a little longer. Dad looked at the clock and realized almost forty-five minutes had passed since mom walked out the door. She would be home in another thirty minutes or fewer. He huffed a little in frustration as he told me to put my clothes back on. He went upstairs for a few minutes and came back down with some pants on. It was a minor victory for me, but there will be repercussions tonight.

Mom finally came home with my brother and sister. They walked in excited and energized, talking about what they did at church. Jason was in the boy scouts' program and tonight they practiced different knots for rock climbing. Deborah had gone with the girls to work on their life skills, like cooking and sewing. Tonight, they wrote a letter to someone who had made a difference in their life. Mom had spent the evening laminating scripture cards for the youth while socializing with the other parents who came through the library. They were excited and happy; I was numb. I turned my face away as an emotionless tear fell.

They were home now though, and I needed them. They allowed the space I desperately needed from dad and the distraction it gave my mind. That night's bedtime was chaotic as we all got ready for bed and brushed our teeth. Jason and I ended up fighting over the toothpaste. I had spilled a bunch all over the counter then screamed at Jason like he made the mess until mom made him clean it up.

As I tried to fall asleep, I tucked myself into my safe spot in the bed, focused on the weight of the water as it pushed me against the wooden side of the bed like a weighted blanket. I had escaped earlier by dragging the game out as long as possible. I already knew this would be an awful night. I didn't know what time he came in, but it was dark outside. I comforted myself by imagining he was just tucking my sister in for the night as any good father would do. A simple kiss and hug. My image was so strong it blocked out reality and I fell asleep desperately believing my own story. until he woke me up. I know I'm awake because I can hear the screaming in my head. Everything is blacked out as he takes what he wants from my body.

I know mom knows. I overheard mom and dad fighting about it one night. Rachael had told mom everything he had done to her, that he had done to us. My mother will never be protection. Eventually, I stopped screaming her name. My mother would never save me. The screaming was replaced with the blackness I gratefully embraced.

The next day, we had to go to work with dad again and on the way home, we stopped to get a milkshake at Dairy Queen. That's the tradeoff. That is what was supposed to make this life worth living through. It was all took to ease his conscious. That is what our innocence is worth to him.

A milkshake.

Chapter Three
Bailed out. Again.

Friday evening, after my father got off work, we drove to Granny and Pappy's house in the mountains of North Carolina in Rockville. They were my great grandparents on my father's side.

To stifle the boredom on our long car ride, we played the alphabet game. It's a game where we find the letters of the alphabet on various cars and signs, calling them out in order. Only one person can use the found letter, the first one to the letter Z wins. We would always get stuck on the letter J until we reach Jonestown, right before the North Carolina border. Jonestown was where we stopped by the same gas station each time and order thick potato wedges and an extra-large diet coke to finish the ride.

After we left the gas station, it was all mountains, forest, and twisting roads. Every now and then we would see a deer, rabbit, or a fox. Most trips included the smell of skunk along the way. When we saw a deer, dad would pull over when it stopped in front of us, allowing us an up-close look at his wiggling nose and regal stature.

We arrived at their house around midnight. Grandmother, who was also staying the weekend, walked out of the side door that led into a partially enclosed carport to welcome us inside. "Hey Grandmother." I said sleepily as I gave her a hug. The door led to a hallway lined with tools and pantry food. I eyed the cans of grape soda as I walked through to the combination living room and dining room. On the left side was a door to Granny and Pappy's bedroom. Along the wall was my granny's chair, her magnifying glass she used as a lamp sat between her chair and side table. A small woodstove sat in the middle of the wall. On the right side of the room was the dining room table with a large picture window showing the front yard. An old-style box TV sat on the floor in the corner. I walked into the open kitchen and saw three glasses of grape juice sitting on the counter for us.

In the back of the living room was another door that opened access to four more rooms and the stairs leading to the garage. On the left side is the room my sister and I slept in, followed by the bathroom door and another guest bedroom with a queen-size bed where my parents stayed. Next was the basement door and then the official living room where my grandmother and grandfather sleep on a pullout couch when they visited.

Grandmother helped us settle in. Our room had twin beds set up side by side with a small table separating them. the slight smell of mothballs drifted out of the closet, leaving traces of its scent around the room. The dresser held an antique brass unicorn standing on its hind legs that played music. I wound it up, listening to its soft melody as it slowly spun in circles while I fell asleep.

Saturday morning, I woke up to the smell of my grandmother's cooking. I rolled over to see Deborah lying awake but still enjoying the warmth of her bed. "Let's get up." I said, stretching my arms over my head to shake off the last bits of sleep. Deborah crawled out from under her covers, and we walked out to the living room. Grandmother was still in the middle of cooking. "It will be at least thirty minutes." she said.

Pappy turned to us and asked, "Do you ladies want to help me in the garden? You'll get to catch all the june bugs." The bright, iridescent, green bugs were fun to catch, and I was excited. We walked down the stairs to the basement and waited for Pappy to open the garage door into the garden. The basement was as large as the house upstairs. It was unofficially divided into three parts. On the right side was pappy's workshop where the walls were lined with rows of screwdrivers, saws, hammers, and other tools organized on peg wood boards. The back was full of sorted boxes containing the memories of their life together. Behind the garage door were all the tools for gardening and a beautiful red tractor. "Can we go for a ride?" I asked Pappy, looking at the tractor.

He replied with a small smile. "Let's get some work done first."

Pappy put on his gloves and sunhat, offering us a set as well. He opened the garage door, and the smell of earth and plants hit my nose. I closed my eyes and breathed in the earthy smell while feeling the sunshine warm my face. I loved it here.

The smell of the cherry tomato plants stood out the most to me. I was ready to eat a few while we worked. He put love and care into his garden, tending it daily. It showed in the neat rows of his vegetables and through the tomato plants growing taller than his head. The snap peas had been carefully placed on a web of strings as they grew taller, and the few weeds were tiny, not even taller than my shoe. He handed me and Deborah a bucket of water apiece. We looked under each leaf for the june bugs to drop in the water until there were so many they crawled on top of each other.

Pappy handed us another bucket and asked us, "Stephanie, will you pick the snap peas? And Deborah, will you pick a few tomatoes for our lunch?" It only took a few minutes before our buckets were full of fresh produce.

When we finished, he took us over to investigate the woods next to their house. He showed us a thicket of blackberry bushes overflowing with red berries, just a month away from turning black. "Y'all can come back next month and then these will all be ripe." he said. "I can't wait!" I answered. I wanted to come back, and I liked there was a plan. I wanted to stay forever.

Inside the house, Grandmother had just finished making homemade biscuits and gravy with scrambled eggs and bacon. The house smelled amazing, and I felt my tummy grumble in anticipation. I didn't really like biscuits, so I skipped them and ate the eggs and bacon. Dad looked at me with a strange expression while he grabbed a biscuit of his own to eat. Granny was sitting in her chair facing the TV She changed the channel to cartoons for us while we ate.

Afterward, the girl from down the street knocked on the door to see if we could go outside and play. We played red light, green light, red rover, and tag for several hours. Exhausted, we laid down on the lush green lawn, heads on each other's stomachs to form a circle, and then tried our best not to laugh, which just made us laugh harder.

Lunch was a bacon lettuce tomato sandwich with a thick layer of mayonnaise served with a side of grape juice. As soon as lunch was done, we started dinner by snapping the tops off the peas and splitting them in half, and then we skinned the potatoes. I used a potato peeler but watched in fascination as my pappy expertly peeled the potatoes with a sharp knife. With dinner prepped and pushed to the side, I asked Pappy, "Will you play spite a malice with me?" It was a card game we played together often. We sat at the dining room table playing the card game while he watched the stock market on TV, writing notes on a piece of paper.

"Can we take the tractor out?" Jason asked. Pappy smiled as he got up. "Let me get you the keys and make sure it's ready." I sat on the stairs that led into the basement, looking down at them as Pappy topped it off with gas and hitched up the trailer. Deborah and I hopped into the back of the trailer, then Jason drove us around the yard. We saw the adults inside, watching us through the window. Jason drove us to the church at the end of the road and around the parking lot a few times. By the time we were done playing with the tractor, Grandmother was back in the kitchen making smothered steak with potatoes and the snap peas from the garden for dinner.

We sat on the floor working on puzzles they kept in a drawer just for us until the table was set. When Grandmother called us over, we piled our plates up with as much food as it could hold. Grandmother gave me an extra spoonful of mashed potatoes because everyone knows they are my favorite! I watched as dad piled his plate with twice as much food as everyone else, then went back for another plate. He then finished up any leftover bits on our plates before going back for his third overflowing plate. I didn't understand how he could eat so much. Jason, Deborah, and I cleaned the table off before heading outside again.

The sun was just setting, and the fireflies were coming out. They lit up the yard like our own personal light show. Deborah went inside and came back carrying three mason jars to put the fireflies in. We ran around trying to catch them, competing to see who could collect the most. At bedtime, we released them back into the darkening sky. In this moment there were no fears. It was just me and my brother and sister playing together in a magical moment of childhood dreams.

"It's time to come inside." mom yelled from the side door. We released the last of our fireflies and put the mason jars in the sink. "Brush your teeth." granny asked us when we walked by her chair. In the bathroom, she kept a toothbrush for each of us to use. It always made me feel good to see my own toothbrush sitting on the counter, a sign I would be back again.

Deborah and I talked for a long time about the things we did that day and anything else that came to mind. She was always there to talk to me when I was too excited or anxious to sleep. We talked until I couldn't keep my eyes open anymore and the memories of fireflies took over, occupying my dreams.

Sunday morning, Grandmother made us breakfast again before we loaded into the car to drive back home. It was the same meal as the morning before. Grandmother had placed a biscuit on each of our plates before we sat down this time. I ate everything else on my plate, leaving the biscuit there. I left the room but could still hear Grandmother and Dad talking about me. "I don't understand why she won't eat a biscuit.", dad said to grandmother. "More for us!" my grandmother replied. "Next time we should make her eat one, then maybe she will realize she likes them." he said. Their conversation continued, but I tune them out to watch TV

"Go pack your things," mom said to the three of us. She came back a few minutes later to ask us again before we turned off the television and listened. Deborah and I threw our dirty clothes back in our bags and carried them to the trunk of the car. We had a few books with games in them and a blanket we set up in the backseat for the ride home. Grandmother gave us turkey, lettuce, and tomato sandwiches for the road. Granny, Pappy, and Grandmother all stood in the carport waving goodbye to us as we began our journey home.

On the way home, we stopped by dad's favorite rock shop. Dad loved to collect rocks and had built a collection. The rock shop had mounds of brightly covered glass piled around the front yard. There was a table filled with thousands of glass marbles and another with a variety of rough stones. The store was located right next to their house. Inside, the shop was filled with amethyst cathedrals, bookends made from dyed geodes, little pewter figurines, and vases made of onyx. The owner of the shop was behind the counter filled with semi-precious gemstones. She usually had a cat riding on her shoulders. Her kids came into the shop while we were there and invited me to go play at their house while dad shopped. Two hours later, dad filled the remaining space in the trunk with all the different rocks he bought, including a five-gallon bucket of uncracked geodes.

We were barely out of town before I fell asleep. It had been a few hours when I felt the car suddenly slowing down, waking me up. We were still on the two-lane highway, just a mile or so from the stop we usually make in Jonestown. Mom was yelling at dad to pull over as steam was pouring out of the engine, making it impossible to see the road. The car was overheating again. The full load of rocks was too much for the engine while driving up mountain roads. Dad rolled to a stop on the side of the highway and rolled down the windows in an attempt to keep us cool from the warm weather. We had to wait for the car to cool down before he could open the hood. We kept a spare jug of water in the trunk just for these types of occasions. About twenty minutes later, dad popped the hood of the car and poured water into the radiator before we slowly drove the rest of the way to the gas station. We ate lunch there while the car cooled down completely. I fell asleep again soon after getting back on the road.

Rachael was in the kitchen eating a bowl of cereal when we got home late that afternoon. She got up and left as soon as we came into the house. She was eight years older than me and barely around us; her absence was normal. I wondered why she didn't want to be around us. A part of me wondered if dad hurt her too. I guess I knew, but I didn't want to think about that, and I push the thought away before I had to acknowledge it.

Mom made us mac and cheese with hotdogs for dinner. We watched a bit of TV, read scriptures and were sent to bed. After the lights were out, Deborah and I talked, creating a language only we knew and laughing about how silly it sounded. With the fun weekend and my sister to talk to, it was an easy night to fall asleep. Safe enough, I didn't even burrow into my spot.

I woke up a few hours later to the sound of mom and dad fighting about Rachael. Dad had checked on her about midnight to discover she was gone; she had snuck out the window to be with friends. I don't want to think about why he had gone into her room to check on her. That image of a caring father, of who I wanted him to be, always took the place of the more intimidating thoughts. The fighting continued. Mom's car kept breaking down, and she needed a new one, she said. Dad complained they didn't have enough money for a new car. I fell back asleep before the argument ended. The next morning, mom was on the phone with a security company to put an alarm on our windows and doors. A set of keys were sticking out of the wall from where they had been thrown during the fight.

∞

It was another Wednesday night. Rachael was out with friends. Jason and Deborah had church tonight. Mom made me stay home last time, so I had a better chance of going this week, I reasoned.

"Mom, can I go to church with you tonight" I asked with a hint of desperation in my voice.

With a stern tone, she said, "No, you're not old enough and I don't want you running wild around the church."

"PLEASE mom," I begged her. "I don't want to stay home with dad."

Dad was standing behind mom, giving me a disapproving look. I refused to look at him, concentrating all my efforts on mom. I hoped she could understand why I wanted to go. She needed her to understand.

"You'll stay with your father tonight," she said, getting frustrated with my pleas.

I glared at her defiantly. *Doesn't she know who she is leaving me with? Doesn't she know what he does when she isn't looking?* I wanted to ask her these things. But, what if she did know?

"Mom, please?" I was holding back the tears.

I am trapped with him. How could you leave me, mom? You tried to hide behind your games of solitaire, but I know you know about him because I've heard the whispers about what happened in Utah before I was born. There had been a court case, and yet you left me to face him all alone.

I didn't ask to be here; I didn't ask to be a part of this family. You brought me into this, mom, and then you turned your back on me as you walked out.

You abandoned me.

I turned around, desperate to find a way out, but as I looked at him, I knew I would not be getting out of anything tonight. "Go sit down at the kitchen table." he told me. "I have something I want to show you." he said as he grabbed a few different-sized batteries and placed them on the table. He brought a chair and placed it so we are face to face, with bits of pink hanging out the holes of his dirty gray underwear. He took two size c batteries and stacked them on top of each other. "This is the size of a man's penis when it's soft." he said. I stared at him, numb to what was going on. "Want to touch mine, and see?" he asked.

"No," I said sulkily.

"It's like bubblegum", he said in a jovial tone.

I sat there glaring at him as he stacked three size D batteries next to the C stack. "This happens when a man is excited or in love", he said next. He was watching me closely to see how I would respond. "Do you want to feel the difference?" he asked.

I can already see he is the size of the D battery. He is asking me questions as if I had a choice. He is trying to make it seem as if I there was a choice. All the anger and terror that has been building up since mom left spilled out of my eyes. I sat there motionless, with silent tears, not saying a word, refusing to look at him. Instead, my eyes were glued to my pink shoelaces.

He sighed in frustration and got up to go upstairs for a moment. "Stay there, we have more to talk about." When he came back down, he was wearing a pair of shorts. He sat back in his chair and stared me down while I look at the floor.

"You know you can't tell your mother, right?" his voice had a dangerous edge to it. I rubbed at my arms to push the hair back down, I hated that they gave away my fear.

I spotted a cheerio on the ground and focused on it. "If you tell your mother, it would tear the family apart, and that would be your fault"

I wondered how long that cheerio had been sitting on the floor.

"You know this,", as he points to the batteries, "isn't your fault. I take the blame for it, as long as you don't tell anyone"

As if that changed anything, I was still stuck here. I wondered if the cheerio is stale yet.

"You can't tell anyone else either, because they will call social services. Do you know what they do to families?" He asked, more of a threat than a question.

I wondered how they made cheerios. What did they make it out of?

"Social services will take you away from us. They will lock me up in prison, take your siblings away from you and place you all in different homes."

I watched as an ant crawled toward the cheerio.

"Do you know how they treat kids in those homes? I'm compassionate compared to what you would go through there."

The ant made it to the cheerio and was trying to take a piece off. What would it be like to be an ant?

"If you tell anyone, they will send me to prison." he said again for emphasis. "Then it would be your fault. If I'm in prison your mom will be all alone. How will she take care of herself, of you guys? You would end up on the streets, homeless."

I got the message. If I told anyone, dad would go to prison, mom would be left alone to live on the streets, and my siblings and I would live in horribly abusive homes. We would be separated forever. At least in this home, in this hell, I knew what to expect. At least in this hell, I have my sister and my friends. In this hell, I know where to find refuge occasionally. To say anything would be to fail my entire family, and it would be my fault. I watched the ant break off a bite of the cheerio and carry it back to his home. I wished I could go with him.

"Go up to your room and think about what I've told you," Dad said.

I rushed up the stairs to my room and closed the door. I went into my closet to the very back corner and climbed the wall to the top shelf. I blocked myself from the view of anyone who opened the closet door. I hid there and cried silently until I heard mom come home. I climbed down and changed clothes for bed, too exhausted from the excessive tension in my body to interact with my family. I wedged in between the mattress and bed once more and fell asleep.

A few hours later I heard dad whisper in my ear, "remember what we talked about." I opened my eyes; it was still dark outside. My heart sank, and I wanted to throw up. "You can't tell anyone", he said again as he took my covers off and pulled me out of my spot. I couldn't move my body as I disconnected. He did what he pleased with my body. It was just a shell right now anyway. My mind was locked up, far away, thinking about those fireflies.

The next morning, Dad left Deborah and me home while he went to work. Mom was in the office, deeply involved in another round of a solitaire. Jason was in his room playing with Legos while Deborah and I watched television. We heard a knock at the door. It was an unusual time of day for anyone to knock.

"I got it!" Deborah yelled. She opened the door to a well-dressed woman who was holding a clipboard. "I'm from social services. Is your mom or dad home?" she asked.

"Mom is napping," Deborah lied.

"Is there anything we can help you with, sweetie?" the woman asked.

I distrusted her immediately.

"No, we are good here," Deborah replied.

"Can I come in?" the lady asked.

"Mom is taking a nap right now." Deborah answered her as she closed the door.

We watched through the window as the lady cast a worried glance, but finally walked away. We had been taught how to behave in situations like this.

We went back to watching TV.

∞

A few days later, dad drove up to the house in a brand new, shiny, silver, Taurus SHO. It was the newest model. "Come for a test drive in our new car!" he excitedly asked us. Jason, Deborah, and I all jumped into the car, breathing in that new car smell of fresh leather. Dad drove to the highway. Each time we yelled faster, he would slam the gas pedal down pushing us into our seats from the g forces. This car was fast. Very fast. Dad loved testing its limits on the freeways of Atlanta.

When we arrived back home, mom was waiting for dad at the top of the driveway. Her arms were crossed, and she was glaring fiercely at dad. I remembered the fight from a few days ago when mom said she needed a new car.

"Go on in the house." dad told us.

We swiftly got out of the car, leaving the new leather smell behind, and hurried inside before we got caught in their war.

Mom was angry because her car kept breaking down, but dad was the one who got a new car. "We can't afford a new car," I heard mom yell. I knew Dad made good money, and we lived in a huge four bedroom house in the nice, albeit older, part of Atlanta. We often went on trips to North Carolina and Dad would bring home a truck full of rocks each time. I didn't understand why they argued about money all the time, as it seemed we had all we needed.

That weekend, Grandmother and granddad drove several hours from their home to bail my dad out of trouble. They brought two cars, a brand new one for them, and their old, baby blue, Lincoln continental, for mom. They only stayed with us one night so that Grandmother could give mom her old car. Mom was grateful for the gift, but the discrepancy between dad's new car and mom's old car made priorities clear, even to my young mind. Grandmother made sure Dad always got what he wanted, and she made sure he never paid for the consequences.

Chapter Four
Eternal

Sunday was considered the of rest. I never understood that because to me it seemed the most stressful day of the week. From the moment we wake up, the entire family was in state of panic to get out of the door on time. Each person looking for that "Sunday best" outfit that the church members will judge us by. Someone was always frantically looking for their lost shoe. We quickly ate a bowl of cereal or an even faster cup of slim fast, which was my favorite.

That Sunday I wore the peach-colored dress mom made for me last Easter. She made one for my sisters too. One was a pastel pink and the other a light powder blue. The fabric was woven with tiny little flowers, where each petal had a hole with the edges embroidered for strength around the edge. I remembered how she had spent hours at the sewing machine, even taking the time to teach us, showing me the different stitches and how the machine worked. The dress had a magical way of making me feel loved.

Church had three meetings back-to-back, each about forty-five minutes long. The first was called the sacrament meeting, in which fifteen minutes into the meeting we would take the bread and water of Christ. After that, there were three talks and two more songs. The talks were broken into three time slots, the first was the shortest at about five minutes, usually given by a youth, the second was about ten minutes and the last could be anywhere from five minutes to what felt like the entire three hours, although it was usually wrapped up in twenty minutes. The speakers were chosen in a sort of rotation by the bishop or his counselors the week before. There was a predictable pattern to each speech. They opened with a halfway funny joke like "I tried to avoid the bishop for three weeks because I figured it was my turn"; Or a blubbered out "I'm really nervous and I hate giving these talks." Then there were the ones that LOVED giving talks. These were the ones that would drone on and on to make sure we knew how smart they were and would make the meeting run late. Sometimes, we were lucky though, and someone engaging would take the pulpit and offer some sincere motivating story that was from the heart.

These meetings were never exciting to a wiggly ten-year-old. My favorite part of church was the fifteen minutes between each meeting when I could run around and find my friends and the welcoming adults waving hello to me in the hallway.

We often passed time by drawing games on a pad of paper like Tic Tac Toe or cross squares in which you build a board of dots and then take turns connecting the dots to form squares and whoever had the most squares when the board was full would be the winner.

When Dad wanted us to settle down, he would put his hand on our legs to try to keep us still. When he did this, he would always move his fingers in a repeated pattern. Pinky, middle, thumb, forefinger, ring. Click, click, click. His hands constantly moved. I hated the constant unsettling click, click, click of his hands and would try to push them off me, but he was much stronger than I was. If I tried too hard to remove his hands, I would be in trouble for causing too much commotion while the speaker droned on about the importance of Joseph Smith and how he had died a Martyr while trying to build up the kingdom of God.

A ward is what we call each congregation. They have been predefined by the geographical boundaries mapped out by the church's leadership. It is expected that you go to the church that is within the ward boundaries. These can be small areas in places like Utah, but in more remote places, the drive to church could be an hour away or more. Inside the center of each ward building is the sacrament room, which is where the main meeting is held. If there are too many people within those boundaries, they will open a partitioning wall in the back that leads into a full-size gym, complete with wooden polished floors marked with court lines for basketball. After church, the kids would meet in the gym to run as fast as they could across the smooth surface until an adult kicked them out.

In the hallway that surrounded the gym, there were about thirty different sized classrooms for the smaller group lessons. I went to room 106, where I met with the kids my age. Today's lesson was on the Plan of salvation. We believed we lived together with God and Jesus before our time on Earth in what we called the pre-existence. During this time, there was a great war in heaven in which both Lucifer and Jesus wanted to carry out God's plan here on Earth. The difference was that Lucifer did not want to allow free agency so that everyone would be guaranteed to make it back to God, taking the glory to himself. Jesus's plan was that he would allow us to have free agency and the ability to sin, but that he would take those sins upon himself in the name of God, giving God all the Glory. One-third of the souls in heaven sided with Lucifer and two-thirds with Jesus. Lucifer, bitter about God's choice, was cast to hell with his one-third portion of souls as Satan and his demons. To thwart God for casting him to hell, he would constantly tempt us with various sins and unbelief to take us away from God.

It was in this preexistence that we could choose the families that we would live with while we were here on earth and into the eternities. This family, my mother, father, two sisters, and two brothers were mine from now until forever. I always thought of my mom and siblings with great joy at the thought of always being with them, but there was also so much fear that I could never escape my father.

Once we are born on earth, it was our mission to live a Christ-like life and to share the gospel with everyone. Once we died, we would be judged and get to go to one of three heavens. The best of the best went to the Celestial Kingdom. To achieve this meant that you had lived righteously, been approved by God, and been married in the temple. It was the gold medal of heaven, and it's where I was determined to go.

At the end of our lesson, we sang a closing song about how families are together forever. I was left with so many questions. What about my dad? Are we going to be together forever? He wasn't going to make it to the highest kingdom. Does that mean we are still family? Did I really choose this life? Did I know I was going to be living with him? Did I know how many years I was going to have to endure his abuse? Why did God allow him to be my dad? Did he know how evil he was? Can't he see the dark shadow that surrounds his soul? What about his lack of compassion for those that live around him? Where is the light of Christ in him? The church is always telling me I have wonderful parents who were kind and dear, according to the songs. They said that my father was my priesthood leader, a mouthpiece for God, and the one I should defer to in all situations. I know the bishop knows about him because that is why he didn't take the sacrament each Sunday.

The youth teachers assured me I chose this, not really knowing our situation, and that God would never give me more than I can endure. Why did I choose this? If I did, then why? Was there a lesson I was supposed to learn? Maybe I chose this family to save another soul from having to endure his never-ending torment? I decided I could live with that answer, that I chose this to save another soul, at least then it has some meaning. Otherwise, it all felt so pointless, so depressing. I had to find something to believe.

The next class was called sharing time, in which the three to eleven-year-olds would sit together. This class started with a prayer, song, and then a child who had been previously chosen would give their testimony of the church. They were all the same. "I KNOW this church is true. I KNOW that Joseph Smith was a prophet and that we have a current prophet today. I know I am a child of God and he loves me. Amen." If the child was unsure of what to say, their parent would be right there to give them the words. Next would be a small lesson from one of our peers, usually only lasting a few moments. Today's lesson was on the Holy Ghost and how he can guide us through this life if only take the time to listen to him and make good choices so that he can be with us all the time. It is taught that if we sin and do not take time to repent, we lose the gift of the Holy Ghost and would be

left in the dark and away from God's love. It is expected that we will make mistakes, but also that we will take those sins to the bishop so we can properly stay in line with the will of the Lord.

Next was another song time. The first song was about preparing ourselves for the temple while we are still young by staying pure, promising to obey God and his prophets, and making sacred covenants. Next was a livelier song about serving a mission when we grow up. So many of the songs were about making sure we stayed on the only path, the righteous path, the church path. I was so grateful to have been born into God's only true church. As we sang these songs, we dreamed of going on missions or getting married in the temple one day to the person that could take us to the highest kingdom.

During sharing time, I sat next to my friend. During song time when no one else would hear, two of the other girls told us to grab our chins as hard as we could, that after five minutes it would feel all tingly and they would do this with us. We were bored and so followed along with them, gripping our chins as hard as we could through one song. When the song ended, they removed their hands where they had only pretended to be gripping and then made fun of us because we had to walk out with red chins.

"I can't believe they fell for that. They are so stupid," the girls said just loud enough for us to hear, but not so loud they would get in trouble with the surrounding adults.

The words hurt; the unacceptance hurt, but it wasn't unusual. These were the popular girls at church, from the popular families, and they knew it. My friend and I were the outcast, we knew that too. But that's just how it was in every Mormon church. We didn't know how to change it and on the few times that we tried, we were just told to "turn the other cheek", or "just to ignore their behavior."

There was a point in our friendship about this time where I knew I would have to make a choice between avoiding harassment from these girls by trying to conform to their world or continuing my friendship with Amy. I longed to be included in the larger group, but how could I act like them? It just wasn't in my heart to be that mean to anyone. Besides, my friend was a far kinder and more genuine person than all of them combined. She was one of the few people who I could be myself around, who I knew would not judge me for the peculiarities of my family. Her house looked lived in; it resembled my own home. It lacked the pristine conditions of a typical Mormon family but allowed a place of comfort, freedom, and no judgments. It was never really a choice for me when I compared the compassion of my friend to the harshness and cruelty of these other Mormon youth. Their treatment of us just brought our friendship closer together.

After church, each Sunday Mom and Dad would take a long nap, leaving the four of us kids to watch TV. That night, our home teacher stopped by to say hello. He was as tall as he was wide, carrying so much weight it was hard for him to walk or breathe. He drove up in his beat-up old pickup truck with the RV-style cab that I think he lived in. I don't remember much about this man, but his presence always left me creeped out. We had to sit on the couch and listen to him preach to us about making good choices and always obeying our parents, even if what they said made little sense to us. He said a prayer and went on his way. I was grateful when he left.

∞

There was a time when dad would take me or my sister out to Taco Bell for a father-daughter date night once a week. He had bought us a poster-sized fuzzy picture and we sat in the restaurant's corner while coloring in the picture for an hour. We didn't have a choice in this, he had decided we were bonding, and this is how he was going to do it. I hated this time with him and always felt so tense. I think he chose a public setting so we would relax knowing he wouldn't pull anything in a public place, or maybe it was more about trying to control his own impulses. It seemed as if he was in a public space he wouldn't be so tempted by his own demons. It didn't matter. I felt the eyes of the employees on me the entire time. Could they see my discomfort? Could they tell I didn't want to be there? Did they know why? Did they know what he did when no one was looking? I could feel the shame creeping up to color my cheeks. After these trips, restaurants always felt like I was sitting in a fishbowl, exposed to the world. I hated it.

Earlier that day, I had been invited to White Water theme park with a friend from the cul-de-sac. On the way home, I asked dad if I could go with my friend. He sat there for a long time and then said I could go if I was willing to do whatever he wanted on the car ride home.

"Just this short time home. It's only a ten minute ride." dad said.

Anytime I wanted to do things with my friends, there was always a payment involved, a quid pro quo. My choices were always to submit to him or never be allowed to do the things I wanted to with my friends, and he would take what he wanted that night, anyway. If I wanted to go to a sleepover or have a friend visit, I had to pay. If I wanted to go to the movies with a friend, it would cost me. No payment meant no escape. Even when I tried to avoid his payments, he got what he wanted anyway and then pretended we agreed to some type of slimy deal. There was no actual choice.

He put his hand on my thigh, his fingers moving in a constant rhythm, click-click, click-click, click. I pushed his hand down to my knee, but he moved his hand back up, with a bit of force this time. I pushed his hand back down. He left it there for a minute click, click, click. Then his hand moved higher up my leg again. I pushed his hand back down with as much force as I could, but I was no match for him. This was a struggle that happened anytime we were alone in a car.

He asked again if I wanted to go to the water park. He made me lay down and put my head in his lap while he drove down Sandy Springs Road toward our house while his hand fought with my underwear. My eyes focused on the power lines outside the car window moving up and down when they met with each power pole. The clouds behind them moved at a slower rate. The song from Sunday came back to mind. "I am a child of God, with goodly parents' kind and dear." How did they get it so wrong? Surely, this isn't what God wanted for me? Was it? Can you make it stop, God? Had I done something to deserve this? 246 power lines later, we pulled onto our street.

I went to the water park that weekend with my friend, and while I had fun, it was tainted with the memory of what I endured to be there. It wasn't worth it. If I could have found a way out, I would have done it. It didn't really matter what I did or what I wanted, he would always find me, corner me, and take what he wanted. I was only ten years old, homeschooled, and secluded in many ways. It was all that I knew.

∞

Summer was fast approaching. I was impatient for the moment that my friends would be available to play all day. I still missed going to school and it was often lonely at home. Every now and then Dad would get so frustrated by mom's lack of homeschooling that he sat us down at the round kitchen table to work on a list of spelling words for a few minutes.

I'm not sure why he did this, but I think it was to prove a point to mom. It wasn't because he cared about our schooling. My lack of daily education proved that my schooling was a low priority. Was it so that he could ease his own guilt about taking us out of school? Was it to show mom he was "helping" her by spending fifteen minutes with us on a spelling list? It felt more like dad saying, "Look at me, look at me, I'm being a good dad." Maybe it was his way of putting my mother down, wordlessly saying, "You're home all day and not getting anything done, let ME show you how it SHOULD be done.

I sat at the table writing the word I had spelled wrong ten times. My legs were folded to keep my feet away from the floor, avoiding the fleas. Despite me efforts, one had worked its way into the fold of my socks and bit my ankle several times. I scratched at the fresh bites.

"Question" dad gave me the next word "Q-U-S-T-O-N" I said. "Wrong, write it down ten times and try again dad said. We worked through the list of fifteen words until I either got them right or dad got frustrated and moved on to other things.

I woke up the next morning and knew dad had already gone to work by the sunlight that filtered in through the window above our bed. I loved watching the dust move slowly across the beam of light, reminding me of the soft way the snow fell on Christmas morning at my granny and pappy's house. In the corner of our room was a built-in reading nook where we played with our stuffed animals and kept two gerbils that Rachael had rescued from the library at her school where she could still attend. As they moved around the cage, I could hear their small snuffles. Deborah snored softly next to me, a soothing sound to me. I love quiet moments like this when my thoughts had the chance to explore in any direction they wanted. The solitude was a rare comfort.

Mom came in, waking us up. she had made us an egg sandwich for breakfast that morning. We were going to a new home school group that day. We met inside one of their churches and gathered in a large room. The moms all sat together while we hurried off to find kids to play with us. There was a group of kids playing on the small stage, but when we went to join them, they stopped their game and stared at us, not letting us join them. I walked in another direction and tried to play with some other kids who were throwing a ball back and forth, but they wouldn't throw the ball to me. On the way home, I asked my mom why the kids wouldn't play with us.

"It's because we're Mormon and they don't believe we are Christians," she responded.

"Why?", I asked. I knew we Believed in God, wasn't that what made you a Christian?

"Because we believe that God, Jesus Christ, and the Holy Ghost are three separate people, and they believe they are combined into one being." Mom answered me.

It was confusing because it just didn't seem like a big difference to me. At least, not a difference means you should treat other people poorly. Can't we believe differently and still be friends? Their actions just reaffirmed that I belonged to the right church.

∞

One afternoon, mom came home one day loaded with bags of candy, chips, beef jerky, squeeze cheese, and crackers. She was preparing to send Jason and Deborah off to two different camps that summer. One was through the church youth program and the other was for the John Birch Society. I was sad, and more than a little jealous, as I watched my siblings load up their goodies into their suitcases. This year, mom was going with Deborah to church camp. I wanted to go with them, but I was still too young. I wish I could have been around the kids my age for an entire week. I knew I was going as soon as I turned twelve because that was the age church camps required, but I wanted to go now. I hated to be left behind.

When Deborah and Jason came back from the camps, they were exhausted from lack of sleep, and yet full of an energy that wasn't often seen in my house. They were filled with tales of campers sneaking out at night and getting caught by the counselors, but no one was really in trouble. They told me about what they learned at the John Birch Camp. Things like how money got its value and the different types of government. In the Mormon church, camps were about the hikes they went on, the food they made, and how the spirit of God was present when the youth gave their testimonies about their beliefs in, and about, the one true church of God over a campfire.

The rest of summer passed in the warm rays of the Georgia sunshine. Mom had bought passes to the water park, and we went to the discovery center a few more times. We also made a trip to Antelope, North Carolina. Mostly, we spent our time riding bikes around the neighborhood with friends and playing hide-and-go-seek in our backyard. We climbed trees and played in the creeks. We made purchases from the ice cream truck and had sleepovers with friends.

My mind had separated in a way. I had gotten good at keeping my nights from destroying my days. I was good at enjoying the moments when dad was at work or away for any reason. The blackness came as soon as I needed it, protecting me, but was always gone the next morning so I could run and play with the unrestrained freedom of childhood.

But he always came back home, and with him came the ever-present fear and anxiety. It was like I had trouble breathing when he was in the house, always on guard for the next attack. I tried to make sure I was always near another person, never alone. His eyes were always on us, watching for any opportunity and keeping us on edge all the time.

As summer turned into fall, we signed up for piano lessons and soccer. Mom helped with the soccer sign-ups, snacks, and in the office. She was there for all our games, actively cheering us on. In this place, I could see that she was happy, like at the library at church. She laughed and chatted with the other adults. She was happiest when she could help other people.

That Halloween, mom worked for hours sewing our individual Halloween costumes. She sat beside me and taught me how to sew and fixed the machine when the thread got tangled. I wanted to be pebbles from the Flintstones cartoon. She sewed a bone-shaped plushie that held my hair straight up off the top of my head and flowered out at the ends. The dress was orange with large brown dots. That fabric reached down to the top of my knees. When my costume was complete, we went out as a family trick-or-treating around the neighborhood with a pack of kids from church.

Mom and dad were fighting again. It was happening more frequently. They fought about Rachael, money, how mom thought dad needed to wear more than underwear around us, and how dad thought mom should do more to homeschool us. They were so unhappy together. For several days after each fight, mom would go to her computer and play solitaire while ignoring us and the animals. The more they fought, the more our house declined. Rachael brought home a couple of cats, covered in fleas, and even though we washed the cats, the flea infestation exploded. Then the dog started pooping in the house because no one let him outside and it was getting cleaned less and less. The pantry moths found a permanent home in our food and the space under the stairs filled with spiders. Mom was spending more and more time on her computer and less and less time with us.

Then dad was fired. I remember hearing the word fire when he told mom, but when he talked about it to other people, he said his contract ended. I'm not sure what the truth was, but either way, there was no more money coming into the house.

The rocks dad had bought were piling up, and so were the bills. My parent's solution was to rent a booth at Yesteryear Flea Market on the weekends. Our booth was set up with rocks like geode bookends, amethyst crystals, pyrite, obsidian, and other varied specimens. We bought some trays full of silver rings to add to the display and increase our profit. Each weekend we made a few hundred dollars.

Once we sold off dad's initial collection of rocks, he came home several large boxes of clothing and other knick knacks to sell at the flea market. Then we went to auctions and bought even more junk to sell.

The flea markets were a mix of fun and work. We could walk around and see the different shops when business was slow but had to work hard when it was busy. Yesteryear Flea Market had a great magic shop with gum that would snap at your fingers when you took a piece and rings that squirted water. I loved to browse their selection, quietly calculating how much I needed to save to buy the next trick.

There was a booth filled to the brim with unpainted ceramics owned by an older lady who took me under her wing. She taught me how to paint the ceramics, and even let me take one home after spending the day helping me. I painted it to look like our black and white dog.

Another booth held several coin pusher games filled with rows of quarters and other prizes stacked up waiting to be pushed over the edge by customers dropping new quarters in. I learned to feel around the edges of the space where the quarters fell and find coins that had been left behind by the previous people. This allowed me to play for free. Occasionally the owner of the booth would smile at me and hand me a few dollars in quarters so I could play a little longer. I watched as some people spent several twenty-dollar bills and walk away with nothing after a few hours. I knew I needed to wait for just the right moment to drop my quarters in, often walking away with a small profit.

One time while I was playing on the quarter machines, a lady pushed me out of the way. She had seen that a large number of quarters were about to fall, and she wanted the machine. I knew she was being rude, but she was an adult so I let her take over my machine. I went back to dad to tell him what happened.

"Why did you let her?" he asked

What do you mean? I thought. I have the ability to say "no" to her? But she was an adult. We were not allowed to tell adults no. I learned this in school, in church, and at home. We were to always be respectful, listen, and, most importantly, obey. Why did I let her? Well, it was all that I knew how to do.

"You didn't have to let her push you around," he said when I didn't answer. "You could have said no."

This thought was left rolling around in my head for years before I could use it. it was so intriguing, so different. What could I do with that information? Could I tell anyone no? Was this just for a stranger? Did it apply to my dad? It was the start of my realizing my own ability to change my situation.

I could have told her no, I thought with wonder.

∞

After having success at Yesteryear Flea Market, we picked up some shows during the week. The night before the markets, we drove for hours to either Hickory, North Carolina, or Pickens, South Carolina. We camped in the backseat of the blue crown Victoria in the parking lot. By 6 a.m., we would set up our booth so we could be done before the show opened at 8 a.m. The shows would only last a few hours before we loaded up the small, red, wooden trailer that dad had bought and headed home.

One day while we were driving home, a car passed us in the adjoining lane. I watched as they drove parallel with us waving and screaming for us to roll down the window. Dad slowed down and opened his window

"Your trailer is on fire!", they yelled at us before dropping back in the lane and pulling behind us again. Dad quickly pulled over, and we put the flames out with the water we kept in the trunk for when the car overheated. The trailer had bounced off its frame and onto the tire, causing enough friction to set it ablaze. Dad tried to fix it, but it happened a few more times before we stopped using that trailer.

∞

Jason was rarely with us on any of the flea market trips. I'm not sure why. I don't think dad liked him very much. He always yelled at him, and even though he didn't treat Deborah and me great, he treated Jason worse. Dad was always picking on him, yelling at him, and never spent quality time with him.

Jason was bullied by the kids on the bus, and it was no different from how he was treated at home. One day, he saw a squirrel fall off the power line. He saved it but got bit in the process. When he got home, we put the squirrel in a box and took it to a local vet who took care of him. That was Jason. He loved animals and always went out of his way to help them. He loved people too, but his huge heart was often bullied into hiding by dad's abuse. Jason turned aloof, even mean sometimes. There was a distance between us because of this. He would pick on me and drive me crazy with his constant sounds and movement. I was up for the challenge, usually throwing it all back at him.

I remember dad yelling at Jason one day, I'm not really sure what it was for, maybe a missed chore, homework that needed to be done, or maybe something got broken, but I remember dad punching the wall leaving a large hole saying that Jason better feel lucky that dad hit the wall and not him.

Rachael was never really a part of my life, at least from what I can remember. I wanted to be around her, to know her better, but she looked like she was always surrounded by a shroud of anger, and I wasn't invited into her world. I walked into her room one night and I saw her and dad next to each other, naked. It was more than I could process, though, so I closed the door and walked away. I understood her anger.

There was another huge fight that night. As much as she loved us during the days, she couldn't handle the nights either. It was too much for all of us to bear the burden of this one man's sins. I don't understand why God can't just make it stop. Is it wrong to wish dad would die? God, can't you just take him home and away from us? How could one person create so much terror and panic for his whole family? He was like a black cloud, a cancer that kept growing and made living unbearable. Did I really choose this God? I mean, that's what we are taught at church. We had been sealed for eternity;

we sang about it at church. He was our literal eternity. Where is the
hope i
    n that?

Chapter Five
Am I Worthy?

Dad came home from work one day when I was twelve years old and told the family that we were moving to North Carolina into my grandparent's vacation house in Antelope, North Carolina. That weekend, we rented a large U-Haul truck and loaded up everything we could. There still wasn't enough room and we left a lot behind, including the family dog and my oldest sister. She was seventeen and didn't want to move with us, so we just left her. The move was rushed, almost like we were running away. We barely had time to say goodbye to some of our friends before we made the drive to our new home.

The house was only used occasionally over the past twenty years as a vacation home. The absence of people allowed the dust, grime, mold, and bugs to move in. However, you could see the remnants of elegance in the beautifully carved dining room table where each chair felt like your own personal throne. The chairs were padded with a thick orange velvet on the seat and backs. The backs were taller than me when I stood next to them. They had thickly carved edges made from deep brown wood that crawled up to the top to form an intricate pattern of swirling leaves that narrowed at its peak. The table itself was a dark brown wood that matched the color of freshly roasted coffee with hints of caramel. The Table was at least twelve feet long. It spoke of large parties and family gatherings.

There was more elegance to be found in the stone fireplace. It had been built by hand by dad and his brothers. Each stone had been carefully placed, reaching from the floor to the top of the twenty foot ceiling. The fireplace was so big that I could have sat inside of it. Now, a few of the stones were coming loose. There was also an old record player that stretched the length of the kitchen counter. It still worked, but we were not allowed to touch it. I was told that these things were made to show off the wealth of my grandfather. Now they had been left behind in a heavy layer of dust and forgotten memories.

Every room, closet, and shelf had been left with evidence of a different era. There were clothes that belonged to my uncle when he was little. The bathroom had someone else's old toothbrush and toothpaste still sitting in the drawer. The closets held a vintage keyboard and accordion, along with an assortment of tools and light bulbs. The cupboards were filled with my grandmother's dishes and unused spices. This wasn't our house. It was just a place to be; Temporary. It was Grandmother's way of bailing dad out when he lost his job. A place to hide, I think.

The main entrance was on the second floor up a set of stairs that were covered in mildew, making them slippery when it rained. The upper deck wrapped around two sides of the house. When you walked inside the kitchen was straight across. It had an island in the middle, and the record player along the backside of it separated the kitchen from the dining room. The kitchen sink was along the back wall with a window that overlooked the unfenced side yard of dense forest. To the right was the living room with the stone fireplace. The floor was covered in a two-inch length, green, shag carpet that was so heavy with dust that no amount of vacuuming could rescue it.

The living room had a couch and an old TV that we could play movies on. I remember joking about watching the great American ant race, which was really just the black and white static emanating from the TV. In the back corner of the house was the dining room that held the antique dining table. All three rooms were together with an open floor plan. The wall along the side of the living room and dining room contained more windows than wall. There was a double sliding glass door that opened onto the massive, covered porch. Above the door, there was a cathedral ceiling with two windows that created a triangle reaching the very top of the vaulted ceiling. The porch had a metal roof, and the ground was covered in a green outdoor carpet. The trees were so thick around the house that we couldn't see the other houses that were close by.

To the right of the front door, there were two closets with a set of double doors on each that opened to old fur coats, suits, and other belongings that had long been forgotten. Next to the closets, there was a hallway that had another set of double-door storage closets and the room I slept in. On the right side of the hallway, there was a carpeted bathroom and my parent's bedroom.

My room didn't feel like a bedroom. It had a large eight-foot table along the back wall that was covered in boxes of unsorted paperwork that overflowed around and under the table. In the other available corner was a computer desk with the family computer that was smothered in more papers and unopened mail that had been moved and then dumped. The closet was filled with old clothes that had been marinating in mothballs and other boxes that I had never investigated. I slept on an air mattress that had been thrown on the ground as an afterthought. There was nothing personal in that room to make it mine; No place to put anything, it was just the place I had to sleep. At least it was upstairs though; the downstairs always felt a bit foreboding to me.

Between the front door and the living room, there was a narrow spiral staircase that led downstairs. The railing was solid metal that had been wrapped in rope, now frayed. The stairs were open risers that always made me nervous that I would fall through, or something would grab me through the steps. As I walked down the stairs, I could feel the dampness of the air increase, and then I was hit with the smell of aged mildew, mold, and dust. It felt like an abandoned dungeon. It expressed, in the dark shadows and hanging spider webs, how we all felt about living here.

At the bottom of the stairs, there was another door facing the driveway. There was an additional living room that was even larger than the one upstairs. A kitchenette was built into the wall on the left side of the living room. The right side had another massive porch that mirrored the size and shape of the porch above it. Between the stairs and the kitchenette was a hallway that had three more bedrooms, another bathroom with carpet, and a laundry room. The living room held a Baby Grand piano and a couch. When my brother sat down on the couch, a huge puff of dust billowed out. It reached deep into his lungs and ripped his breath out, smothering him. He was coughing and gasping for air as he walked outside to try to catch his breath. It took over twenty minutes.

Once we moved in, you couldn't see the couch and piano anymore because they were covered in boxes, turning the space into nothing but storage. The boxes were stacked on top of each other, floor to ceiling. The only way to move around was to snake your way around the boxes and the mess left behind from rummaging through them, and hope that nothing fell on you.

More of our boxes were stored outside on the downstairs porch. The porch had been covered in a green, artificial grass carpet that, over the years, had built up a layer of mold and algae, creating a slimy, slippery film across the carpet. We built shelves to keep our boxes off the ground, but it didn't protect our things from the rain that the wind that blew through or the humidity and the sun that filtered through the trees. I guess in the end, it didn't matter, as we never unpacked the boxes. The contents were trashed the moment we packed them in Georgia.

The carpet downstairs seemed to hold even more dust in its short, orange, fibers than the green shag upstairs. I'm not sure if the carpet ever had padding underneath it, but if it did, it had been worn away leaving the carpet to sit on the hard cement below. The back half of the downstairs, where the bedrooms were located, had been built below ground level and was not properly sealed. Water from the ground outside seeped in through the painted cement walls, leaving trails of black mold that reached into the carpet, mingling with the dust and dirt. On a good day, the carpets were only a little moist. The dampness was about the same as when you just had your carpets cleaned. On the bad days, the water sat just below the carpet level so that if you jumped, the water would splash up and hit your knees. It wasn't the kind of place where you walked barefoot.

My sister's bedroom was in the far back corner of the downstairs. The water damage was the most severe in her room because two of her walls faced the outside ground, allowing the moisture of our rainforest environment to accumulate there. The trail of mold reached from her windows down into the carpet and onto her mattress that laid on the floor for the entire year and a half that we were there. My sisters soft snored had turned into consistent, hacking cough that, like the white noise of a fan, blurred into the background of our daily life. Her room was almost empty except for her bed and headboard. I remember she had a green sandcastle made of rock and was covered with a beautiful sparkling glitter on her headboard. There was a sliver of natural light that came in through the small one-foot-wide window that sat five inches below the ceiling and a few inches below was the ground outside. The other window sat below the backyard deck, which blocked the light.

My brother slept in the room across from Deborah, but he stayed in his room, and I rarely saw him while we lived in this house. I can't even remember what his room looked like. He might have slept on a couch. I remember the deep hacking sounds of his coughing that intertwined with Deborah's and then faded into the same background.

The smell of this house wasn't the worst part for me, it was the bugs that lived inside with us. We would have to watch out for the camel crickets, flying ants, spiders, and oh so many fleas. The camel crickets were at least twice the size of a normal cricket with brown and tan spotted coloring on their body. They had an enormous set of legs that would jump farther than I was comfortable with and long antennas that would wave at me when I turned the lights on. When we moved into the house, these crickets were there to welcome us, especially in the showers of the carpeted bathrooms. It felt like they were just waiting for the right moment to jump out of the dark to attack me. They were harmless, I was told, but I feared them anyway. There were also millions of flying ants that almost blacked out the cathedral windows in the upstairs living room. I had never seen ants that flew before, much less thousands of them in one spot. They mostly stayed in the windows, except when we found them in the fibers of the shag carpet while we watched TV.

Then there were the fleas.

So. Many. Fleas.

We had taken them with us, packed in our boxes and clothing from our previous house. They loved me, and they thrived in the moist environment that we provided them. I was their self-serve meal ticket for gourmet blood. My scalp itched as I felt them walk around in my hair. My arms and legs were covered in scabs from the incessant scratching of endless bites. We could never get away from them. Even after we moved, they traveled in our clothes and in our car, like an unwanted passenger itching its way through our world. We could be at the grocery store and feel one biting us through our socks, or at the flea market and have one under our shirt. There was never an escape from the fleas.

Survival is a weird thing. You're literally struggling to breathe every day and terrified of what the night brings. We lived in a state of fight or flight with no idea how to fight and nowhere to go if we fled. We were stuck in this house, in these situations, secluded from the world. My mind was always looking for a way to cope or a reason to open my eyes the next day, because, wanted or not, the next day kept happening. To survive, my mind looked for all the good things in the world, for any sign that I was going to be ok today, for any hope of a good future that I could count on. Even the smallest things can make a difference when you live in this state, and we found joy in simple things.

Outside was filled with beautiful, tall, vibrant trees that included all the shades of green. There were tall pine trees, twisted rhododendrons, and magnolia trees. The area we lived in rained almost every day. It's considered a temperate rainforest, one of two in North America. My brother, sister, and I spent hours turning over every rock we could find on to reveal salamanders, hundreds of snails, and all the centipedes and rolly-pollies you could imagine. I stood on the top deck looking out into this magnificent dense forest, breathing in the fresh air, and admired the view many times.

One time when my sister and I were on the deck calling out for a kitten that ran away, we made meowing sounds, and then we heard a voice meowing back at us through the trees. We never met this man, but he was always there to meow back at us through the trees. It comforted us knowing we were not alone in those woods. After dad caught us meowing back and forth with the man, he told us the man was dangerous, and that we needed to stop.

In July and August, there were more blackberries than we could pick. They were all bigger than my whole thumb and so plump that the juices leaked out just by touching them. Our palms would be stained purple by the time we had gotten our fill of them.

School had quickly fallen out of our life; I wasn't even pretending to work on it anymore. There were laws in Georgia that kept track of what we were learning. We were supposed to pass state exams to show proof that we were learning. In North Carolina, there were no applicable laws forcing us to stay on track because no one knew we were here.

My father was working about five hours away in another city and was gone most of the time. He only came home on the weekends. Often, he would disappear downstairs for long periods of time. I was so busy trying to hide from him I didn't realize it until later in my life, but he was spending time with my sister. The nights that he was home, and after mom was asleep, he would still slip into my room with his vindictive ultimatums. I would slip into the darkness, blocking out all of my emotions except the pure hatred I had of this...man?...demon?... Monster? That I called Dad.

If he wasn't directing his unwanted attention at us, then he was in the bedroom fighting with mom. I remember overhearing once that no one knew where we were, and that the bills for the house were still in my grandmother's name. When I asked about going to play with some of the neighborhood kids, I was told no, that no one should know where we lived. They fought about our schooling and how the state of North Carolina did not know that we were here. I had a feeling that we were hiding from more than just missed schooling. We moved too fast; our house had not sold. We didn't move TO anything, no job, just AWAY from something. Dad worked over five hours away, which also seemed suspicious to me. Why did we not moved to where he worked? We were being careful not to make our presence known. We were hiding, I just didn't know from what.

Sometimes during the week, Mom would drive us back down to our house in Georgia to finish packing up the remains of the house and clean it up enough to sell it. My older sister stayed mostly with friends, but she used the house to throw parties for her friends. She left it all for us to clean up. We were left to clean the condoms found on my brother's bed, the red solo cups, and food covered in ants. Under the back porch, the black trash bags were piled almost a story high, a 5ft long black snake had claimed the pile as his own. The dog had been left at the house. He had gone into the bathroom to drink some water and must have closed the door; he had scratched and chewed a large hole through the door to get out. With the house being mostly absent, the flea population had exploded. When I first walk into the house, my legs would be almost black from the fleas. You could hear them make little clicking noises as they jumped around, desperate for food. We put down water bowls filled with water and dawn then watched as the fleas jumped in, drowning as they tried to climb on each other.

∞

After several months, we began attending church in Rockville, thirty minutes away. We had been to this church a few times over the years as we visited my granny and pappy's house who lived down the road. I made a few friends here, but most of the girls were distant, or maybe I was. I'm not sure anymore.

Around this time, a missionary in the Rockville church had recently been caught molesting several of the members' children. This created a lot of upheaval in the ward. I was told to babysit the younger children in the primary room while the adults met to talk things over. It was a tiny congregation, less than a hundred people. Several families left the church permanently, disappointed with how the church handled the situation. The Elder went to jail for a small about of time. Afterward, the higher leadership sent out a nationwide e-mail that missionaries could no longer be around children without the supervision of their parents.

We started going to church in Camden, an hour away from where we were currently living. I guess all the commotion was too close for Dad's comfort. Camden Ward was my home church for the next eleven years.

Now that I was older and a part of the Young Women's, a program for girls ages 12-18, the lessons had changed a bit. When they talked about eternal families. the focus was now on who we would marry and what we needed to avoid be pure. We learned the important skills needed to be a good wife one day, like sewing, good manners, and crafting.

Most of the lessons, both on Sundays and Wednesdays, were about keeping God's covenants and staying pure for the person we were going to marry. Through marriage, we could continue our eternal family in the Celestial kingdom, the highest of all the heavens. To stay pure meant that I would wear modest clothing, no dating until I was sixteen, and then only in groups. No Single dating until I was eighteen because then it's time to date with the intention of getting married. Being pure meant no making out, no sex, no masturbation, and no porn. My clothing had to go down to my knees, and cover my shoulders. We were to follow the words of wisdom presented in our scriptures that mention no tea and no coffee. It also meant living a Christlike life like by serving our fellow men, reading scriptures, and praying multiple times a day. We were to always Keep in mind that we were the example of what a Mormon was, especially in our rural town where there were very few Mormons. The pressure to be the perfect Mormon "at all times and in all things, and in all places" a quote from the young women theme we had to repeat any time we were together, was very real.

At the age of twelve, I would be interviewed once a year, or more if I had broken any of the rules, in a worthiness interview with the bishop. He would sit behind his large desk and overstuffed padded chair, while I sat on my side in a smaller chair, similar to one found in a waiting room. The chairs indicated who had the authority in this situation. This was God's literal mouthpiece, and he was going to let me know if I was worthy to be in God's house, or if I needed to repent for my sins. Even when I had done nothing wrong, I still found these interviews to be intimidating and scary.

He would specifically ask if we had been intimate with anyone, and wanted specifics. Did we masturbate? Did we pay our full ten percent tithing? Did we believe in God? Do we promise to obey and support our local leadership and those in Utah including the prophet? Did we associate with anyone who was against the church? These questions are almost impossible for an abused girl to answer. I can't tell the truth without losing my family, but I can't lie either, because God would tell the bishop. Wasn't he supposed to know everything? My father was always right outside the door for these interviews, watching my face when I walked out for signs that I had talked. I answered the questions all the right way, carefully separating the things I had done from the things that were done to me. A careful balance that I had to maintain to keep my family together and God happy. I passed. I was found worthy and was successfully issued a temple recommend. The recommend is a small piece of paper that has been signed by both the bishop, and the leader above him called the stake president before entering the temple.

There was a temple dedication happening for the Atlanta Georgia temple that they were broadcasting to the churches that were too far away to attend in person. All that I knew about the ceremony was that I needed to have a little white handkerchief for something they called the hosanna shout. I didn't know what that was, but I brought my white hanky. The ceremony began with prayer and then a talk about the beauty of temples, about the work for the dead that would be done there. I imagined baptizing everyone in the world that had died without the chance to be baptized for themselves. This is done so that they have a chance of going to heaven. I listened as he talked about eternal families and pictured my family, as a whole unit, having made it to the eternal realm together, healed.

For the dedication, we had to hold the hanky high and say in unison together, Hosana, Hosana, Hosana. It came out in a united, monotonous tone that set me on edge. We continued, "To God, and the Lamb. A-men, A-men and A-men" on the amens we waved our little white hankies around. On the "A" sound we held our hankies high, on the "men" sound we bring them down. Three times. I'm not sure why, but that chanting sent a trickle of fear down my spine and throughout my body. It felt unholy and wrong. Something was off, but it felt like a distant memory too far back to remember.

∞

I was finally old enough to attend my first church dance. It was for the youth church members that lived in western North Carolina. I was excited about this opportunity, but also nervous because I had to ride with the members from the Rockville church, and I didn't know them very well. We met at the church with about five other youth. I saw a girl my age and walked over to talk with her. She seemed nice and helped ease some of my anxiety. Our leader, Brother K, arrived in his white minivan. I was uncomfortable riding in a van with people I didn't know very well, but I was too excited about the dance to back out.

The anxiety I felt leaked out in nervous, but eager chatter with Brother K. He didn't carry the same air of arrogant authority that some of the other men carried. He felt more down to earth. He talked with me like I was his equal. He asked me questions with genuine interest and answered my many questions. My guard slowly dropped away as I relaxed, feeling safe in his presence. It was unusual for me to relax around older men, especially those from church. Why was he so different? Why did I feel safe around him? It was more than just a friendly conversation; he had a presence that just made you feel loved and accepted. I felt compelled to get to know him and his family better.

The next time we went to church in his ward, I met his wife and children and each of them glowed with a type of happiness that stood apart from the other members. They thought and acted differently than the rest of the church members. They didn't judge other people; they didn't carry with them that air of being better than everyone that is common in the Mormon faith (although no one at church wants to admit that). They were down to earth and worst of all to my parents, they were democrats in a world of republicans. I wasn't completely sure what that meant, but I heard my parents complain about it a lot.

All I knew for sure was that they exuded a sense of calm, kindness, and love. I wanted to be around them. I wanted to soak up that goodness, to pull it in and make it a part of who I am. I wanted to know what made them feel so different. How could I make my home like that one day? They were the picture of the family that I wanted to recreate in my own life, where the kids are safe and supported in their dreams, free to be uniquely themselves. Where it is ok if you think different, or to just be different. The type of house you were excited to come home to. They were my example that it was possible, and they gave me hope.

Chapter Six
Pawns

The true history of my extended family is a mystery. We were told a variety of stories that consistently reinforced that they were dangerous people, and we had to stay away from them. The stories felt fabricated, like the truth had been twisted and reformed to create the reality my parents believed.

My mother's father was an alcoholic who abused his children. At least, that is what I heard in the whispered rumors. Except for a one-week trip to Florida when we were younger, we never met, saw, or even talked to her family. They never existed to us.

The history of my dad's side of the family was more complicated. His mom, who we referred to as Grandmother, was very particular about the way we addressed her. If we tried to call her an informal name like Grandma, we would be corrected instantly. Grandmother's name just felt formal, distant, and cold.

Grandmother took us for weeks in the summer and spoiled us on the holidays. She created crafts for us to do at her house and let me play with the miniature figurines on her wall. However, she still had that formality like her name implied to us. For example, we were to wear a dress if we went out to eat, we were to be polite no matter what, and we were never, under any circumstances, to show disrespect to our father.

Grandmother and Dad's relationship was full of constant defensiveness for each other. If I said something to Grandmother such as "I don't want to wear this dress.", Dad would be there to tell me I had to listen. If I disagreed with Dad, Grandmother would quickly come to his defense, it made no difference who was right or wrong. There was no logic to it. Dad used Grandmother for her money, constantly "borrowing" money, a need created by his own poor choices. She was always there to provide it for him. He was the favorite of her three sons, and it was noticeable. Around the time I was born in Utah, Dad had gone to court for abusing my siblings. Grandmother hired the very best lawyers to keep him out of jail.

There was a weird energy between them where the other could do no wrong, ever.

Grandmother had three boys, one of whom was adopted. From I heard, he was a gifted to her from her first husband, as a distraction. My grandmother and biological grandfather divorced before I was born. I was told that He was cold, mean, and ill-tempered. He was a successful lawyer who thrived on using words to manipulate the people around him for fun. I was told how he could convince you that a bright blue sky was purple. He was dangerous, and therefore we were never supposed to meet him. He didn't even know that I had been born for fear that he would kidnap me like he did my siblings.

I was told that my older three siblings had gone for a visit to see my biological grandfather and his new wife. During the visit, they sent my sisters back home, but tried to kidnap my brother and keep him as their own. They sent my sisters back and kept Jason. I was told they kidnapped him. This was during my father's court case, and it is rumored that my bio grandfather spent his time with Jason filling him with lies so that he could gain custody of him. My mom explained that Jason was never the same after that. All I knew was they were dangerous and a threat to our family. What kind of person intentionally breaks up a family? They were the enemy.

Grandmother married Grandaddy Roy, and he is the grandparent that I grew up with and loved. He was Grandaddy, a warm and inviting soul. The kind of Granddaddy that you could curl up next to and he would wrap his arm around your shoulders and give you a hug that you feel all the way to your heart. He was brilliant and would talk about things I never understood, but that didn't matter because we loved him. Sometimes he would have a prickly side, especially if we disagreed with grandmother. He was always there to defend her in an overbearing irrational kind of way.

My dad's brother Gary, and his wife Carolyn, were people we only heard about; they had two kids. We were told by our parents that Gary and Carolyn were part of the extended family that had tried to destroy ours in and that they were just out for Grandmother's money. However, Grandmother used to talk to Carolyn on the phone a lot, which was strange to me if these were bad people. I don't remember the details about those stories, just the overall feeling that they were supposed to be dangerous.

We were also told that when they came to visit our granny and pappy's house, our pictures would be taken down so that they would not know about us. If they knew I had been born, it would have been dangerous for us as they would tell my biological grandfather and he might kidnap me too. When we went to Granny and Pappy's house, their pictures would still be on the walls. I spent hours studying them. There were pictures of them fishing, school portraits, and family outings. The photographs that I love the most were of the beautiful and graceful dancer. She was elegant; her hair was in a perfect bun, and she wore the most gorgeous dresses. I wanted to be the girl who got to dance like her.

They appeared happy in these pictures. They didn't look like the kind of people intent on destroying another family. I wanted to know them; I wanted to have these cousins in my life. I wanted to have Christmas and thanksgiving with them. My heart told me that these were good people, but the adults said that they were too dangerous to meet.

The only time we ever met in person was at the funeral of my great-grandfather. There was the beautiful dancer I had only seen in pictures and her quiet, almost shy seeming, brother. They were standing within reach, but I didn't know how to interact with them. I could not think of what to say to them with the words of my parents and grandparents flowing through my head. I didn't trust them, but I also wanted to know them so badly. We were all together but also looking for an escape from this awkward situation.

Gary and Carolyn divorced, and Gary married Vandy. Vandy was just a name I heard now and then, always in a tone of disgust. I had never even seen a picture of them together. I knew my mom hated them fiercely. She could barely spit out their names, as if mentioning them caused her great pain. The only story I really remember was something about how they stole a house that mom and dad were supposed to rightly inherit. When Grandmother and Harold split, Gary went with Harold, and that was all that we needed to know to understand that they were evil and dangerous.

Jon, the youngest of my dad's brothers, had a few different wives over the years. I have a vague memory of one Christmas together with his first wife and their children. I remember Tammy, his second wife, the most. When we saw Tammy, she gave me the best hugs; she took the time to talk with me and made sure I felt loved. She was happy, and she joked a lot, making the people around her laugh.

When they divorced, I never talked to Jon again, but I kept Tammy as my aunt. I didn't care what the adults said about her, which was a lot. She was good to me, and I could feel her warmth each time we saw her.

Together, they had four kids that I only saw a handful of times. When we were really little, we had a few holidays with them. I remember the fun, the chaos, and the feel of an extended family. But as we got older and years passed, it

felt awkward around them because they were family, but we didn't really know each other. I desperately wanted to have cousins and those built-in friendships that I associated with the idea. I thought about them all the time and I dreamed of all the adventures that we could have gone on together. Our families were never close to each other. There was just too much awkwardness, too many years of Grandmother talking trash, and Jon giving off weird vibes similar to my father.

There were so many people that could have been a part of our lives, but the past kept us all apart. I was told that it was to keep us safe, but it just didn't feel truthful and so I was left with a constant yearning for all the memories that could have been made. A family that I never got to know.

∞

After five months of living in Antelope, dad's contract ended with his company in Burlington, and now he was home full time with no money coming in. Consequently, we began working a flea market forty-five minutes away. We had a booth for a few weekends before creating a permanent shop inside the main building. At first, we sold rocks and silver rings that we bought from wholesale shows. Then, customers started asking for repairs. As a result, dad bought a few tools and learned how to size and repair jewelry.

Dad wanted to diversify the things we sold and some of the other vendors had been talking about an auction on Thursday nights. At these auctions, another side of dad's controlling behavior showed up. When mom wanted to buy an item, Dad would shoot her ideas down saying it cost too much or wouldn't sell. It was like he felt threatened by mom having her own ideas. However, when he wanted something, he would get caught up in a bidding war, paying more than the item was worth just to win. We would go home with random boxes of Knick knacks, figurines, and pictures to sell. Our booth kept expanding as we went to more auctions. We also added more jewelry and a jeweler's tool bench to repair them.

We were at the flea market for two years. During that time, there were a lot of other vendors with kids that we spent time with. There were three kids whose parent's sold carpets; they had been at the flea market for the longest amount of time. Another kid whose parent sold funnel cakes, consistently taunted us. There was a German couple with a daughter my age who I related to the most. We would walk up and down the entire flea market socializing with the other vendors. We owned that place in a way, with few people telling us what to do and few rules to follow. The flea market was backed against the Tuckasegee River, and we would spend the warm summer days playing in the water and catching tadpoles when we were not working.

There were a variety of other vendors that included a guy who had a trained monkey that would take coins from your hand. He would let us play with the little spider monkey as long as they were not busy, and we had a few coins in our hands.

There was a couple who sold exotic birds. The cost was much lower than the pet shops and we took home a baby green conure. He was still getting his feathers and needed to be fed with a pipet. We took care of him for a few weeks before he died.

There was another couple set up near our booth that also owned a shop on the old strip in Camden, North Carolina selling leather goods. We became friends with them for a little while and they let us set up a booth inside their shop on the busy weekends after the flea market closed for the day. There was a live band across the little two-lane road and a mini arcade that I love to play in. The traffic was thick with tourists looking to take photos of the Native Americans posing in their headdresses.

There was a lot of work to do, especially on the weekends when the flea market would get inundated with tourists. We would spend most of our time working with customers and repairing their jewelry. Deborah and I had to learn how to use a torch so that we could repair and size rings when needed. Other work included rearranging the booth to make room for any new products and making sure the booth stayed clean.

One day, dad decided to build an indoor gem mining operation. The day was over ninety degrees in the middle of the humid southern summer. We unloaded all the heavy pine wood into our booth to start construction. When a piece of wood needed to be cut, we carried it back outside and across the blazing hot gravel parking lot into the grass. Deborah and I spent several hours carrying the lumber back and forth as Dad cut the wood to the specified size. Deborah said that she wasn't feeling good, and she looked pale. We could never be sick though, there just wasn't time for that. Dad told us to keep working and that we could have a break later. Deborah was acting lethargic and had quit sweating. We continued to carry the lumber back and forth until Deborah passed out. Dad seemed more irritated than concerned. When Deborah regained consciousness just a minute later, He gave her some water and a slight break telling us to get back to work.

∞

At church, I had made a few friends in the Camden congregation. There were four girls who were my age and whom I still consider my friends to this day. Sometimes on Sunday after church, I would go home with Christina. We formed a strong bond while we commiserated on how unfair life was at this age. We sat in her room and listened to different types of music. I was only allowed to listen to country or new age music like Yanni or Enya. I wasn't sure how I felt about her taste in music because it was so different from what I was used to, but I loved her sharing it with me. On sunny days, we walked around the woods at her house to escape the ears of her parents. Her life of school and boys fascinated me, and my life of flea markets and the deceptive freedom of no school intrigued her.

There were a few older girls at church. One of them was nice, but the rest of the girls were mean to us. They walked around with their nose in the air, pretending they were more important than us. They rarely said anything nice, preferring to lift themselves up by putting us down. It felt constant and Christina and I worked to avoid them.

The flea market kept us busy, which lowered the frequency of dad's nighttime visits and unbearable car rides; although he never passed an opportunity to create "payment" out of normal activities with friends. If I wanted a sleepover, I still had to pay for it. As a result, I rarely slept over at my friend's houses. He would still insist on putting his hands on my upper thigh anytime we were in the car, regardless of how often I pushed his hands away.

59

One morning, dad and I drove the forty-five minutes to the flea market. it was Monday, which meant the market would be very slow today. I had been invited to spend the night with a friend the following weekend. I wanted to ask him if I could go, but waited until the flea market was in sight so he wouldn't have time to create a deal.

"Dad, can I spend the night?" I asked him.

Without responding, He pulled over to the side of the road, next to a sunflower field across from the flea market. My stomach clenched up. I didn't think he would attempt this with so much traffic and a few buildings around us.

"Let's make a deal." he said it in a deep throaty tone that suggested where his mind was at. I was fourteen now; I had never found a way out before. I had tried several tactics, but it didn't matter. Not waiting for me to respond, he reached over to me as I sat frozen. I stared out the window at the bright yellow sunflowers as he groped my breast, reaching for the protective feel of the blackness and the only escape I knew.

The darkness didn't come this time. Where was it? I panicked as I felt the onslaught of emotions that I had previously blocked out. I was unprepared to feel so many things all at once and they tore through my mind like a tsunami that had just reached land, leaving me wrecked. I felt lightheaded; I couldn't take a breath. My lungs felt as if they had turned to solid stone. Was it always going to be like this? Where was the blackness? Why did I have to feel his hands on me?

The car spun as my vision lost focus, blending the sunflowers and blue sky, making me dizzy. I finally inhaled a small gasp of air. I had to get control, I thought. I can't let him see my fear. Time paused as I attempted to stop the questions that controlled my panic-driven thoughts. I just needed to breathe; I told myself, taking another small gasp. As the questions left me, I could recognize the individual emotions. I felt hate, anger, discouragement, fear, despair, and rage. Each emotion brought an assault of memories that had been deliberately suppressed.

Breathe; I told myself again, trying to keep control. I was so focused on just breathing that I could not stop my feelings from forcefully running out of my mouth on instinct.

"STOP IT!" I screamed the words out with a ferocity that demanded he listened.

He stopped, staring at me, shocked. I stared back at him in defiance on the outside, but on the inside, I was terrified of what he would do.

What the hell had I just done? Why did I do that and why didn't the darkness protect me? I wouldn't have yelled those words had I been in the dark; I wouldn't have to feel all this overwhelming rage that suffocated me. What was he going to do to me? Fear replaced the rage and as it rushed over me. My heart beat louder than the words he had been speaking. I had acted on impulse; I didn't mean to let the words out. Can I take it back? I'm not strong enough to fight him. There was no protection for me. I was already so broken. What would he do?

His words slipped through to my awareness. "Remember, you can never tell your mom. If you do, you will be the one responsible for breaking her. She isn't strong enough to handle the truth."

His words echoed the thoughts I felt about myself. I knew what it meant to be broken. I was broken, every part of me shattered and torn from the years of abuse. I managed to smile through it all because it was all I knew to do, My coping mechanism for survival. That didn't mean I wasn't in constant pain, constant fear, and exhausted from being in a perpetual state of intensified fight or flight. I just wanted to go to sleep and never wake up, but the sun kept coming up without my permission. I had no control over my life, over what happened around me, or the things that happened to me. I see my family hurting and I don't know how to help them. It feels as if I'm being sliced apart one incision at a time, day after day, year after year. There was never a way to escape. I tried to find hope, and sometimes I could believe in it, but I had been taught that my family was eternal and that even death was no escape.

I knew what it felt like to be broken and I couldn't pass that on to my mom.

Stop.

The word repeated in my head, filled with the terror of what would happen next. What had I done? I asked myself again. Every cell was warning me of danger, every hair was standing on end. I felt paralyzed. I had never been able to say "No" outside of my own head. I could never push back, to take a stand. I was too little; he was too powerful. I was suffocating, stuck in this car on the side of the road, his glare pressuring me to give in. The sunflowers were still there. I wasn't sure if they were mocking me with their bright friendly yellows or trying to give me confidence.

What else could he take from me?

He wanted people to believe that he was lovable and successful. He would never let us leave because we were that image of a decent family that made him look good. We were useful to him as free labor for his business. I didn't think his threats of social services were viable anymore.

Then what could he take away from me? Friends? I will give that up to end this. I already mostly had, but I don't think that threat is real either. Friends were allowed because they promoted his desired image of happy kids. He wanted everyone to view him as the perfect father with the perfect homeschooled family. He looked successful, and he wasn't going to mess that up.

"If you tell anyone, you'll break the family up." He looked at me sternly, adding more pressure.

I glared back at him. I let my body speak for me since my words were absent.

I could not think of any more threats or punishments that could affect me. My body stiffened as the realization dawned on me that he had nothing to take and consequently, he had no more power over me. Something in my own face must have changed because I saw the first crack of fear in the slight twitch of his eyes. I recalled the lady from Yesteryear Flea Market who had pushed me off the quarter machine; I could say "no" to an adult! My fear transitioned into unwavering defiance that allowed me to stand firm in my words. I could finally tell my father no, and there was nothing he would do about it.

We continued to stare at each other. I could see he was hoping I would relent, scared that I wouldn't.

I wasn't going to back down this time or any other time in the future. I know why the darkness didn't come; I was finally old enough, strong enough, that I could protect myself from this disgusting excuse of a father. I was repelled by his face, his smell, and the slimy layer of his gray sweat mixed with jewelry dust that always covered his body. I soaked in all the hate, relished in it, enjoying the strength it gave me. I immersed myself in the anger as separated me from the cruel bond of a malicious father. I had discovered my own power.

I was going to be the person who protected me, the one that stood up for that abused little girl who hid in her waterbed with the green satin sheets. I was going to rescue the little girl who screamed for her mother but was left abandoned over and over. It was going to me who protected the little girl who endured car ride after car ride of humiliation and shame. It was time for me to be the person who I needed everyone else to be, the who saved med me, and I was ready.

He was still waiting for me to respond, pressuring me to break.

I looked at him defiantly. I was no longer a scared little girl afraid to tell her father no.

Instead of blocking out all the bad things he had ever done, I used the torment, destruction, chaos, fear, and hate that he caused, and I let it fuel me with a new determination and strength that had never been there before. I loathed this decrepit old man who, for years, had systematically torn me and my family apart piece by piece with no remorse. Unless, of course, he was caught and then he cried his fake tears. I was infuriated even more as I realized it was all just a chess game to him. We were nothing more than disposable pawns, and he saw himself as the king. I wasn't playing anymore.

Chapter Seven
Rocks

Grandmother wanted to sell the Antelope house, and she asked us to move out. My father had found a brick-and-mortar storefront in Sylva, another small town in North Carolina. The building shared a parking lot with the only movie theater in town, three restaurants, a flower shop, and a few other businesses.

I watched as the wooden sign with the letters "ROCKS" was placed above the storefront, sealing our fate for the next several years. Through the double doors, in the back of the spacious showroom, was a set of stairs that led down to a dark, damp basement where we would live.

I looked around windowless space and I thought about calling child services right then and reporting the situation myself.

"Is this a joke?" I asked. This can't be real; he has to be joking.

"Maybe we could go live in one of those trailers," I said, pointing over to the run-down mobile homes that were in view from the back dock.

Dad tried to sell us on the idea. "We can finish building the walls and put in some carpet, we can make it nice," He voice was overly cheerful, "No point in making two payments when we can make just one"

Dad's voice resonated in my head endlessly. If I told anyone, I would lose my family. He made sure we understood. I had thought about calling child services many times hoping they would fix my broken family. Maybe they could have made dad go to jail, and mom could get therapy. Looking around the store basement, my new home, I knew if I made that phone call, they would have no choice but to take us away. It simply wasn't inhabitable. This place was just another secret we had to keep.

"We will fix it up," Dad promised.

I looked around, looking for any kind of silver lining. This place made the house in Antelope look like a palace.

There were two ways into the basement. One entrance was from the loading dock through an old set of double doors decaying from years of weather damage. Several layers of paint were flaking off, showing the worn wood underneath. Each door had a small window with rusty metal bars covering them. The bars made me feel unsettled.

The second entrance was a staircase leading to the storefront. When I walked down the stairs, at first all I could was a long storage area to the left that was eventually filled with old food storage, paper towels, toilet paper, and other leftovers from the Y2K scare when the world was going to end. To the left of that was another fifteen feet of hallway that lead to the dock.

Across the back doors and to the right of the Y2K storage area, a sheet hung on the unfinished framework that hid our living area from anyone looking in. The main room had a couch and an old TV that we could watch movies on. The floor was covered in dirty leftover carpet squares that had been thrown over concrete to form a mismatched carpet. We had to keep readjusting them when they slid around. Two of the walls in this room were solid, covered with wood paneling, and the other two walls had sheets stapled over the framework to form the semblance of a wall.

Straight back from the living room was my brother's room. He had three sides with solid walls and the last one was another that faced the living room. It was hard to care in a place like this, and Jason expressed his emotions in the high piles of trash and clothes that enclosed his room. Even if he cared, there just wasn't a place to put anything.

To the left of my brothers room was my parent's room, the only room that had four walls and a proper door. Their mattress sat directly on the floor. It was supposed to be temporary; It was all supposed to be temporary. In the corners of their room, they had packed boxes and piles of paper just lying around.

To the right of my brother's room were two more rooms filled with packed-up boxes from when we moved from Georgia. This room didn't have any carpet, which was good since it was also the room that our dog would use as a bathroom. We would clean the messes up once a month or so, if we remembered.

The room I shared with my sister was off the left side of the living room. We had three walls covered in thin paneling and a sheet separating us from the kitchen and bathroom. There were old closet shelves on one wall that we filled with trinkets and homework. I had a desk on one side and a dresser on the other. We hung our clothes in the only closet in the entire basement, which was also where the water heater was located. Even though the floor was perpetually damp, at least a place where I could put my things.

The kitchen was just an open space where we built rustic shelves to store dry food. We also used some leftover cabinets, placed on the floor against the wall to create a countertop which held the microwave. We did eventually get a double plug-in electric burner that also sat on the counter. For water and cleaning dishes, we used the tiny sink in the bathroom. Eventually, we bought a full-size electric stove, but I don't think we ever got around to setting it up. A refrigerator was plugged in on the other side of the wall in the hallway.

The bathroom had one little window with bars that were covered with a small opaque curtain, a tiny sink, and a small standup shower. You could reach the toilet and the shower at the same time if you spread your arms out as far as you could. The bathroom, kitchen, and my room were all covered in a dark green berber carpet that seemed to hold almost as much filth in its short fibers as the shag carpet from the last place we lived.

If this was my reality, then I had to find the positives and focus it. I had a place to put my things and I shared a room with my sister again. We lived in town, and I could walk to any of the restaurants or gas stations near us. The only bugs we had here, were the fleas that we brought with us.

Upstairs, the storefront was a large open room with double glass doors in the middle and two large display windows. We used glass cases to form a u-shape display. Behind those, we had bookshelves that lined the walls filled with colorful geode bookends, amethyst cathedrals, onyx décor, and the random junk we had picked up at auctions for the flea market. We separated the store into two sections by a row of rustic shelves covered in sheets to form a dividing wall.

In the back of the shop on one side, there were four desks, two of which had computers, and the other two were set up for my sister and me to do our homework or to pack up orders to ship. On the other side were two eight-foot tables set up with six different jewelers' stations where we created, cleaned, and repaired jewelry for customers.

Time passed in a repetitive schedule. Monday to Thursday, we worked in the shop helping customers and building inventory for the show the following weekend. Friday to Sunday, we traveled in rotation to some of the biggest monthly trade shows in the south.

∞

STOMP! STOMP! STOMP!

The sound of three stomps shook my roof as dad stomped upstairs. This was dad's way of telling us to go upstairs without having to yell for us. Anytime we disappeared for more than a few minutes and he didn't know why, we would get the three stomps.

We had gotten in at 2 a.m. the night before from a trade show and I was exhausted. There was no morning sun to wake us up, no beams of light to dance around and welcome us to a new morning. Just a dark room and his three stomps demanding that we start another day of work. I kept my shoes by the bed so that I could put them on soon as I got out of bed, avoiding getting my feet wet from the damp carpet. I slipped them on and quickly dressed, then walked upstairs to check the ground for dog poop before opening the store. Mondays meant we had to unpack our beat-up blue utility van from the most recent tradeshow. This week we had just gotten back from Birmingham, Alabama.

Jason and dad carried in one of the glass display cases while Deborah and I carried in the other. We unloaded dad's wooden jewelry workbench and set the jewelry back into the display cases for the week.

Today we would be creating more jewelry for the next show and work on the repair orders. We made most of our jewelry from scratch, starting with a wax mold. When dad found a design that he liked, he would buy the rights to copy the ring, or sometimes he would just illegally copy the design by making a rubber mold of the original. Then we could make as many wax replicas as he wanted.

We would cast several times a week. Deborah and I worked side by side using a wax injector on the rubber mold to create the wax replicas. We used a hot temperature prod to attach the wax to a stem, creating a wax tree of pendants and rings. Each tree would hold an average of thirty rings or pendants and we would make about five of these per casting session.

We placed the wax trees into a metal canister, and then poured in plaster of Paris around the tree, gently shaking it to release all the bubbles and then placed it into a sealed vacuumed dome to release any remaining bubbles. Once the plaster had dried, the canisters were placed into a high-temperature oven that would melt and burn away the wax, leaving behind a strong burned smell that filled the entire building. The customers would occasionally ask about the burned smell.

Mom and Dad went to local pawn shops and bought unsalvageable jewelry to be melted down and recycled. We placed the gold on one side of a centrifugal casting machine and heated the canisters on the other side. Using a torch, we heated the gold until it was molten liquid, then we released the latch holding back the metal canisters and watched as the centrifugal force of the rotations forced the gold into the space left behind from the wax.

My favorite part of the entire process was when we took the canisters, now filled with molten metal, and plunged them into cold water, dissolving the plaster in a fit of hissing, spluttering bubbles. The leftover plaster was dumped outside in the parking lot onto a growing mound of disregarded white goo. The remaining plaster on the rings was washed off in the small upstairs sink. I'm sure we sent pounds and pounds of plaster down that sink. The last steps were to cut the rings off the tree, tumble them in a rock tumbler to remove any extra plaster, polish them with a handheld drill, and then set the stone.

Dad sat at his workbench, and Deborah and I worked across from him, setting stones into the jewelry. I grabbed the pair of pliers that Deborah and I were sharing at the same time as Deborah. She looked at me with a gleam in her eye; it was a challenge. We both gripped one handling twisting our arms and hands in a furious attempt to gain control. We were laughing as she jerked her arm around, knocking me to the floor and I pulled her down with me. Her nails dug into my flesh, and I clawed her back in a friendly wrestling match. She was getting the upper hand pinning me to the ground. I looked around for a way to regain the lead and saw a bottle of water. With one hand still fiercely gripping the pliers, I grabbed a full cup of water and dumped it all over my sister, taking our wrestling match to the next level. She grabbed another container of water and threw it at me, soaking me instantly.

"Get back to work." dad said in an annoyed tone.

We looked at each other knowingly and put the pliers down. We filled our water cups back up in the sink and walked back to our workstations. As we were about to sit down, we threw our water all over dad. He looked at us for a minute, calculating his response as we grinned at him, water dripping down his face. He grabbed a gallon of water and tried to douse us both as we ran away laughing. By the time we ran out of energy, we were all soaked, and so was everything around us.

A customer walked in and mom, still dry, walked up front to help them. Deborah and I went downstairs to shower and put on dry clothes. Before I showered, I looked out the sheer flimsy curtain to make sure no one would watch us. There was a guy with a long-ratted ponytail and a dirty denim jacket sitting on the back dock drinking a beer, his back to the window. I went back upstairs to get dad.

"Dad, there is a guy on the back porch. Can you please ask him to leave?"

Dad walked down the stairs and opened the creaky back door, making the guy jump in surprise. I listened on my side of the door.

"Hey man, you gotta leave. This isn't a place to hang out," my dad said in a firm tone that left no room for arguing.

The guy apologized as he walked away, muttering something under his alcoholic breath. I walked into the bathroom and waited to hear the door close, signaling that dad had walked back into the house. I assumed I must have missed the sound after about five minutes and jumped into the shower. After my shower while I was getting dressed, I finally heard dad come back into the house. I wasn't sure if he had walked back in, or if he had been outside the entire time. I wondered if the bum, who was oblivious to us showering, would have been safer.

We went back upstairs to work a little longer. Work would wind down around eight or nine o'clock, but the store was open until after the last movie was over at the theater in hopes of catching a few more customers. On those nights, we would be open as late as 11 p.m. Deborah and I spent those hours in AOL chat rooms and messenger. We stayed up later than mom and dad most nights enjoying the quiet freedom of no parents until one or two in the morning.

∞

The next morning, Deborah and I woke to the sound of three loud stomps.

"And good morning to you too," I grumbled to Deborah. She gave a small snicker. We grabbed a bowl of cheerios to eat for breakfast and then walked upstairs to create inventory for a few hours.

When a customer walked in the store a few hours later, I went up front to help her. I loved selling and I knew I was good at it.

Assessing her body language, I thought she looked friendly enough, a little snooty compared to most of our customers though.

"Hey! Welcome in," I greeted her.

"Hello, I'm just looking."

"No problem. Let me know if I can help you."

"Ok," she said.

"Where are you from?" I asked her to create a conversation. The longer I could keep a customer talking, the more likely they were to buy something.

"Raleigh" she replied.

"Where is that?" I asked. I had not heard the name of this city before.

She looked at me, dumbfounded. I could tell she thought I was stupid by the way she looked at me.

"You don't know the capital of our state." she asked me in what felt like an accusing tone.

The capital of this state? Was I supposed to know that?

"Do you know any of the capitals?" she asked, almost sarcastically.

Another customer walked in at that moment, and I took the opportunity to exit the conversation. Mom came up and finished helping the lady until she left the store. She didn't buy anything, figures, I thought.

There had been other situations where my lack of school was evident, and I didn't appreciate it. I had been trying to work on school when I could, but it was a challenge.

"Hey Dad, can I work on schoolwork for a while?" I asked.

With an overdramatic sigh, he complained, "We have so much work that needs to get done today. We have to cast more jewelry and your mom and I have to go buy gold from the pawn shop. We need to make at least fifty rings to stay on track."

Dad's frustration at how inconvenient my schoolwork was to his personal agenda hung in the air. Mom stood up from behind her computer and silently glared at dad from across the room. She never directly objected to dad's opinions, but with the looks she gave dad, she didn't need to say anything more. This silent battle lasted for a solid minute.

"Fine," he snapped. "Do whatever you want, I'll just have to do all the work by myself since you think your homework is more important than the success of our family." He sat back down with a huge harrumph.

Did he mean family? I thought. Wasn't he talking about the success of the business?

"If you can bother to take the trouble of interrupting your homework when a customer walks in, you can at least help them." Dad said sarcastically, letting one last lash out before he jerked his jewelry glasses down over his head and went back to his own work.

I walked over to my desk and sat down to work on schoolwork. The same power play of conversation happened each time when I asked Dad if I could work on schoolwork. The results depended on who won the silent feuds.

I thought the abuse was over. Turns out his obsession had just changed. He went from focusing on us to focusing everything on the business. Maybe this was his coping mechanism. It was certainly his new drug. A new game of chess where we were still the pawns but now the rules were shifting and changing into an emotional battlefield. He viewed the world in two separate parts; people and things that support his business, and those that didn't. Although I consistently worked for him for years, I also pushed back when the frustrations went too high, often putting me in the opposing category. Living in the Sylva store was the turning point where my education went from an annoyance to a threat to his business. It was like a little parasite for him that crawled under his skin, and no amount of scratching would make my schoolwork disappear.

∞

On Wednesday nights, I paced the store waiting for mom to finish another card game on her computer so she could take me to church for activity night. This was the first time in my life that I can remember having an entire group of friends that I could see regularly. I was always eager to get there as soon as possible. It also looked as if it was going to rain, and I wanted to leave before I had to get wet getting in the car.

I had several friends from church, but I spent most of my time with Christina. We slipped out of class every chance that we could. Her mom was the teacher, and she had always been good to me. I always felt a little guilty when we slipped away, but it was so rare for me to be around anyone my own age, and I needed that kind of bonding more than another lesson on modesty.

I cannot say that church was a safe place, it was just different than home. The older girls were always making snide comments to us when the leaders were not looking, and I didn't want to be around them more than I had to be. Betty was the worst of them all, she seemed to take great pride in being as mean as she could to us without being caught. She walked around the church with her nose stuck in the air showing us how superior she was. I think she got a sense of euphoria out of being mean and putting other people down. She never grew out of it either.

Christina, Rhianna, and I skipped class again. We found an open classroom, slipped in, and locked the door. We kept the lights off so no one would suspect that we were there. One little kid had heard us talking and grabbed an adult. They came and rattled the door, but because it was locked, they didn't believe the kid and walked away. I thought it was odd that the kid was telling the truth, but the adult was so quick to tell him he was wrong.

The three of us sat in the dark together, talking. I listened to Rhianna and Christina talk about their school assignment. They were talking about a guy who had been shot named John F. Kennedy. I had never heard of him.

"Who are yall talking about?" I asked.

I could feel the silence as they stopped talking and even in the dark, I knew they looked in my direction.

"Are you joking?" Christina asked me.

"No, I just don't know who he is," I replied.

"He was the 35th President of the United States," She said.

My lack of education showed several times in our friendship, but they never talked down to me and never judged me for it.

"Are you going to the football game this weekend?" Rhianna asked, changing the subject.

"Yes! Where do you want to meet up?"

As they continued talking, I got lost in thought. I wanted to go to the football games, I wanted to know about the presidents, and I wanted to be a part of their world and know what it felt like to walk down the high school hallways waving hello to my friends and complain about how much homework the teachers had assigned us that day. I loved these moments with my friends because for just a minute, I could pretend that I was normal.

"I hate waking up so early in the morning for seminary." Christina said with a tinge of anger, or maybe resentment, in her voice.

"Why don't you come to seminary Stephanie? Rhianna pulled me back into the conversation.

"I don't know. I guess I haven't thought about it.

Seminary is a weekday hour-long class for high school-aged children that starts an hour before school. I had never considered going because I didn't think my parents would wake up that early.

"I don't have a ride," I said.

"My dad could probably give you a ride home. He takes all of us to school when seminary is over, and you are not that much further"

For a short time, I thought about it. "I'll ask my parents and see what they say." I was interested in the lessons, but mostly in just having another opportunity to be with friends.

We talked more about the boys at church and school, about how our parents made us feel that week, I talked about my dad and our current frustrations. The youth leaders were working on a week-long camp to go to Washington D.C and we talked about our excitement over the upcoming trip. We heard more people in the hallway signaling that classes were ending. We walked around the church building meeting up with the guys who had been in a different class and hung out as long as we could before our parents said it was time to go. It was a twenty minute drive home and the rain had picked up its intensity as we drove home. We stopped by Taco Bell to grab dinner for the family.

∞

It rained all night. I used to love listening to the rain in Antelope as the rain hit the tin roof. In the basement, I couldn't hear the storm. The next morning as I went to turn the lights on in my bedroom, my feet hit the soaking wet carpet. Anytime it rained more than a few inches the rainwater would collect in our room and in the bathroom. I listened to the splish splosh sound of my walking as I turned the lights on. There was at least an inch of standing water in the corner of my room, probably more. The entire carpet was wet. In the bathroom, there was even more standing water in one corner and the entire carpet was soaked in there as well. The carpet never really had a chance to dry completely, and the bottom of my desk, dresser, and the bed had all warped from the constant moisture. I grabbed my clothes hanging next to the water heater and got dressed on my bed to avoid getting them wet.

I went upstairs to work for the rest of the day.

I spent the night before thinking of my church friends and their life. I wanted to go to high school, even though I didn't think it was possible, and I wanted to see how dad would respond to the idea of me going to seminary in the mornings.

I put the ring down I had been working on and looked at dad "I want to go to high school." I told him.

He assessed me for a moment, trying to figure out my motive. "You are too behind in your schoolwork, you could never catch up." he said as if to end the conversation before we could even have one.

Sidestepping his answer, I changed tactics.

"Can I go to seminary?" Without waiting for an answer, I tried to deflect his complaints. "Brother McLachlan could give me a ride home so all I need is a ride to his house and I would just go on the days that we were in town."

He stared at me, trying to see how this new idea would play into his interest.

"It would just be maybe three days out of the week," I added.

"If you can wake yourself up early we will give you a ride." You could tell he didn't think I was going to take him up on the offer.

The following week, I set my alarm for 5:30 a.m. I quickly got dressed and knocked on mom and dad's door to wake them up. I was apprehensive about seeing if they would follow through or not. Mom got up to give me a ride.

Our teacher was brilliant and taught church in a way that made it interesting. That didn't stop us from falling asleep on his couch a few times, though. He was a rare type in the Mormon community, he understood things differently and didn't spend all his time telling us all the rules and doctrines that controlled our lives. Instead, he was elated in making connections between different points of doctrine and comparing those to theology outside of Mormonism. He taught us the history of religion in and out of the church in depth. He taught Philosophy of Religion at Western Carolina University, and he brought his education into our seminary lessons.

When Seminary ended, he would give us all a ride to the school. I watched as hundreds of kids walked around campus, jumping out of their cars, meeting with friends, and then hurrying into the building with an air of excitement. I held back the tears and slinked down in the backseat wishing I could have jumped out, that I didn't have to go back to the basement.

I knew I would never be allowed to go to high school. I wanted to go to the football games, and the dances, I was even willing to do all the homework that my friends complained about. I wanted to be with my friends, eat the crappy cafeteria food, and even go to gym class every day. I wanted the eight hours to escape from my life every day. I wanted different priorities than how much work we can fit into a day. But I could only get glimpses of a life that I could never live. After a while, it just hurt too much and I stopped going to seminary.

Chapter Eight
Forgive and Forget

I couldn't let it go.

I was so tired of people looking at me like I was stupid. I wasn't stupid. I just didn't have the opportunity to go to school like everyone else. I wanted to get an education, and I knew college was the way to get out of here. Maybe that's why dad fought me so hard on it.

Deborah had just gotten her GED and applied to go to the local community college. If she could do it, so could I. Deborah and I sat at the workstations together and Dad was across from us.

"Dad, I want to get my GED" I stated.

He looked at me hard for a minute, calculating. He was always calculating.

"You will never pass the test, it's too hard." he said.

"I can pass the test; I can buy a GED book and pass just like Deborah did," I countered.

He looked at me frustratedly. He hated when I brought things like this up.

"You're better off working for me. Those tests are impossibly hard for someone with your education. You need to get more years of homeschooling under your belt before you can even try."

I tried again. "There is no age limit on the GED, I can try to take it now. It doesn't hurt to just try."

"Listen," his voice was rising, "We have to get the van loaded for the next show today, and I still have about twenty orders I'm trying to fix, plus we need to make wax molds for one last cast. I don't have time for this and you're never going to pass the test, anyway. I need you to get back to work"

"Dad, this is really important to me, and I think I can pass it." I said in a measured voice. "I can pay for the test myself and figure out what I need to do to take the test. All I need from you guys is a ride to the testing center, but I am going to study to take the GED."

It was a statement. I wasn't arguing with him, I was telling him. It was a bold move for me.

He realized I was not going to back down and his temper flared. He started screaming, "I do so much for this family all the damn time and all I'm asking is for you to get back to work and all your doing is wasting my time."

I just stared at him, not responding.

He screamed at me. "If you are so intent on focusing all your energy on your schoolwork instead of on the business where you are needed, then YOU ARE FIRED." His face turned red from his anger and frustration.

There was silence for a minute. I couldn't figure out if this was a good thing or a bad thing. I mean, on one hand, if he really fired me then I was free to do what I wanted. Did this mean I could go to school, seminary, be an ordinary kid? On the other hand, it was like he was literally kicking me out of the family. The business and the family were synonymous for him. Our status in the family depended on how good of an employee we were. Jason was still living with us, but he didn't work with us. He didn't travel with us. He had his own world, and he wasn't really part of anything that we did as a family anymore unless dad needed him to lift something heavy. Did I want that? Did I want to be on the outside?

I looked at his face full of anger and knew I was being kicked out of the family. This wasn't just being fired, this was him being tired of me pushing back on him, tired of my fighting for my education. I could feel tears forming from my own frustration and fear.

No, I told myself firmly, I can't cry. Crying is a weakness, and he will use that against me. He will think I am giving up. I covered up the tears with my own anger, staring back at him.

He screamed at me again, "Just go away, we don't need you here anymore and I'm tired of looking at your face. If you will not help this family you need to leave."

"FINE" I screamed, pushing myself away from the work desk and stomping down the stairs into the dark basement. I was hurt and angry and I felt alone. Everything felt heavy all the time, and I was tired of it. I was living a life that I hated, that revolved around his obsessions, and I was losing my ability to tolerate it. Firing me was his last threat when he had nothing else to lose, his way of saying I don't matter to him. At that moment, and others like it, I really didn't matter to him. I was just an employee and if I wasn't doing my job, then I was taking away from the business. If I took away from the business, I was a problem to be dealt with, just another obstacle in his way.

I saw education as my way out, and so did he. He has no investment in me growing, expanding, or evolving because each chapter I studied, each fight we had, and now the GED, it was all an attempt of me growing up and leaving him. He wanted me to stay in his world forever and I so desperately wanted out. Each one of my successes was his failure.

"We don't need you anymore."

"You'll never pass."

"It's too hard."

"You're wasting your time."

"You would be better off spending your time working for me."

"You're not smart enough."

"You're fired."

His words were always in my head. I did my best to block them out, but they were always there in some form. Sometimes they were just so overwhelming.

There were other words too, like

"You need to lose weight."

"Your clothes are looking too tight."

"Why can't you just do what you are told."

"When I say jump, I expect you to say how high without questioning me."

"Why can't you look like your sister."

"Your voice is annoying."

"You should just be grateful I don't hit you with a belt like I did your siblings."

I read a poem one time about two faces. The face we showed the world and the face we hide. I pulled the poem back out and reread the words a few times, feeling them at the very bottom of my soul. I was mostly happy; the negative things were looked over as a survival trait. But there was a part of me that was slowly being torn apart and dying. A struggle between where I am and where I wanted to be. I looked around my room, at the moldy green carpet, at the water heater closet where out clothes hung, and the sheets that we had instead of walls. The pictures I taped up of all the things I wanted in my life but didn't know how to reach mocked me.

When I was around people, I smiled and joked because it was the only way I knew to survive. I was constantly told how bubbly and charismatic I was by customers. If I made myself be happy, then I didn't have to see my reality for what it truly was. I could keep the negative things away.

As I read the poem, it made me acknowledge that other face, the side of me that no one else got to see. I felt separated from this girl. She was broken. She protected all my secrets, helped me to forget the darkness, and she knew all my pain. She kept all that ache and understanding hidden from everyone, including me. The burden was too much, and she held them. Until she broke.

It was just too much. Too much abuse, neglect, denial, and an overload of emotions. I spent a lot of time praying to God for help and guidance, but there was just no way to process all these things that happened to me from such a young age.

There was no way to process all the things that were still going wrong in my life. Just for a moment, I let out that hurt little girl, and I sobbed as I felt all her pain, her anguish, her memories, her feelings of betrayal. I heard her voice screaming for help. She wanted out, she needed out and I cried for her. I cried as I allowed her to acknowledge all those missed opportunities of playing, dancing, and swinging on the swing with friends. I just wanted to be a little girl free of all the darkness that enveloped my world. I cried as I asked God to help me through this as I wrapped my arms around myself and hugged her deeply as I gently put her back in her place where she guarded me against all those things I couldn't handle.

I ripped the poem up, but that wasn't enough, there was too much truth in it. I took the torn pieces and watched them dissolve into a glass of water. Fearful that it would be found in the trash and somehow readable, I flushed the wet torn words down the toilet. I leaned against the bathroom wall, trying to regain my composure. I stayed in constant prayer with God as I asked him to take away all this pain, it was too much for me. Eventually, a calmness took over, and I could take several deep breaths. I walked back into my bedroom and straightened my room for a minute while I waited for my tears to dry up and the redness on my face to disappear.

Dad walked in through my bedroom sheet.

"Look," he started saying.

"I'm sorry I fired you; we have a lot of work that we need to get done today and I need you to get back to work."

I thought about the look that lady gave me when I didn't know about the capital of our state, or of any states. Like I was stupid. I didn't want anyone to look at me like that again. I didn't want to feel that about myself again.

"My education is important to me and it's something I'm willing to fight for." I told him, not willing to back down.

He gave me his calculating look again; it was like I could read his thoughts. "*What do I have to give her to get her back to work?*" his look said to me.

"If you work for me until you start college, I will buy you your first car and pay for your education," Dad said.

"My entire education, like all four years?" I asked.

"Yes, but I need you to get back up to work right now," He answered.

Was he serious? Could all this be worth something? I calculated the amount he was talking about. I knew the car he would buy may cost about a thousand at most, still better than nothing. The community college I planned to attend was about $1200 a semester times a minimum of four semesters plus another two years at a university, which would cost even more. It was a valuable offer. I could handle a few more years of this if it meant that my college was paid for.

"Is that a promise?" I asked him. Dad didn't make promises often. He was already planning on paying for Deborah's classes next semester. It could be a genuine offer.

He sighed, annoyed at my disbelief. "Yes, it's a promise. Now get upstairs and get back to work."

There were many times that I wanted to walk away from his business, but I remembered the promise. When we worked long days, I remembered. When dad yelled at us because production wasn't enough, I remembered. When he constantly changed how he paid us to benefit him, I remembered. That promise was the only thing that kept me working for him as long as I did.

I put the smile back on my face and went back to work.

That didn't stop dad from becoming irritated every time I chose to do schoolwork or study for the GED. As dad's dismissal of my education grew, so did my resolve to prove him wrong. It was a constant battle of wills that fueled me to work even harder. Every time he told me I could never pass the GED, or that I wasn't smart enough, it become a mission for me to prove him wrong. It made me unwaveringly determined. I studied every chance I had.

The front door of the store jingled. I walked up front to help the customer. It was the owner of the flower shop next door, and she was angry. As soon as she saw me, she yelled in rage. "I told you to stop walking your dog on my property. I just walked through a pile of dog crap and I'm sick and tired of having to clean up after your dog. That's MY property and if you don't stop walking…"

"Can I help you?" Dad walked around the corner, cutting her words off.

"I'm calling the police on you if you don't stop walking your dog on my property. I've been nice and I've given you plenty of warnings. What else do I have to do to get you to listen to me? I own that property, not you, and you have no right to be walking your dog over there." She continued "I wouldn't mind if you cleaned up the messes, but you never do, and it has been MONTHS of this bull and I'm just done with it." She raged on.

Dad interrupted her again. "You don't have to yell. I'm sorry. I've asked the kids not to walk the dog over there." he said, blaming us to sidestep her anger. "I'll make sure that it's no longer a problem and I'm very sorry"

He has told her this before.

She walked out of the store with a huff.

I don't blame her. She had asked us several times not to walk the dog on her property, but Dad didn't seem to care. I know he blamed us, but he was the one who told us to walk the dog over there. After that transaction, the piles of dog poop downstairs built up even more.

The dog's name was Charlie; he was a Pekingese we had picked up from a flea market. To solidify that he was mom's dog, we were not allowed to play with him the first few weeks. Charlie loved everybody and we played fetch with him and his favorite brown bear occasionally once we were allowed too. He was a friendly dog most of the time, I guess. He didn't have any hair on his back because he would bite and scratch incessantly, making a chewing sound that made me feel like I was going insane. The constant chewing and fleas made it hard for me to truly bond with him, so he was in our life, but never a comfort to us. He was just mom's dog.

Mom and Charlie got in the van to run some errands. When they came back a few hours later, I heard the van pull in, but they didn't come inside. I went outside to mom eating a taco. I was hungry and excited that she brought us some food.

"Hey mom! What did you get us?" I looked in the van to see what food there was. Charlie was in the passenger seat eating another taco but there was no other food. Maybe it's in the back, I thought.

"I didn't get any extra," mom said.

Wait, what? But she bought food. Why wouldn't she buy us food? I thought.

"You didn't get any for us?" I asked, looking at Charlie nibbling on his taco.

Mom looked at me guiltily. With an annoyed sigh, she said, "I'll go get y'all some food. I'll be right back."

These types of interactions happened often. That dog was mom's favorite, above us. I tried not to get jealous of him, but it was hard sometimes when the discrepancy between our different statuses was so noticeable.

∞

Food was always weird in our family. Dad's idea of buying food left us questioning if we were going to get sick every time we ate some new mysterious item he got from the secondhand shop. I'm not talking about a grocery outlet store where the food is simply close to expiring. I mean the place food goes after that. Where the labels have fallen off the soup cans, leaving them a mystery and the expiration dates were last month at the earliest on cereals and other dry goods. The meat was the sketchiest part of all of it. It was frozen, but it had unhealthy sheen implied it has been been frozen and unfrozen a few times. Other mean had been frozen so long it had freezer burn on it. Goldfish was the safer option and that is what we ate most of the time.

Neither of my parents knew how to cook. Dad would always try to experiment with food. Once we would end up with a sandwich filled with apples, peanut butter, and horseradish. Often, he would eat an uncooked hamburger patty with some salt and pepper on it for flavor. He liked to experiment with food storage that we had bought from the church. So sometimes dinner would be dehydrated hamburger mixed into a shelf-stable soup with enough salt to make your mouth pucker for a week.

Mom tried to cook, and sometimes it would turn out ok. I loved her spaghetti and when she made chicken and dumplings. But those weren't meals you could make in a microwave, so we didn't get to eat those kinds of foods anymore.

Fresh fruits and vegetables were never a part of our life except for maybe the occasional lettuce and tomatoes to go on a sandwich. So, we would drink a SlimFast for breakfast and then snack on goldfish crackers or have ramen until dinner time when we would get food from the Mexican restaurant across the parking lot or Taco Bell.

∞

My life felt unstable and out of control. I wanted to go to school because I knew it as my ticket out of here. I needed a place to pull the strength from that I needed to make it happen. There were so many things I needed like a source of peace that I could rely on, someone I could talk to when the emotions were just too much, someone who believed in me. I had my sister, and I know I would not have made it without her, but I needed God too. I prayed and read scriptures every night. I spent hours in prayer just talking to God about how we were going to make it through this. I asked him a million questions, and I felt his presence guiding me to make decisions that would improve my life. He gave me hope and let me see the light at the end of all this chaos. We were so close that even when I wasn't praying, I could hear him telling me it was going to be ok. I was going to make it out of here and I was going to have a better life. That this was just a small part of my life and he had better things in store for me. He knew everything I had gone through because he was there to help me through it.

As my relationship with God grew, so did my belief in the church. The church gave me a community of friends, it gave me an occasional refuge from my dad, and it provided a roadmap for my life if I just followed the rules. There were so many promises that if I live by God's law, if I just do my part, then I would be ok. My family would be ok.

The church showed me a path where I could live with all my family, even dad, as perfected beings. It showed a life where Dad had gotten better, and my parents were happy. If I could just live the way the church taught, I could live with my perfected family forever.

I wanted that. I really, really wanted that. I wanted to be that family you saw in the church magazines where they glowed because of the happiness that radiated from them. Even though it was not my reality, it was something that I hoped for; I hung onto it.

Thinking about my parents, I knew it was up to me to be an example for them. They talked about being good church members, but it seemed they only lived the teachings that were convenient for them. We had stopped going to church on Sundays a few years ago because we were always traveling or working. Family scripture time had faded out as well after we moved away from Georgia. The only time we prayed as a family was over a holiday meal.

I don't think that my dad really believed in the church. He used its teachings to control us and to keep my mother from leaving him. He seemed to use his worthiness status in the church as a measuring stick for how society viewed him. Like it somehow validated that he was a good person, despite his past actions. As for genuine faith, the kind that makes you a better person, I don't think he has that.

I hoped that if I could just be faithful enough, if my parents could see that I could be happy despite our history, that maybe, just maybe, they would understand and be better in this life.

I wanted them to see how hard I was fighting to keep us together. I wanted God to know that I was willing to put in the work. So, I prayed. I prayed every morning, every night, and on the more stressful days I prayed all throughout the day. I studied the scriptures reading through the entire old and new testaments. I read through the Mormon Scriptures which include the 'Book of Mormon,' 'Doctrine and Covenants, and 'The Pearl of Great Price' several times. I paid my full 10% tithing on every bit of money I made. I went to every activity that I could go to unless I wasn't allowed because we had work to do. I went to seminary and when I could, and when it was too hard, I did the work at home. I never used curse words or took God's name in vain. I stayed away from coffee, tea, and drugs. I wore shorts that reached me my knees and shirts that covered my shoulders. I followed all the rules and fought for God's love so he would know I was worthy enough for him to fix my family.

∞

I was downstairs studying for the GED, sitting in the chair with my legs folded to avoid the damp floor and fleas. The workbook was explaining how to graph out a math problem. I could hear Dad walking down the stairs and feel the hair on my arms raise in alarm. Even though it had been a few years since the sexual abuse stopped, his presence was never good. My breathing would still stop, and my muscles tensed up when he came into my space. He pushed past the curtain to my room.

I hated how my heart heartbeat would stutter, like I was being assaulted all over again just by him touching the curtain. I didn't want him here, but had no control over it. I was fourteen; he was my parent. The look on his face was pensive, his shoulders slightly slumped. He looked alarmingly humble, which was not something I had seen in his expressions or body language.

Something is wrong, I thought as the alarms went off in my head.

He just stared at me, trying to find his words.

That's not normal either, he almost always had a well-thought-out calculated plan. After a minute, he looked me in the eye and spoke quietly. "Part of the church's repentance process is that I need to ask for your forgiveness for the past"

He was asking for my forgiveness? I heard his words, but I couldn't respond. How do you respond to something like that? How can he just come in here and ask for forgiveness like it was nothing? Doesn't he know all the damage he created? That he is STILL creating? He can't just undo everything he has done with those words. Why was he asking me this?

"I have to have your forgiveness before I can be re-baptized," He looked at me pleadingly, and softly added, "Before we can be an eternal family."

The church was making him. This was just a show so he could go back to the church leaders and check off a box. It wasn't true or genuine, he had never shown true sorrow for what he had done, only acted his sorrow when the situation warranted it, but it was all an act and so was this. He hadn't changed, only his obsessions had.

I could feel the bile rising in my throat. It was a moment I had desperately longed for. If he was truly willing to change, then it was everything I had hoped for. But I knew this was just a mockery of that deep hope.

He stood there waiting for my reply, knowing that there was only one answer that I could give. He had always used the church teachings to his own advantage, and this was no exception, forcing me into a forgiveness I didn't want to give.

I stared back at him and trying to control every one of my muscles to stop them from showing how angry I was. I'm not supposed to be angry, not when he is saying sorry. I know deep down that it is a mockery, but he hasn't done anything in this moment to prove it. It was just a knowing that I had and that isn't enough to let the anger out.

I had to forgive him. It was clear in every church lesson that those who didn't forgive held the bigger sin. I thought about the horrible things my dad had done over the years and knew that I could never allow myself to be worse than him. If God saw me as worse than Dad, then my dreams about making it to Heaven and having a perfect family would never happen. They say it's a choice, but there was no choice here. I was being forced into a forgiveness that I didn't feel ready to give.

I felt God watching me to see what I would decide. I couldn't just say the right words to say them because that was lying, which was not ok either. If I said the words, I had to follow through and mean them. I didn't want to forgive him, he had hurt too many, he was still hurting so many. Why did I have to forgive him just because he asked me? Why did I have to be the worse person if I could not forgive him?

Dad was still staring at me, and I felt God judging me. Both seeing if I would say what I was supposed to say, mean what I was supposed to mean. My thoughts swirled in a repeated whirlwind. If I lied right now, then God would continue to judge me. I would be diminished in his eyes, not worthy of his love anymore. The connection we had been building would be gone. If I lied, would I even be able to keep my family for eternity? Everything I had been working for would be gone in that instant. If I fail this test, then I'm no longer going to be the person I strive so hard to be every day. I can't lie.

I knew I must forgive him, and I have to mean it. It doesn't matter what I'm feeling inside because I must do what God is telling me to do or I'm going to be the one who suffers eternally under the weight of my father's sins. I can't be like him, I can't take that, but I don't know how to forgive him either. Why did he have to ask for my forgiveness?

A solid minute has passed while I try to contain my composure. Keeping my body still, my face without emotion, willing the little hairs to lie back down. The thoughts were spiraling too fast for me to even know what they were and the emotions were so close to erupting that it took everything I had to just stand there.

I heard the words slip out of my mouth against my own will, through the mouth of a religion that betrayed me in that moment, I had to decide between being true to myself and the religion I held so dear. I could no longer be true to what I felt.

"I forgive you." I whispered.

I meant it, I had to mean it. The words had slipped out, and I would not let myself be a liar. I felt a weight had lifted off my shoulders. I'm not sure if this was because of the forgiveness or just that the moment was over. He said thank you and left the room. That was it. He took what he wanted and left.

Now I had to live the words that slipped out of my mouth. If I did not forgive him, God would hate me. I had to forgive him, or I would have been worse than him. I fell into my own pile of tears as the weight was simultaneously lifted and now felt a thousand times more burdensome. I lived in a duality of what I felt was right and what I felt my God thought was right. Shouldn't they be the same? shouldn't right be right? But it wasn't. I was angry at God, myself, and at the world for putting me in this position. The sexual abuse never happened to me again, but the torment of my soul was far from being over, it has been ripped open in an entirely new way.

The problem with forgiveness is that the memories always come back around. Right when you think you can heal and move on, something will trigger the memories and the anger and rage come back just as strong or sometimes stronger. It's worse now because I'm not just angry about the past, but I'm irate at myself for being vulnerable enough, blind enough, naïve even, to think I could put it all behind me and forget about it. Now I must face the anger all over again and forgive him again and again with the anger building each time because I didn't want to forgive him in the first place.

I had already set the precedent for my choices when I said the words "I forgive you." Every time the anger would rage within me, I had to forgive him over and over, and over. God was there each time, watching to make sure I would make the right choice. His choice. There was so much resentment, disgust, sorrow, and hopelessness that I had to lock away and forget about it. It was the day that the lost little girl, that broken part of me that just wanted someone to stand up for her, fight for her, to tell her story and share her truths, was silenced. The hope was gone.

I was taught through the church that to truly forgive someone you must forgive and forget, it meant that I couldn't tell anyone what happened, because if I did, I would not be honoring the forgiveness. I had to compartmentalize the past from my current reality. I knew I had to separate myself from that broken little girl because I could not fight for her in a way that would honor her; so, I had to lock her up. I couldn't fight for her and stay true to the religion that had provided hope and guidance. But I could still hear her tears as she cried out in my dreams. I could still feel her fear every time my father walked into a room. I felt her sorrow every time an opportunity was missed to tell her story, to break free. I had chosen a family. I had chosen the idea that I could fix the abuse that happened in my family for generations. I had to forgive and forget because it was the only way to honor God and he was the one who was helping me to survive every day. He was the one who could make my family perfect. I HAD to be the best Mormon that I could be. I chose to do this God's way and not mine. That meant that I needed to throw myself into this religion with no room for doubts because I desperately needed it all to be true.

Chapter Nine
Trade Shows

I still felt betrayal and relief, even though I had forgiven myself. I tried to sleep, shifting my weight on the waterbed to create gentle ripples that would rock me to sleep. It seemed to take forever as the words and feelings from the previous conversation continued to invade my thoughts. Forgive and forget. I wish I could forget, then maybe I could get some sleep, I thought cynically. I wondered if the church understood the damage their teachings caused in my life. Would my family be ok now? Amidst the constant stream of thoughts, I eventually fell into a deep, dreamless sleep, a result of pure exhaustion and concealed depression.

It was Thursday morning; we were packing for another trade show this weekend. We had a repeated monthly pattern with each weekend spent in a different city. The first weekend of every month was at the Nashville, Tennessee fairgrounds, and the last weekend was at the Louisville, Kentucky fairgrounds. We explored new venues on the other two weekends; Clarksville, Tennessee, was the most common. This weekend we would go to Louisville, Kentucky, which was my preferred trade show because many of my favorite vendors would be there, and the booths had higher-quality merchandise.

My morning alarm woke me up, playing a familiar song. It was from a CD I received from a past church camp and the uplifting words helped start my day on a positive note. I walked upstairs, scanning the floor for dog poop before unlocking the front door and flipping the closed sign to open. Mom was working on one last casting session while Dad finished a few jewelry repairs for the customers we worked with at the Louisville show last month. Deborah and I were setting stones and polishing jewelry to increase our inventory.

We stopped the last bit of hustling to pack the van. The light blue utility van was past its prime. The exterior of the van was covered in old paint and growing rust spots. It ran most of the time, which was better than past vehicles we owned. A twin-size mattress was placed between the front seats and the bench seat so we could sleep or just have a place to stretch out. The back of the van was filled with two, six-foot display cases that were stacked on top of each other. We filled the remaining space with the jewelry workbench, tools needed to repair jewelry, and two stools.

We finished loading the van, but mom had more work to complete for orders we had received on eBay. Dad and I got in the van to drive to Taco Bell. He moved out of the parking spot in front of the shop to the exit. A stool shifted in the back of the van, making a troubling sound.

"Do you think we need to rearrange stuff in the back?" dad asked me

I looked back and saw that the stool had moved into a stable position and that it wasn't able to move further.

"Nah, I think it's ok," I said.

Dad turned back into the parking lot and sat there for a minute, like he was waiting for something. I looked at the stool again and it was still in a stable spot.

"Why aren't we going?" I asked, confused.

"I asked you to rearrange the stuff in the back," he said in a frustrated tone laced with a hint of anger.

I didn't understand, he asked a question, and I responded to him. "Why are you getting angry?" I asked, uncertain.

He barked back at me in a harsh tone, "I was trying to be polite. I wasn't asking you about your opinion; I want you to stop being lazy and get out of the car and rearrange the stool in the back before it hits one of the display cases and breaks everything."

After getting out of the car, I opened the back door. The stool had fallen in such a way that it was in no danger of hurting the display cases. I wiggled the chair and pretended to move some stuff around, but it had settled into a better position and was best where it was. "If you wanted me to move things around, you could have asked for that, but you asked my opinion and so that's what I gave you." My anger pushed against his.

"I was trying to be polite," he stated.

"It was misleading," I countered.

He put the car in drive and sped through the parking lot, letting me know he was angry through his speed instead of arguing with me. We drove to Taco Bell, where he ordered ten soft tacos, ten hard tacos, and ten burritos. He never asked us what we wanted because that was too complicated.

When we got back home Deborah and mom were ready to go. Mom grabbed the dog and got in the front seat while Deborah climbed into the back seat with me. An hour into the trip, I asked dad if we could stop to use the bathroom.

"I'll stop soon," dad said. He handed me a book to read. This was before books on tape, and dad wanted us to read out loud for the entire eight hour trip. It was our job to entertain him while we drove. We didn't even get to choose what book we would read or for how long. I didn't feel like reading, I got car sick and I still had to pee.

"Do I have to read right now?" I asked.

"This is part of your homeschooling. You want an education, don't you?" I knew he didn't care about my education; he was just twisting my needs for his purposes. I learned to read out loud well, and I learned math because those things benefited him. He paid for my sister's education because she was majoring in accounting at his request, and so he encouraged her higher education.

I read the Cat Who series book out loud. We each took a turn reading a chapter. It had been a little over an hour and I still had to use the restroom. My stomach was hurting from the constant pressure.

"Dad, I really need to use the bathroom!" I asked him again.

"Yeah, just a few more minutes," he said dismissively. I lay down on the twin mattress, trying to sleep through the increasing discomfort. Mom was reading now, and I drifted in and out of consciousness. I could not fall into any kind of deep sleep for fear of peeing. I was willing to use the side of the road if he would just pull over, but it was another hour before he finally turned into a gas station. He didn't pull over for me, but because the car was running low on gas. I climbed out of the car and raced into the gas station to use their restroom. We stopped at this same gas station often on our trips. Dad had certain places where he would stop, and he refused to pull over at any other time, regardless of the reason. I learned to avoid drinking water other than a few sips here and there to keep my throat hydrated while reading.

Back in the van, Deborah was taking her turn to read, and dad was snacking on pork rinds, the crunching sound filling the vehicle. I struggle with the sound of people eating and I was doing my best to tune it out. I sat on the mattress with my back against the side of the van, snacking on goldfish and reading my own book. It was getting dark outside and there were fewer cars on the road. Dad driving in the middle of the two-lane highway.

"Why don't you stay in your own lane?" Mom asked dad.

"I pay taxes on both sides of the road; I don't see why I can't drive where I want to." He said while driving over the dotted white lines. Dad was getting tired, drifting from lane to lane and shaking his head every few minutes to stop his vision from going blurry from exhaustion.

It was my turn to read again. I put my book down and sat on the bench seat, leaning forward so that Dad could hear me while I read his book. We got to Louisville at about eleven pm that night. Our booth was always on the third row back from the check-in booth. We drove into the building and carefully navigated the other vehicles and booths who were setting up. Sometimes there would only be an inch or two between our car and someone's pottery booth. This part always made me anxious, but dad was phenomenal at navigating these tight situations. We unloaded the van into a pile in our booth and parked the van outside. We worked to set up the booth as much as possible before they kicked us out that night. I think it was about 1 am by the time we made it back to the hotel. We stayed right outside of the fairgrounds with most of the other vendors. The hotel staff was always excellent, going out of their way to accommodate the trade show guest. We woke up the next morning and ate breakfast, the staff bustling about to keep up with the high demands of so many people that morning. We chatted with them and with each other about how we thought the show would turn out that weekend. Deborah and I made a bagel with butter and cream cheese, making sure that the cream cheese made it over every part of the bagel. Deborah's precision spreading of butter and cream cheese would drive dad crazy because it took extra time.

I loved the shows; getting to see thousands of people every day. I enjoyed the freedom of walking around the booths and chatting with the other vendors. We were like a family that met together every weekend. When it was slow, we walked around and chatted with the vendors. I would always find things to spend my money on. Deborah saved hers, and mom would hit up the bins of food and get us some chocolate treats for the weekend.

The traffic in the show picked up after lunch and while we were busy, we had to stay at the booth. It took Deborah, mom, and I to keep up with all the people who stopped by our booth. We were all good at attracting potential customers and turning them into sales.

"Hello!" I called to a woman walking by. She was holding hands with her significant other. "I love your shirt," I complimented her. The compliments I gave varied but were always truthful. It helped to make them smile and be more open to talking.

"Thank you!" she said, taking a second look at what we sold. I assessed her jewelry and clothing to see if she was someone who would be interested. She had on two rings. One was her wedding ring, and the other was a cheap ring that showed where the plating had rubbed off. She wore a necklace that looked like it was gold with an amethyst in it and a small diamond on top.

"What were you guys looking for today?" I asked to start the conversation and to stall them from walking on.

"We are just looking," they said. This was the response I got most often, and I enjoyed switching out how I replied to see different reactions.

"Aww man, you're giving me that line." I said jokingly, "let me at least give you something good to look at. What's your favorite stone?"

"I don't know, I don't have one." The customer replied

"Well, what's your favorite color?" I asked

"I like blue, I guess; I don't have a favorite," she said.

She had not walked away yet, which means she was just being polite or was slightly interested. I knew I didn't have her full attention, and her husband was tugging on her arm to move her away from the booth.

"What month were you born in?" I asked her.

"March," she said.

"I have a gorgeous ring for you to check out!" I brought out an aquamarine ring and handed it to her. She let go of her husband's hand and grabbed the ring. She was now facing the booth and fully engaged with me. She tried the ring on, unsure if she liked it. I took the entire tray of gold rings out and placed it in front of her. I love this tanzanite, I mentioned to her. The deep purplish blue sparkled at her as her face lit up. "Here, try it on", I said, handing it to her. She kept trying rings on and I turned my attention to her husband. "Have you found anything you like yet?" I asked. He held up the bag he was holding. "I got this knife," he said excitedly as he took it out of his bag.

"That looks awesome!" I encouraged him as he showed me the knife. I opened and closed it a few times and felt the edge of the blade, showing appropriate praise while giving his wife time to try on more rings. She had found another ring, this one a blue topaz. Blue topaz was good because the price point was within most people's budget.

"How much is this one?" she asked me. I knew I had the sale at this point.

The ring did not have a price tag on it; I approached dad and asked quietly how much it would be.

"Eh, I guess about $125." He told me.

I loved to barter; it was part of the sales process for me. I also liked the challenge of selling things for more than Dad thought they were worth.

Turning back to the couple I said, "The gold itself comes to about $150 and the stone is about $50, making it come to $200." I knew it was still a reasonable price compared to a regular jewelry store, even if I upped the price. She looked hesitant; I needed to change tactics.

I looked at her husband and asked, "When is the last time you bought her something meaningful that was more than $20?" He thought about it. "She just got some clothes," he said.

"That's a necessity," I returned, "what about something that is for no other reason than to let her know you love her?"

She was looking at him, watching what he would say. I took the heat off him and turned my attention to her. "What about you? When is the last time that you bought yourself something that was just for you?" I asked her. This line always worked. I had learned that most women I talked to put everyone else in front of their own needs and rarely bought things for themselves, which made it an excellent selling point.

"I don't need it," she said and took the ring off.

I looked at her husband again. "What if I dropped the price to $180?" I asked him.

They looked at each other. He was giving in to the idea. I could tell she still thought it was too much money by her hesitation. I waited for them to counter my offer. "Would you take $160?" she asked me hesitantly. I wanted to make her feel confident about her purchase and I love it when people countered me. "Tell ya what, I want to make sure you are comfortable with this ring. I'll drop the price to $150 and I'll throw in a free ring sizing to go with it."

Her face lit up, and she beamed at her husband while he nodded his consent. She was happy with her new ring, and I was happy to have sold it for more than Dad said. I added the tax in my head and took her credit card to complete her purchase while scanning the crowd for the next person who may show some interest.

We worked hard for a couple of hours until my stomach growled. Mom gave me a few pieces of chocolate and I ate goldfish. Mom and dad always had a couple of 64 oz thermoses filled with diet coke. I knew we didn't have time to stop for food right now. When it finally slowed down, I made us sandwiches from the ingredients we had in the cooler. I took out the white bread and put on a thick layer of mayonnaise. The package of meat held about ten slices, but they were cut so thin you could see through them and were nearly impossible to separate into individual slices. The package had enough meat for maybe one sandwich, but we made it last for four. With the goldfish and other snacks, we were not starving, but we were never really full either.

When the show ended for the day, we would go out to eat at a decent restaurant with a few other vendors. The Chinese buffet was the favorite because of the all-you-can-eat crab legs. I filled my plate up with a few crab legs, rice, and some beef and broccoli. Mom and Dad both filled their plates with about five sets of legs each. An hour passed as we cracked open crab legs and chatted with the other vendors. We talked about how much money we each made that day and ways to make it better. There was always a friendly competition of who made more, but we were also a community and shared ideas on how to increase sales and traffic. Mom and dad both returned to the buffet for another heaping pile of crab legs. I had consumed all that I wanted and out of boredom, helped them to crack their crab legs to speed up the process. When dad finished his second plate, he ate the rest of the rice and beef and broccoli off my plate and my sister's orange chicken and noodles before getting his third plate of crab legs. I think he had about three pounds of crap legs per plate. It was usual for dad to have at least three heaping plates of food plus finishing our food. It was as if he didn't have an off switch when it came to food. He just keeps eating at everyone else's expense. At the end of the third hour, dad was considering another plate of crab legs. However, the Chinese couple who owned the restaurant came out and gave us our bill saying that they needed the table. It was a polite but firm dismissal. Deborah and I were just grateful that we could finally leave the restaurant and get back to the hotel room.

Saturday morning, we stopped by to grab a continental breakfast in the hotel lobby. At the show, dad had a few repairs to finish, so Deborah and I went for a walk around the market before it got busy. One of my favorite booths had hundreds of small figurines and collector cards I loved to buy. We stopped to talk to Nick, the knife guy. He always took the time to talk and joke around with us. We avoided the baby clothes guy because he gave an unsettling vibe and always stood too close to me. We said hello to the carpet guy and the leather belt guy. There was a lady who painted portraits we said hello to as well. Then we stopped to pick up the delicious sugary lemonade before heading back to our booth.

The crowd picked up at about eleven am and we engaged with the crowd. Each person was a new puzzle, and I loved working different angles to make the sale. I drank the entire oversized lemonade between each person and needed to use the bathroom. It took about five minutes to snake through the crowds to the bathrooms and another five to get back. That was if there was no line. It could take upwards of twenty minutes to get there and back to the booth on a busy day. We had been working for a few hours when I needed to use the bathroom.

"Hey Dad, I need to go to the bathroom," I told him. He looked up at the thick crowd, rolling his eyes at me.

"We don't have time for you to leave right now." He said, annoyed I was asking.

I had already waited as long as I could, understanding how busy we were. I turned to mom, "Mom, I really need to go." She looked at dad as they silently went back and forth.

Dad huffed, sounding like an indignant teen who wasn't getting his way as he jerked his jewelry glasses down and got back to work. I could hear him telling mom how I purposely picked the most inconvenient times to go to the bathroom as I walked away. I felt guilty, but didn't know what else I could do. I dashed to the bathroom and back as fast as I could and got back to selling. The show didn't slow down until about 7 p.m. that night. we did not have the opportunity to eat more than a handful of goldfish crackers since breakfast that morning.

We were exhausted and just wanted to go back to the hotel room and relax. We grabbed fast food and drove back to the hotel, where we watched the TV show Pretender while taking turns showering. When Pretender ended, dad took over the TV while he sat on the edge of his bed scratching his feet for the next hour, the flakes of skin looking like snow on the ground. He left a pile of dead skin from his feet on the floor of every hotel room we visited. The rest of us were always careful to walk around the space or wear shoes.

It was frustrating when dad took over the TV, He would choose something only he liked, instead of finding something we could all agree on. It was just another small area where he could insert his dominance. Deborah and I both loved to read. She was reading the Wheel of Time by Robert Jordan and I was reading the Myth series by Adam Asprin. When it was time to sleep, Dad still wanted to watch TV and refused to turn it off. I put a pillow over my head to block out the light and noise. Once he assumed we were sleeping, he would switch the channel to whatever late-night porn he could find. If we moved or twitched at all, he would quickly change the channel and yell at us to go back to sleep.

I brought the sheet up over my pillow, leaving just enough space for my nose to stick out so I could breathe. He was selfish and unaware, or uncaring, about how others felt in his presence. He expected us to jump at his commands but hated any rules imposed on him. Rules were just personal challenges made to be broken. Porn was one of the major sins in our church. They consistently preached about it, yet here he was, breaking God's law because even God was his pawn.

At least the TV was quieter than his snoring, which was often compared to a freight train. The other vendors joked about making sure they were in a different hallway than us so they could sleep through his snoring. The goal was to fall asleep before he did, but when that didn't happen, we would just have to deal with his loud noises. We had tried to find different solutions; I asked for a separate hotel room. He was offended by that question. We tried waking him up to get to sleep before him, but he fell asleep faster than I could. He defensively told us to put a pillow over our heads. Thinking about this just added to my anger. He saw it as a personal offense against him instead of trying to work out a solution. He expected to sleep through the noise and didn't care how it affected us.

That part of him that feels for other people, it was just broken, or maybe he never had it. I wiggled under the covers just to irritate him. He changed the channel in a panic, like we didn't know he was watching porn. It was childish, but I was angry about who he was and how he treated us. It took a few more times of shuffling around before he huffed and turned off the television. I had about five minutes to fall asleep before his snoring started. He was my prime example of everything I never wanted to be.

On Sunday, the show ended earlier to give all the vendors a chance to pack up their inventory. After working the show that day, we packed up and drove out at about 8 p.m. Once we were on the road, we counted to see how much we had made that weekend, about $3,500, which was average for this show. Dad paid us $150 each for our work that weekend. It was nice to get paid, but we had to buy anything we needed, like clothes or summer camps out of that money. I was trying to pay dad off for one of the church camps I had coming up and handed him $50 to pay for the camp. We read out loud to dad for a few hours until he said we could sleep. My sister lay on the bench, and I slept on the mattress until we arrived back at the store at about 2 a.m.

Chapter Ten
Stay Positive, Stay Alive

The next weekend we were traveling to Clarksville, Tennessee in an older RV that we borrowed so we could save money on a hotel. We were now selling a variety of onyx rocks shaped like obelisks, vases, and spheres of all sizes.

It took us most of the day to load up all the onyx, jewelry workbench, and display cases. By the time we were ready to drive out, it was later than our normal routine. We stayed the night at my grandmother's house located halfway to Clarksville. We would just get to the show Friday morning and set up our booth as much as we could before the show started.

Friday morning, we woke up around 6 a.m. to the smells of bacon, sausage, and biscuits. My grandmother had been in the kitchen for an hour already, making sure that we had a hearty breakfast before we left. She always made sure that there was a glass of grape juice sitting at the table just for me. We gathered around the table to eat. I filled my plate with sausage, eggs, fruit, and bacon, skipping the biscuits. While we ate, dad kept looking back and forth between me and the biscuits with a mixture of disappointment and confusion.

"Why aren't you eating a biscuit?" he asked me.

"Because I don't like them," I said

"I don't understand how a girl from the south can't like biscuits," he said in a confused tone

"They're dry," I said, picking up a fresh strawberry to eat.

"Then put butter or jam on it," he said as if that would magically make me like biscuits.

"I have before, and I still don't like them. There are plenty of healthier foods here that I like. Why does it matter to you so much?." I was pushing back against his words, and I knew he felt my irritation.

"I just don't understand," he said, irritation slipping into his words as we stared each other down.

"You need to listen to your father and eat the biscuit," my grandmother interrupted.

"I don't like them and there is no nutritional value here" This was a pointless argument, and I was getting more frustrated. Why did it bother them so much?

"I want you to eat a biscuit at every meal we have at your grandmother's table. It's rude to not eat them and it doesn't make sense that you don't like them." Dad said in a voice that left no room for arguing.

"You need to show more respect for your father," Grandmother said.

They did this a lot, backed each other up even when it made no sense; especially when it made no sense. This wasn't about food. Dad had already repeatedly proven that he didn't care what we ate or even made sure we had enough food. This was about control. Dad did not like the idea that I didn't like biscuits and because he could not understand, he was determined to force me to eat them. I was furious. He had Grandmother backing him up, and she was the most stubborn woman I had ever met. She was fiercely defensive about making sure her son got everything he ever wanted. It was an unusual relationship that extended beyond rational thinking. She was also particularly spiteful when things didn't happen her way and she would ensure I understood who was in charge. They both stared at me, and I knew I didn't have a choice. They wouldn't let me leave the table if I didn't eat a damn biscuit.

"If you don't eat the biscuit, we will wrap it up and send it with you," Grandmother said.

Dad chimed in, "you won't be allowed any other food until you eat the biscuit."

It was a standoff, and I was losing. I knew if I talked back there would be some sort of consequence. I also knew they truly meant I wasn't going to be allowed to eat anything else. When these two teamed up, it amplified both of their stubbornness.

I picked up a biscuit and began nibbling. It was so dry it made me choke, or maybe it was the tears I was holding back because it all felt so hopeless. I hated being fifteen. I hated not being able to control my life. I hated that these two people had the ability to take my control away and used that power for ridiculous reasons. Where was the logic in this? How did eating the biscuit benefit me in any way? If this was about respect as they said, then why didn't it apply both ways? Why was grandmother backing dad up on this? All these questions combined to form the bottom-line answer to all of it, it was about control. It left me feeling helpless, infuriated, and resentful. There was nothing to do with all these overwhelming emotions but to control them so that none of it showed on my face. If I pushed back, so would they, and I would be in an even worse situation.

They saw that I was eating the biscuit; that they had won this battle. Dad headed outside to the RV parked on the street. He removed the rock placed under the tires and tried to put the RV. into drive, but instead, it began to slowly roll backwards onto the main road. Dad grabbed the steering wheel and used it to lift himself up, putting his whole 375 pounds on the brakes. The RV continued to slide into the street below. It finally came to a stop when the road leveled out, blocking an entire lane of traffic. It was still early in the morning, and fortunately, there were not many cars out. He managed to put the RV in the right gear and pulled it forward.

"It will be fine," Dad said in response to the look on mom's face.

Deborah and I apprehensively got into the RV. A few hours into the trip, we were traveling up a long steep hill when the RV began to overheat. Dad pulled off to the side of the road to let the engine cool down. The RV slowed down quickly but then rolled backward down the hill. This time we were on a major highway and although we were on the side of the road, there was a lot more traffic. Mom began screaming at dad as the RV gained backward momentum. She frantically searched for the button to turn on the emergency flashers and warn other drivers. Deborah and I searched for the buckles buried deep in the pull-out sofa without success. Dad was standing on the brakes again while simultaneously steering the RV in reverse. I looked out the side of the RV to watch the traffic slowing down and moving into the left lane to give us space. The road leveled out, and the RV finally came to a stop. We sat there for a minute in silence as we realized how close we were to death. It would have been a serious accident. The RV was old and already falling apart. We had not been able to buckle up and the heavy load of rocks in the back of the RV would have added to the impact. Mom sat in the front seat, furious. She refused to look at or talk to my dad before entering a complete shutdown. Deborah and I looked at each other, making sure the other one was alright. We were both pale from fear, but otherwise unharmed.

"We're ok," dad's words hung in the air. "The RV will cool off and then we will drive on. This is the steepest hill on the trip, so we will take it slow and gentle up this hill and the rest of the drive will be cake."

We didn't say anything. What could we say? He was willingly putting our lives at risk. Was he that oblivious to the danger?

"We have a show to get to and we are running out of time," he said.

We sat in silence as we waited for the engine to cool down and then dad restarted the RV. He slowly climbed the hill in the emergency lane and although the RV indicated it was running hot, it didn't overheat again. Once on the other side of the hill, the engine began to cool off.

We made it to the show without another problem. I don't know if that's good or not. When things work out like that, it just encourages Dad's poor choices, enforcing that he was right. But he wasn't, he had put us in danger. Just because we arrived at our destination didn't mean he had made the right choice for us.

When we arrived at the show we could not drive in because it was too late, so we had to use a dolly to bring everything in. There were always people around with their personal dollies to help load and unload vehicles. We hired a fifteen-year-old boy with a larger cart to speed up the process. Inside we worked twice as fast to unbox all the rocks and create the display before the show started.

The show opened to the public while we were still unloading the RV. There was one large onyx sphere left. It was a major attraction that brought people to our booth. It was two and a half feet in diameter and weighed about 300 pounds. Dad asked me and the boy to get the sphere. I thought it was too heavy, but the boy was a showoff and wanted to take on the challenge. We wheeled the cart out to the RV and positioned it under the back door. The box that held the sphere was dilapidated from being moved so much that it barely contained the sphere. The boy got in the RV and scooted the box to the edge of the back door. He jumped down, and we positioned ourselves on either side of the cart. We grabbed the box, planning to let it fall on the cart in a controlled manner. It would have worked, but the box was too far damaged, allowing the sphere to roll out. It was like slow motion watching the sphere slip out of the box. I imagined how angry dad would be if the sphere broke; it was an expensive item. I reacted quickly, catching the sphere just as it hit the concrete. It took a moment to register that the tip of my ring finger had been jammed between the 300-pound rock and the pavement. Blood was pouring out from under my nail making it hard to see the damage. We worked to put the sphere back in the box that was sitting on the cart and pushed it inside. Tears were rolling down my face from the pain. I immediately showed dad my injury and asked if we could go to the doctor to have it checked out. The tip of my finger was flat and deformed, my nail was pushed down into my finger. The entire finger was swelling up leaving me scared about permanent damage.

Dad looked at my finger to assess the damage. "It doesn't look that serious," he said to brush me off. "The doctor won't do anything besides wrapping it up which we don't have time for right now." Mom gave Dad a dirty look but didn't say anything, she gave me some medicine to help with the pain.

Halfway through the day, my entire finger was a deep purple and hardened from the swelling. The throbbing had intensified as did the pain. Dad was repairing some jewelry; I interrupted him to ask if we could go to the doctor again. He looked annoyed for a minute and then covered up his expression.

"Let me see it," he said

I held my hand out to him and he looked at it closely for a minute.

"All we need to do is drill a hole through your nail so the blood can be released and then you will be fine," he said while grabbing his Dremel.

"Can't a doctor do that?" I asked eyeing his Dremel with trepidation.

"Yes, but we don't have time. Just give me your hand, this will only take a second."

"What about all the dirt?" his Dremel was filthy, covered with gold dust and grime from the jewelry, and the buildup of oils, pork rind dust, and other food from dad's hands over the years. It was an infection waiting to happen.

He sighed, annoyed that I was taking so much of his time and that I had insinuated he was dirty. "The dirt isn't going to kill you," he said as he reached out for my hand. "I'll heat the tip of the drill bit with the torch to kill any bacteria"

The pain was getting more intense, but I knew he wouldn't take me to the doctor. It was just too inconvenient. I was terrified but gave him my hand; he drilled into the middle of my nail. The heat was instant, and I yelped in pain, but dad only held my hand tighter. He stopped drilling for a second to let my nail cool, then continued. He got through my nail and blood poured out of the hole. Mom had found Neosporin and band-aids at another booth that she put over the hole. Dad wiped the blood off with his dirty leather apron he wore while working and returned to repairing jewelry with the same bit on the Dremel.

It lessened the pain, but I still wanted to go to the doctor. I was still worried about an infection and if my finger was broken. I needed to relieve the pain. I wanted to quit; I wanted parents who cared about me. I wished that my safety mattered, but the evidence was clear. I remembered Dad's promise of how he would pay for my education and buy my first car. I didn't say anything further, it would not have made a difference. With my stomach growling and the crowds picking up, I grabbed a handful of popcorn and got back to work.

When the show was over, we walked out to our RV. in the parking lot. We made a simple dinner of baked beans and hot dogs. I made up my bed and curled up in the corner to read. With each throbbing sensation of my finger, the futility of my situation melted away the thread of positivity I had been able to hold onto. Depression was edging in, with bouts of anger at dad for his dismissal of anything he saw as problematic to his own agenda.

∞

The next morning, I heard Dad's alarm go off. He rolled over to press the button. I felt sick to my stomach and had an awful migraine, I didn't want to move. He must have pressed the snooze button because his alarm was going off again. He didn't usually push the snooze button. I looked over at Deborah through half-closed eyes; she looked pale. I wanted to fall back to sleep but the pain in my finger wouldn't let me. I lay there for a few minutes when Dad's alarm rang the third time. That NEVER happened. I heard him and mom talking in muffled tones in the back room of the RV. When Dad walked out, a shiny gleam of sweat covered his whole body and he looked like the color of an off-white onion. Deborah darted past me into the bathroom and threw up. That created a chain reaction and we all threw up.

"We could have food poisoning," dad wondered out loud.

Mom came out of bed looking as terrible as the rest of us. "I don't think I can work the show like this. I have a migraine," she told dad.

"We have customers that want to meet us at the booth right when the show opens, and we can't be late or we will get in trouble with the show host."

We were still a few minutes late despite our best efforts that morning. Dad and I arrived at the show first, and then Deborah and mom followed thirty minutes later. There were a few people already at our booth waiting on repairs from the previous day. We quickly removed the sheets covering the displays and grabbed their orders.

As the day wore on, we slowly began to feel better. My finger was still a dark shade of purple, but the swelling had gone down a bit. I could see that the tip of my finger was misshapen, perhaps permanently.

Dad was talking to one of our customers about what happened.

"Do you think it could be carbon monoxide poisoning?" they asked.

"Huh, I hadn't considered that," Dad said.

"You can easily buy a test that will let you know if you have a leak," the customer informed us.

I had a friend who died of this when I was younger, and the idea was disturbing.

That night after the show, we bought a carbon monoxide test. It had been ten hours since we woke up that morning. The test read 400ppm. Anything over 150ppm is enough to cause disorientation, unconsciousness, and death. We should never have woken up that morning, and from the way we were feeling, we almost didn't. If dad had pressed the off button instead of the snooze or If we had gone back to sleep giving into the migraines and stomach aches, we would have died. The only reason we were alive was the customer who we had to meet that morning.

"Are we going to stay in a hotel tonight?" Mom asked dad.

"No, we can air out the RV and we won't use the generator tonight. Besides, we have the test now and it will let us know if the levels get bad again.

Sometimes, I just didn't have the words to describe how I felt. I could have raged, I guess, I could have refused to sleep in the RV. I know I should do something, and yet no words would come out of my mouth. He was so stupid and reckless with our lives. You need to be more positive, I told myself, trying to hold off the deep anger that I had to constantly keep in check. It was difficult to be positive when your life means so little to your parents. Revealing my thoughts would do no good.

"It would be safer in a hotel," I said, with the only controlled voice I had left.

"There is no point in spending money on a hotel when we've already spent so much on the gas to get us here," he retorted.

My dad is a genius, I know this. I see his mind calculating everything. He can solve math problems instantly, find a solution to any problem, and he remembers everything. His eyes are constantly moving as he observes his environment. He was savvy too, I've watched him frequently outwit others, talk himself out of every police ticket, barter any price down, and convince everyone with words that he was a decent person. So how can he be so incredibly stupid? I worked hard to control my thoughts. I try to forgive and forget when I need to. I aim to honor my parents as the church teaches. I strive to be positive even when things are rough. I tried to think of life after I move out, of my education and future family, and how happy I can be in the future. But will I even make it that far in life when someone so irresponsible and heartless is making decisions for me? I wanted to fight, but at the same time, I was exhausted from all the stress in my life. I was tired from the carbon monoxide poisoning, my finger still throbbed, and I was terrified of sleeping in this death trap another night. If he was willing to make us sleep in the RV another night, it could only mean that he didn't care if we lived or died. Did he think he could outwit God? He probably did. Maybe it was just another move in his game. We all die together, or we all live together but at least we are together.

I wish I could have known what passed through his head sometimes. I wanted to know why he thought these kinds of things were acceptable when clearly, they were not. I wanted to understand why he would take such casual liberties with our lives. It reflected in everything he did, in all the choices he made for us. He never

106

considered what was best for us, only what benefited him. Like forcing me to eat a biscuit the day before, there was no logic, only the thoughts in his head, only control. Is that what this is about? Seeing if you can control us? Watching us sleep in these beds of death even though every part of us is screaming that this is wrong? Do you make yourself feel better seeing how powerful you are over your wife and teenage daughters? Does it make you feel more like a man? Do you get some weird kick out of putting us in dangerous situations? How can you make sense of putting your family in an unsafe vehicle that almost killed us three times in one weekend and here we are again sleeping in the same place that almost killed us last night? How is this ok with you?

It makes you worthless in my eyes and I hated every single fat, gray, greasy, slimy part of you. I hated looking at your calculating face knowing it never meant anything positive. You're just a useless piece of trash to me, just as I am to you. Maybe it would be better if we all slept in this RV tonight and died, because then you would be taken out of this world. It would be a better place for everyone. No more abuse and no more damaging words and controlling mannerisms. There would just be peace where there used to be torment and pain. I could live with that idea, or not, I scoffed. Either way, I didn't get to decide.

Why were you so awful? Who made you this way? At what point in your life did you decide to molest your children? When did you think it was ok to cross every boundary ever made? Why do you think the rules never apply to you? You want to control our food, our education, and when we use the bathroom. You limit our reach into society and silently watch our every move. Now you are taking risks with our lives, AGAIN. Why do you see life as some chess game where you are always the king of your realm delegating others to their death and demise?

Do you realize you could have been different? I asked who made you this way, but it doesn't matter because you make your own choices now. You chose to be this horrible person every single day, in every single moment. You get to determine who you are, yet you always choose to be a perverse kind of person. Your choices are on you. It's not based on anything that happened to you; I'm not willing to let you off the hook like that. I don't care if anything has happened to you, because I have been through hell and back because of you, but I don't use it as an excuse to hurt people. I understand how disgusting your actions are, and I think you see it too.

You are responsible right now, at this moment for making a choice that has the potential to get us killed, and all you can do is talk about how we need to save $100 on a hotel as if our literal lives are not on the line. We know the full danger here. My best friend died from this when we were eight years old. I am terrified of having the same fate. I just couldn't believe how indescribably foolish you were at this moment.

I had found my words, just none that could leave my mouth. Sometimes hate isn't a strong enough word. Egotistical, arrogant, conceited, proud, vain, irresponsible, idiotic; all words to describe you, I guess, but not how I feel about you. Despise, loathe, dislike, detest? They didn't feel right, they didn't feel strong enough. Vile, evil, disgusting? Getting closer, I thought, but still not enough to describe the depths of my rage, my desperation to get out, my terror of sleeping tonight while breathing in my own death.

I slept that night thinking that maybe, just maybe, we would all fall asleep tonight and never wake up, Then I could watch your face as you explain your actions to God. I imagined the sorrow, pain, and misery on your face as you had to face judgment for, molesting and then killing your family.

Maybe this was just my mind's way of making peace with the death that I felt for sure was coming for us that night.

∞

We did wake up the next morning. Was this a good thing? I had come to terms with my death last night. I was ready to leave this earth and now here I am having to face the light of another day. I am having to go in and work a business I hate while staring at your repulsive face. I was still angry. Now I can't figure out if I'm angrier with dad for his control and manipulations or at me for allowing myself to be controlled and manipulated, or at God who didn't let me die last night. This nightmare could have been over.

Think positive, I told myself. I needed to get through this. The fact was, we are at the show today, we are alive, and we have customers to help. I threw myself into talking to as many people as I could, trying to make all the sales. If I didn't have time to think, then I wouldn't have to deal with it. I wish it worked like that, but thoughts always creep in.

He was ok with us dying last night. I squeezed my eyes shut, trying to block out the words. Stop it, Stephanie. He genuinely believed we would be ok, and he was right.

He is such a bastard. Stop it, Stephanie, he is doing the best he can with the knowledge he has…

Does he even want us alive? Of course, he does, who else would work for him for practically free…

Stop it, Stephanie, be grateful he pays you at all.

I should quit…

Stop it, Stephanie! This is paying for your college. It will be worth it when you get to leave.

What happened in his childhood to create this monster? The thought both taunted and enraged me because he would use it to excuse his behavior. Stop it, Stephanie! Identify the positive.

Monitoring every thought was a chore as I tempered the negativity. I remembered the hate that came with the insufficient words I used to describe my father. It was a path I had chosen not to take again. I didn't see how it would do me any good. I forced my thoughts to contemplate the future again. I dreamed about passing the GED, being accepted to college, graduating, and creating a stable family of my own. I thought about summer camps coming up and Wednesday nights with my friends at church. I thought about my bedroom and even though it flooded every time it rained, it was at least a space I could call my own.

I took a break and walked around the market intentionally connecting with each person and appreciating them. They had no idea what our life was like, and I liked it that way. I loved them for the little breaks they allowed my mind to take. We bantered and joked and eventually, I felt my body relax.

By the time I got back to the booth, I could look at his face and not want to vomit. That is progress, I guess.

I still wanted to please my Heavenly Father and he could hear all the thoughts that went through my head. I hope that he heard all the pain that was associated with them too. I hope he understood how desperate I was to be a better person. I know that each day and each moment I was also choosing who I want to be, and I had let my thoughts slip the night before. I didn't have that type of freedom if I was going to survive; if I was going to be different than dad. I was going to have to guard my thoughts more closely, pray more often, read my scriptures so that I can let go of all the rage, or at least keep it locked up so I can focus on being positive.

That night we slept in the RV again. We took it on a few more weekend trips before Dad decided it was cheaper to drive the van and stay in a hotel.

Stay positive. I just had to repeat those words to block out everything else. Stay Positive.

Chapter Eleven
Obsession

We were in a constant flow of packing, unpacking, selling, and prepping. This weekend we were back in the rusted blue van driving to Nashville, Tennessee. This flea market was the largest and took over the entire fairground once a month. It was the only market that had booths both inside and out. The vendors were a mix of brand-new goods, antiques, and yard sale booths.

The momentum of this show typically picked up around midday, which gave Deborah and me more time to walk around. We ventured outside to visit with the mother-daughter duo who sold flowers. They gave us a welcoming hug, and I sat down on one of their stools to hang out and watch their antics. When they were not busy, they were in constant playful banter with each other and other vendors around them, and they let us join in on the fun. It was one of my favorite booths to visit simply because of how they showered people with their love.

We walked by the knives booth and said hello; glad to see him at this show as well. We worked to avoid the shoe guys because they were a little too interested in all the wrong ways and made us uncomfortable. There was a guy we had not seen before who had a booth right down from ours. He sold pewter necklaces and other cheap jewelry. I wanted to buy a figurine of a sea turtle that was $10.

"Would you take $6?" I asked him. I started low, giving him room to raise the price while still getting a better deal.

"How about $8?" he said, sizing us up.

"$7 would be a reasonable compromise. Look at his face; the turtle looks lonely and needs a loving home." I joked around with him.

He laughed with me. "$7.50" he countered.

"Man, if only I had an extra 50 cents that turtle wouldn't have to look so lonely and underfed," I said with a playful gleam in my eye while taking a step away, implying he was losing the sale.

"Alright, alright, alright, $7, but only if you promise to feed him well."

"Sold! I handed him a $10 bill with a smirk. He laughed as he handed over my new turtle figurine and $3 in change. I loved to barter. It was more about the challenge of battling back and forth, a sort of mental sparring, and I thrived off it.

Our break was over, and we had to be back at the booth. A customer was talking with my mom about having a chain cleaned. I watched for a few minutes to see where I could help the best.

"Will you make a jeweler's bomb?" my mom asked me.

"Ok," I replied. I measured out the right amount of cyanide and poured it into an old coffee pot, placing it on the single stovetop burner with the necklace inside. I waited for the small amount of liquid to boil. We made several of these each day, mostly to clean chains, but sometimes it was just a fast way to clean up a piece of jewelry. The jewelry bomb would take off a micro-thin layer of gold, leaving the piece looking brand new. Once the cyanide was boiling, I dropped in the peroxide and stepped back as the smoke and bubbles whooshed up to the top of the pot, and sometimes out. I grabbed the chain with pliers and dropped it into the sonic jewelry cleaner to remove any remaining chemicals. The left-over solution would be poured into a container to be saved and refined one day.

I worked for a few more hours making sales when I felt my stomach grumble. We didn't bring a cooler this time, so I took a handful of popcorn that Deborah had bought earlier. Dad said we could buy hamburgers in a few hours when the foot traffic slowed down. I would have been angry, but this is my normal. I reminded myself why I was here; that my college would be paid for. I made sure I focused on being positive and that my thoughts were in check. I had a long-term goal, and I wasn't about to let a few stomach pains stop me from achieving the ultimate goal of a college education.

The bathrooms were located closer than usual to our booth. I asked mom if I could go to the restroom. I tried to avoid asking dad anymore as his answers came piled with negativity. When I walked away from the booth, I noticed the guy I bought the turtle from exiting his booth at the same time and walking in my direction. I thought it was odd for him to leave his booth when it was crowded with customers, and he was the only one working. I slipped through the thick crowd, leaving him behind.

On the way back, he came up behind me and tried talking to me. He was walking too close to me, and I felt uncomfortable. Maybe it's because of the thick crowds, or he has a hard time hearing, I told myself, trying to shake off the uneasy vibes.

∞

That night at the hotel, several vendors sat in the hot tub exchanging conversations. Most of the time, we were all too tired to do anything but eat and go back to our rooms. We never even considered bringing our swimsuits with us. We walked outside to say hello and greet our friends. They were chatting about the newest beanie baby craze. The trade show had to have police officers at the door that morning to control the crowd of people waiting to get in to see the vendor that sold beanie babies. We talked with the beanie baby man at the end of the day as we walked out of the show together. He bragged the entire time about how he had made several thousand dollars that day. He pointed to his socks, "This is where I put all of the money I made today, can't no one steal from me" he laughed. I looked at his socks. They were bulging out over the top of his shoes by a few inches. It looked as if his socks were bragging with him rather than hiding his money from thieves.

In the hotel room, I gathered my things to take a shower, being careful to walk around dad's white pile of dead foot skin. While I was showering, I could hear mom and dad talk about how much the shows were making and if this was the correct way to go forward. We began to sell jewelry on eBay and that business was picking up, meaning we didn't necessarily need the shows to survive anymore.

The next morning, we grabbed McDonald's on our way to the show. We were in more of a rush than usual because Dad had repairs to make that morning. When we drove in, I noticed the police stopping all the shoppers at the main gate until the show opened. They were all there for the beanie babies.

I walked over to say good morning to the flower lady and noticed the turtle guy trailing behind me. He made me nervous, he felt like bad intentions. I didn't wander around on that break, just quickly walked from one place to the next, keeping my eye on him as he followed me.

It was very busy that day and we worked for several hours without a break. When I finally did get a chance to walk away from the booth again, I checked to see if the turtle guy was at this booth. I didn't see him and thought it would be ok to leave. I walked in the opposite direction hoping to get out of sight quickly. He came up behind me and tried to grab my hand. I yanked my hand away and told him to stop. He was trying to talk to me, asking me why I was playing hard to get. I walked over to the lady who painted portraits and stood by her. He made another move by putting his arm around me; I told him sternly, to stop. He was unsafe, I needed to go back to my booth. I saw a couple of police officers walking in the same direction and if I left now, I would be in their sight most of the way back. Turtle guy tried to put his arm over my shoulder again. I spun out of his grip and yelled at him to stop touching me. He got mad at me and asked why I was making such a scene. I glanced at the officers behind us. He was bold to act like this in front of them. I knew I was in danger. I yelled at him to go away while watching the cops. I needed to make sure they were paying attention. Turtle guy huffed, "I'll see you later," he said as he walked off.

I quickly returned to my booth and did not leave for the rest of the day. I told my dad that he had been following me and how he had tried to put his arm around me. Dad blew it off. "You'll figure it out," he said putting his glasses back on.

"What?" I was exasperated. I'm fiercely independent; I had never asked my dad for help with a person. I could handle the occasional creeper just fine, but this guy was different. He was no longer just giving off bad vibes or making inappropriate comments, he was actually putting his hands on me. Why was dad just blowing me off?

"You'll be fine," he said again in response. I figured I was on my own.

The next day I watched turtle guy at his booth. When I needed to leave for any reason, I took Deborah with me. I saw him follow us; I looked at Dad to see if he would do anything. He was intensely watching the situation, eyes crinkled in concentration, but never moved from his spot. Deborah stayed with me as we bought hamburgers for lunch. He didn't approach us that time. When we got back dad was talking with a customer while surveying the crowd. I looked down at the turtle guy's booth and he wasn't there.

Over the next few hours, I helped customers while trying to keep an eye on the guy. He hadn't returned to his booth, customers kept asking the surrounding vendors how to pay for their items.

When it came time to pack up at the end of the weekend, we were always one of the last ones out. We usually had one or two customers still shopping so we would break down what we could without disturbing their shopping. The last customer of the day at any show was always worth a couple of hundred dollars making the time well worth it.

Mom was helping the customer while Deborah and I packed the little things and clutter from the weekend. The other vendors were in full swing breaking down their booths. The smaller booths were already empty. The turtle guy's booth still sat there untouched; he had not been back since that morning.

The customers made their purchase, and then we took down our displays. Dad walked outside to drive the van in so we could load it up. It took about an hour to pack up. We got into the van and drove out of the building with only three booths left. Two booths had people packing and the last booth was turtle guy, still untouched from that morning. We never saw him again at that show or any of the other shows.

I asked my dad about it on the way home, and he said it was strange, that he didn't know what had happened either. However, I got the feeling that he had stepped in to manage the situation. Did he just protect me?

We stopped off at a truck stop to fill up on gas and snacks. While we were looking around there were some books on tape for sale. They had books from the "Cat Who" series by Lilian Jackson Braun, the same books that we had been reading out loud to dad.

"Huh," dad was thinking out loud "I didn't know they made these." He bought the tape and we listened to it the rest of the way home, grateful to give our throats a rest. Deborah and I sat in the back of the van making fun of the turtle guy and laughing about the different things that could have happened to him. We talked about our goals and school. She attending the community college on Tuesdays and Thursdays, so it didn't interfere with the business, and dad had paid her tuition last semester. Watching dad pay for her tuition reinforced the idea that he would pay for mine as well. We talked about the other vendors, and I showed her the things I had bought. She always saved her money, keeping a stash for emergencies. We talked and giggled until we fell asleep together on the twin mattress.

STOMP! STOMP! STOMP!

The sound of dad's stomping upstairs meant that it was time to wake up. We had gotten in late the night before and dad said he would let us sleep in, so I had turned my alarm off. It was 10:30 am, and dad had opened the store already, but we had not unloaded the van. After getting dressed, I pushed past the sheets to climb the stairs. Dad was talking with a customer about her jewelry repair. I noticed a pile of dog poop on the floor and tried to clean it up without the customer noticing. She gave me the side eye and I knew she had seen it. My face turned red. I knew most people didn't have to clean dog poop off the floor every morning and it was embarrassing.

Deborah, Mom, Jason, and I worked to unload the van while Dad continued helping the customer. We set the workshop in the back and arranged the display cases in front. Dad invited the customer into the back to watch him work and keep her entertained while she waited.

As soon as the work was done, I headed downstairs to work on my GED. I still wanted to take the test and studied whenever I could. Dad wasn't concerned, he didn't think I would pass the test and it appeased mom, so he let me study without as much resistance in the down times.

Each summer I attended a variety of camps. The majority were church related except for the John Birch Society which was based on political education. John Birch was my favorite: it was the only camp that I went to with Deborah and Jason. During the day we had to attend different classes about government and conspiracy theories. I only half paid attention as I was more interested in handing notes back and forth and talking with friends until a counselor asked us to pay attention again. We had plenty of free time to hang out and get to know the other kids. There was one family with several kids who had been at camp for several years and felt like the unofficial mascots. They always made everyone laugh and were adept at including anyone who was feeling out of place. The sisters showered everyone with kindness, and you could count on the brothers to cause playful havoc. They would sneak out at night and the next morning they would walk like a crab around the flagpole as punishment for being caught. One time, they found an unused bunk bed, toilet, and taxidermy squirrel and set them up on the lawn for the morning flagpole ceremony. They were the heart of the entire camp for me.

At night we would sing familiar campfire songs and Mr. P would have us belting out the lyrics as loud as possible until we were exhausted. At the end of the night, he would play Taps as we quietly filtered into our cabins.

On one of the first days of camp in my second year, I was sitting on a wall talking with friends and watching the other kids play volleyball. A new kid walked past me. "Y'all know him?" I asked my friends. "No, but he's hot, you should say hi to him!" One of my friends replied.

"Hey!" I shouted at him with confidence, knowing I would never see him past this week. "What's your name?"

"Jason," he replied, taking us in.

"Come sit with us!" I spoke. He looked nervous but walked over. We talked for a minute, getting to know each other, where we were all from, and what grade we were in. We joined in on the volleyball game, kicking sand at each other and talking smack. We spent the rest of the camp together talking about everything that came to mind. I asked him a million questions and he asked me a million more. After camp was over, we would talk on the phone for hours while I cleaned the store. I never told him about my history of abuse; It was better to keep that in the past. He was my best friend, and his phone calls were a lifeline to me. He was the first boy I ever had a deeper connection with, that I confided in, and the first one I ever loved, although I never used those words.

I attended another camp that summer at Southern Virginia University, which emulated Brigham Young University. It was a church camp and the most expensive of all the camps, which I thought was inconsistent with what a church should stand for. It took me a long time to save up enough money to attend. This camp also had a lot of classes during the day. These were mostly about living the principles of the church, choosing to wear modest clothes, and abstaining from things like coffee and sex. There were also classes on how we were the chosen generation and that we would live to see the second coming. In one class, the school

117

administration came in to encourage us to apply to college on their campus. I looked around at the old architect and felt intuitively that I needed to come to school here, almost like God was telling me directly. This school was a part of my life journey, my jump into the world. I knew I would need to get here, no matter what. There would be some difficulty in reaching my goal, but I also knew that I could do it.

Afterward, I talked to the staff member about how strongly I felt I needed to be here. He walked me over to the tiny gift shop and picked up a poster. "Here, you can have this," he said. It was a printed copy of a hand-drawn picture of the school.

I returned home and hung the poster up on my wall. It was my constant reminder every day that I was going to get out of here. Nothing was going to stop me. It added fuel to my already burning desire, and I set up the GED test later that month.

With the test date set, my studying intensified. We were selling our jewelry on eBay more and traveling less, allowing more time for studying. As the test date approached, dad started tearing down the idea of me attending school even more. He wanted things and people that he could control, that he could manage; I was fitting into that category less and less. Our fighting increased as I dared to push back. I was unyielding to anything that did not further my agenda to get an education. It was an obsession for me to pass this test.

Chapter Twelve
Southwestern Community College

Today I take the GED. My anxiety had kept me up all night. What if I failed? What would that mean for me? Would that prove that Dad was right? What if he was? Could I even pass this test? A pulsating pain started in my neck and reached through my shoulders, caused by the tension and stress I felt. I tilted my head from side to side to release the pain, but it didn't work. It felt as if my entire life depended on these next few hours. The idea that my father was right, that I wasn't smart enough to pass, made my stomach turn. I had spent every second I could spare in the past weeks studying the GED prep book. If my mind was busy, I could silence the negative thoughts, at least for a few moments.

The test was at Southwestern Community College, three miles down the road. My sister had classes that day, so mom dropped us off at the same time. Deborah walked uphill to her class, and I walked down the large hill to the building that housed their admissions and testing office. I gave the clerk my information, and she reviewed the rules. I sat down to wait with the other participants; It was a hodge-podge of about thirty people. I was the youngest one there at seventeen. There were a few in their mid-twenties, a gentleman with a mullet and a goatee who looked to be in his early forties, and a handful of people who looked to be a few years older than me. Most of them avoided eye contact, looking at their shoes or the ceiling. I understood them because I felt the same way.

We entered a room that had several rows of desks evenly spaced to prevent cheating. They gave us the rules again, then allowed us to look at the test. This was it; this was the culmination of the past few years of work. I took a deep breath and tried to shake off any negative thoughts. I can do this, I told myself. There just wasn't any other acceptable choice.

I carefully looked over each answer before moving on; I didn't want to go back over them and second guess myself. Once I was done with an answer, I was done. There were four different sections: math, Science, literature, and writing. My education had not been tested since I had finished the second grade. Why did I think I could do this? What if I failed? My thoughts were straying. I needed to pull them in; I needed to focus.

A chair scraped loudly, catching my attention. The first person got up and walked away from the test. I was only halfway through; I think he gave up. It was another thirty minutes before the next person stepped out. I was close to finishing, but I felt unsure because the other twenty-seven people were still working. Another person walked out; this one looking confident. I had finished, but it felt like it should have taken longer. So many people were still working. Was I done too early? Did I get them all wrong? Maybe I should have spent more time on the long essay. I waited for a few more people to walk out before I left my seat. It would be a week before the results came in the mail.

Deborah was still in class; I had another hour to kill before she would be ready to leave. I walked over to the admissions secretary and asked her what I needed to do to enroll the following semester. She told me about the placement test and information on what classes I could take and the cost of enrollment. For two classes, it was going to cost about six hundred dollars. I took the information and walked up the hill to where I planned to meet Deborah. I felt like I had done ok on the test, however, the fear was gnawing at my stomach.

She was in one of the smaller buildings. Inside was a lobby with two ping-pong tables and two offices off to the side. I sat down in the chair next to her and watched a couple of guys playing ping-pong. One office had an older man seated behind a mound of paperwork and the other had a few people sitting around a large table joking around and laughing.

"How did you do?" Deborah asked as she sat down next to me.

"I did ok, I guess. They said it would take a week before I can find anything out."

"I'm sure you did great," she said, confident in my abilities.

We walked outside to meet mom who picked us up, stopping by a fast-food place on the way home. I talked to my mom about taking a placement test next and what classes I wanted to enroll in. Maybe I would just take a couple of classes my first semester to make sure I wasn't overwhelmed with having a teacher and a set schedule to follow.

When we got back to the shop dad was in the back at his workbench. I walked over to him and handed him the paperwork from the admissions office. He looked it over with a frown. "How did you do?" he asked me.

"I won't know until next week." I replied.

"We won't worry about all of this until after you have passed the GED," he said, handing the papers back to me. The disinterested look he gave me implied he wasn't worried about the next step because he still didn't think I would pass.

The next week dragged on in slow motion. I cleaned and organized the store while I listened to books on tape, dusted off all the knick-knacks on the bookshelves around the edges of the store, and revamped the window displays. Next, I sorted through the boxes we had shoved under the display cabinets with leftover goods from the flea market. When I had done as much as I could, I moved downstairs and cleaned up the space we called a living room, and then tackled the kitchen. I rearranged the food on the shelves and got rid of any expired foods. Anything I could do to keep my mind off the test.

I watched for the mailman each day. I hurried outside to meet him, and we talked for a few minutes. He laughed with me as my impatience grew over time. A week later, with a small smirk on his face, he handed me the envelope. I snatched it out of his hands, excited to read my results. I ripped the envelope open, then paused before grabbing the paper that would determine my future. What if I had failed? I thought about all the arguments and negative comments I had to overcome and about the lack of education I had compared to my friends. I had studied my GED book, but I had not completed any schoolwork past the sixth grade.

My hands shook just a little as I pulled out the piece of paper and read through the numbers. It took me a minute to process the numbers; I wasn't sure I understood. If what I was reading was true, I didn't just pass, I had scored high!

I was a seventeen-year-old misfit who had been denied a decent education and yet I had graduated a year early. I could see myself sitting in class at Southern Virginia University in a crowd of other people my age. I could see myself working a great job, getting top grades, finding the man of my dreams, and getting married in the temple. I would live in the perfect house with fresh carpet, large windows, and no bugs. This was a happy future family where all the cousins would get together often, with no hint of our past on their cute baby faces. If I had accomplished this, I could do anything, and I was tingling with possibilities of my future.

The bells on the store door jingled as I excitedly pushed into the store elated to show my family the results. Deborah jumped up and gave me a hug and mom smiled at me from behind her computer with a sparkle in her eye. She had always had a bit of faith that I would make it and I could tell she was happy for me.

"Congrats, I guess," Dad said in a defeated voice. "They must have made the test easier than when I took it."

I could feel the disappointment from him before I saw it on his face. I thought for sure that once I had passed the test, he would have been proud of the work I had accomplished. Instead, it was another opportunity for him to tear me down. I ignored his grouchy attitude and sour face; this was my ticket out of here and there was no way he could stop me.

The positive energy was running through my body, making it nearly impossible to stand still. As I planned for the next few months and years of my life, I was all but dancing around the store. "I need to take a placement test; I can start next semester!." The possibilities were endless!

"We can't afford it right now," dad said. I just stared at him; positive I had heard him wrong.

"What do you mean?" I asked, giving him a chance to correct his words.

"I didn't think you would make it, so there is no money to pay for your education. Besides, I don't think you are ready for college." He was giving me a pointed look that said there was no room for an argument. My face paled as the joy of the moment instantly evaporated. At first, there was just shock, no thoughts, no emotions, the calm before the storm. There is no way this could be my truth. Then I felt sick to my stomach. Why was throwing up always my body's first reaction? A trivial thought to calm down the dam of emotions that was about to break. I grabbed the chair in front of me to stop myself from falling as a wave of dizziness swept over me. I

122

felt my face getting hot and there was pressure building inside my skull. There is no way he would break THIS promise.

"So… you lied about paying for my education?" my voice had a harsh but controlled edge to it. I could feel the seething anger in every part of my now tense muscles. Hold it together, I told myself. I can't change this if I lose control. Keep it together. I focused on maintaining the rhythm of my breath, not letting my fingers curl into a fist, and relaxing the muscles in my face. I did my best to keep the anger contained, packaged up, and controlled. I was skilled at keeping things packaged up. This was too much, though, he was messing with my entire future and the anger just kept building up.

Dad responded, but the words were a string of incomprehensible lines of betrayal, deceptions, lies, and manipulations. I had done everything I had promised. I worked for him for years, giving up high school, my freedom, and overriding my intuition. My education was supposed to help me get out of this hell. I forgave and forgot over and over, and this is the compensation?

It was suffocating to look at his face made of broken promises. He was hiding behind his jeweler's glasses as if he didn't just destroy every dream I had permitted myself to believe in. Everything I forgave and forgot assaulted me, blow after blow. I couldn't figure out which memory sickened me the most. The times I returned to work after he fired me, the times he wouldn't let me eat or use the bathroom because it was inconvenient for him, the times I wanted to hang out with friends but the business took precedent, the times he cut me down with his words saying I was fat or stupid, or the countless times he twisted the religion I loved to fit an agenda in his perverted chess game. Maybe it was all the times his ego and self-interest overshadowed everyone else. The list of things he did to hurt others was always growing.

How could I have ever let myself trust you? A panic attack was coming on. I needed to get out of this nightmare before I hyperventilated or threw up because both were a possibility. I threw my GED scores on my desk and ran out of the store, the bells jingling behind me. How could I have let myself fall for his promises? Didn't I know how selfish he was? Didn't I see the evidence of that every single day? He wrote checks three months in advance, promising they would be good, only to extend them again. He repeatedly changed our pay so that we would get less money for more work. I saw him avoid the law when we moved, and how he kept us under the radar so no one would check on our schoolwork or the abuse. He talked down to mom, tearing apart any confidence she had in herself one ruthless dismissal after the next. He was dependable for only one value, to twist the truth to suit his purposes. I saw him, and yet I let myself trust him. Fear, anger, and regret turned inwards as I blamed myself for trusting my father with something so critical as my future.

I walked for hours as I processed the rage, sadness, and desperation I was feeling. I needed a plan and I needed to get my thoughts and emotions under control. I had made the mistake of depending on him and now I was paying the consequences. Focusing on the negative emotions would not get me out of this situation, so I put those aside. There was no way I could succumb to his broken promise. I needed to figure out how I was going to do this on my own. I was going to take the placement test and start saving what money I could. As I walked past Papa's Pizza To Go across the parking lot from the store, I walked in and asked for an application. I will not allow my future to be placed in your hands again.

∞

Later that week, I asked Mom if I could get a ride over to the community college when she dropped Deborah off. It was time to figure out how to do this on my own. I walked down to the admissions office and talked to them about my situation and asked them what I needed to do. She asked for my transcript and when I explained I didn't have one; she set me up to take the placement test. It was only an hour long, and they had a computer available now.

Taking the placement test was not nearly as stressful as the GED had been. This one would not stop me from getting into the school. It simply assessed the level of classes I should begin with. That was fortunate because the math part of the test had symbols that were foreign to me. They used dots and slashes between the numbers where the multiplication or division signs would have been. As a result, I could not understand the questions and answered every question wrong. A failing of my homeschool.

When I walked out of the testing room, the admissions lady looked at me with a sad look on her face. She let me know I scored right into an entry-level class for English but that I would need to enroll in their lowest possible math class. I was bummed about the math part for a moment, but she said I could take classes! I didn't care what I had to take as long as I could get in.

I asked her how I could take classes when I had no way to pay for them. She introduced me to FASFA, a financial form to receive government aid, and walked me through the entire process, leaving me confident that I could do it. She introduced the idea of scholarships and how they worked. It was obvious by the way she spoke, that I should have known what a scholarship was, and how it worked, but I didn't.

That night, I filled out the FAFSA form. I was approved for enough to cover the entire tuition, including a little extra for books and supplies from the school bookstore. Energy and hope returned as I figured things out on my own. The next day, I registered myself for classes in English and math for the following semester. I was creating my own future in spite of my dad and I felt confident in my ability to succeed.

∞

On the first day of class, I walked down the hallway to where my math class was. The teacher was waiting outside of the classroom and pulled me aside. She asked if I had been homeschooled and if I knew how to take notes, or if I had ever been in a classroom before. Her questions were genuine and did not show any sign of judgment. I was grateful for her kindness, although I wondered if they had told her about my poor testing results in advance.

The classroom was mostly filled with people who looked to be in their forties. I was by far the youngest one in the crowd. The teacher began the class with, "What is a whole number?." My heart sank as I realized how basic this class was. I knew how to do algebra and how to graph equations. The teacher moved on to how to add and subtract using a number line. This wasn't the right class for me at all. I knew this, but I didn't know my options.

After class, I talked to the teacher. She said I could test out if I wanted to. However, since I was already signed up, I could use this class as practice to understand the routine of a classroom. I was apprehensive about meeting the expectations of college classes and her idea of staying in this class eased those feelings.

My next class was English 101. I walked in and chose to sit three rows back. I didn't want to be in the front because I didn't want to get called on, but I didn't want it to seem like I was hiding in the back either. This class mostly had people my age or a few years older in it. They were all talking to one another while we waited for the professor to arrive.

five minutes after the start time, an older frazzled-looking man with hair like Albert Einstein and a long white beard walked in. He stood at the front of the classroom for a solid minute without talking as he took in his class of new recruits. He then held his hand up and flipped us all off saying, "Sit and perch you guys."

What had I gotten myself into? Was this how all teachers were? He was rude and crass; I did not know what to think about this. The other students snickered and finally, the teacher burst out laughing and handed us our syllabuses. He talked to us about social norms and taboos that day. He believed that everything that was considered taboo should be talked about until the weirdness of the topic no longer existed. He was thought-provoking. As we wrote different styles of essays for him, he graded us only on how we wrote, not our viewpoints, even if they differed from his. He quickly earned my respect.

A week into my classes, the math teacher had a family accident and had to leave. Two substitute teachers took over the class, but they were so lost in the curriculum that they could not solve the basic problems. I was grateful that it was information that I already knew because they made it confusing, and the other students were getting lost.

∞

In between classes, I would meet with Deborah in the lobby with the ping-pong tables. The older man who sat in his office came out and introduced himself as Steve. He was head of the Student Government Association (SGA) and they were looking for volunteers. He pointed to the larger room that had an executive table with several people sitting around talking and laughing. One, in particular, caught my attention. She had brown hair in a ponytail and a white oversized sweater on. She appeared to be the leader of the group. She moved the conversation around, making sure each person was included. I looked at Deborah and could not think of a reason why not, so we followed him into the office. They stopped talking when Steve walked in and greeted us. "Hey, I'm Hope, I'm the president," said the woman who I had been watching before. She moved around the table introducing the others "This is Tim, Sarah, Rob, Chris, and Jason." Everyone said hi as we took a seat. They asked us several questions to get to know us before the conversation moved on to the food Chris had been making in his last culinary class, and then how Rob spent his last weekend.

They were so comfortable with each other. It was obvious that Hope was the glue that held this group together. Tim was quiet at first, but would always crack a joke with impeccable timing. He was the brains of this group, and his skills showed when it came to planning and implementing ideas. Chris was passionate, and either loved you or hated you with all of his heart. Jason was the joker, always going above and beyond to make sure that everyone was laughing but was also emotionally intelligent and took care of those he loved.

I was at Southwestern Community College for a year and a half. Those years were spent with the people of SGA. Steve was consistently pushing us to do more activities and to be better people. I found myself in his office on more than one occasion talking about my life. He would give me a few things to think about and then pitch a new activity he wanted my help with.

Once a week we would meet officially using Roberts Rules of Order to create and plan ideas for the campus. We brought in a blacksmith who showcased his forge and wares on campus, generating a lot of interest. We brought in a comedian and other entertainers. We set up parties with bounce houses and food for the students and their families.

One weekend, we took a group road trip to Charlotte North Carolina for an entertainer's event. We attended show after show of entertainers to pick out the ones we wanted to bring back to our campus. They had a dance one evening that required that we dress up. I had never worn makeup before, or at least not much, and I didn't know how to put on eyeliner. Hope took me under her wing and helped me look beautiful for the evening. One guy was following me around the entire weekend, and Chris was always there to save me, pulling me under his arm and away from the unsettling follower. I was safe with these people.

It was obvious that I was new to the world in so many ways. These people allowed me the freedom to move and grow. They took me in without hesitation or judgment. They were just happy to have another person to add to their family.

∞

I was still trying to get to Southern Virginia University (SVU) and needed to take my ACT. It was going to cost me eighty dollars, and I didn't have the money. I asked my parents if they would help cover the cost of my testing, but dad refused because he thought it would be a waste of money.

Of course, he wouldn't help me. I don't even know why I bothered to ask him. I guess I just keep hoping that one day he would step it up. The disappointments never got easier. In fact, they got more difficult as the frustrations stacked on top of each other. I was still upset when I arrived at school that day. The moment Hope saw my face, she jumped up and gave me a hug that released all the pent-up emotions. When the tears stopped, the rage and frustrations of the past few years took its place. She already knew most of it, but she listened anyway until I had to go to class. It felt empowering to talk about dad and to be validated in my emotions. While sitting in class, I thought about how I could save money. The deadline for the ACT was approaching fast and I was running out of time if I wanted to apply to SVU the following fall.

I walked back down to the SGA lobby after my class. When I walked around the corner, everyone was standing in a circle talking quietly, but animatedly. When they saw me, they stopped talking, and all stared at me, then at Hope, and then back at me again with huge smiles on their faces. They were up to something. I didn't know what was happening, but their smiles were contagious, making me laugh.

"What are ya'll up to?" I asked them curiously.

Hope walked up to me and handed me an envelope. "What is this?" I asked her in surprise.

"Just open it!" she said, her eyes brimming with excitement. I opened the envelope and pulled out a card filled with words of encouragement and the eighty dollars I needed to take the ACT. I was stunned. They all came in and surrounded me in one large group hug. I covered up my tears of appreciation and love with laughter. I just couldn't believe that these people, my people, would believe in me more than my family. They would support my dreams with such solid faith in my ability to achieve them. It was one of the first moments when I knew true love and acceptance from a group that wanted nothing in return. They loved and accepted me for who I was, all homeschooled awkwardness and weird ideas included.

I took the test and then submitted my application.

Dad was still fighting me about attending Southern Virginia University in the fall. Each achievement I earned just made him more vocal about the next move. "You'll never get into a four-year school. You only got into the community college because they will take anyone." "Four-year schools want to see a list of achievements and since you don't have any, they will not want you." I couldn't believe he was still tearing me down.

∞

Deborah and Jason had begun attending a group at church for young single adults called YSA a few years ago. The group got together several times a week, officially, and a few more unofficially. It was a requirement to be eighteen to join them, but because I had already obtained my GED and was attending college, they let me in early. On Sundays, we would sit side by side in the same pew at church paying more attention to each other than to the speaker. On Mondays, we would get together for what Mormons call family home evening. It includes a small lesson, a snack, and an activity. Most of the time it would end with a game of twister and watching the show Veggie Tales. That was until we were told by the bishop that twister was not of God and we could no longer play that game. Thursday night was institute, taught by my old seminary teacher Brother McLachlancLachlan. In this setting, he was even more interesting because he combined all kinds of ideologies in his lectures. The other nights we would hang out at Western Carolina University.

Kyle and Johnathan from the YSA got a job working for dad making jewelry for eBay. That business was now taking off so we only did a trade show occasionally. Instead of going home for the summer, Kyle asked if he could move in with us and continue working. He had seen the downstairs and knew how we lived. He cleared out one of the storage spaces and moved in his bed and a few other belongings. We hung up another sheet to partition his space and give him privacy. Kyle left on his mission a few months later and Johnathan asked if he could live in Kyle's space. He moved in the following week and stayed for a few years.

After a while, we had another YSA member, Felicia, move in with us. She spent her own money to hang the sheet wall and added a door to her room so that she could lock it. I was a little jealous of her solid walls and locking door, but I was also grateful to have her there with us. She was only with us for one summer before she moved out and another YSA member moved into her space. I loved the ins and outs of these people. It gave us someone to talk to and share our experiences with. They saw the craziness of where we lived and chose to be there with us. It wasn't some big secret anymore. I'm sure social services would have been appalled at the conditions still.

As my world expanded, I didn't mind the basement as much.

∞

My life has changed dramatically in the last year. I progressed from working for my parents with barely a life outside the walls of the store to being in school full time, having a job, and having a community of loving people through school and church. I had my first boyfriend, and I still talked on the phone occasionally to friends from the summer camp. It's as if all the things I ever wanted, came true at the same time. Where I lived just didn't matter anymore. Dad's negativity was easily overlooked as I realized how little impact they had on my future. I was in a space where I could honestly forgive him for the past so that I could move on. He had not changed, but I had.

I had just finished working a shift at Papa's pizza and headed to the basement to get some homework done. I walked into my room to see Deborah sitting on the waterbed with a serious look on her face.

"What's wrong?" I asked her, concerned.

"I'm moving out," she said tentatively.

We were close, really, really, close. She was the only person in my entire world that had been by my side in life. She was the only one who knew the darkness of our early youth and the stress of living with Dad and his business. We knew each other's thoughts and feelings without ever saying a word. We talked every night before going to bed and she was the first person I spoke to each morning. She was the reason I had held myself together over the years. I couldn't imagine how lonely my bedroom would feel if she were gone. Yet I couldn't be sad because I was thrilled for her.

"Josh asked me to marry him and I said yes!" she told me with a sparkle in her eye.

"That's AMAZING, CONGRATULATIONS" I squealed, giving her the tightest hug I could. She has been dating Josh for a while now and he had been working for my dad as well. I didn't realize it had been so serious between the two of them, and it seemed a little fast, but I could tell she was excited.

"I was afraid you would be mad at me for leaving." She said, her voice laced with a bit of concern.

"I'm going to miss you, you're my best friend, but I'm so excited that you are making it out of here," I reassured her. She was my proof that I would make it into the world on my own.

"I'll still be here every day working, and I'm only moving a few miles down the road. When I finish my school at the community college, I'll go to school with Josh at the University." Her plans were spilling out as her excitement built up. My plans to study were forgotten at the moment as I shared in the joy of my sister. We also talked about my plans and life beyond this moldy basement, filling each other with new hopes and dreams.

Chapter Thirteen
Love and Hate

My life was so busy now that time passed quickly over the next year. Deborah and Josh married and had their first baby. I finished my first year at Southwestern Community College and was preparing to go to school at Southern Virginia University in the fall. I still work for dad occasionally but only in my spare time. My job and school were my priorities. Everything changed after he broke his promise about paying for college. He still talked about buying me my first car once I had my license, but I had no incentive to believe him.

My parents inherited the house from my great grandparents, where we caught fireflies in the summer. The shop was never that busy, and it didn't make sense to stay there anymore. We packed up the basement, the shop, and the fleas, leaving behind a chemical smell from years of casting mixed with old dog feces and urine. I was not sad to leave this place behind.

The house was pleasant, with soft carpet and actual walls with doors that locked. Dad set up a shop in the basement and hired about six employees from the local church to work for him. His eBay business had boomed.

My brother and I spent more time together lately. Our friends from YSA were still back in Sylva, thirty minutes away and he was my ride to see them, or anywhere else I wanted to be. We spent the drives listening to 80's music and getting to know each other as adults. Even though we had lived in the same house, we were never really in the same space at the same time.

Just a few miles down the road from our house was a skating rink. We would meet there once a week with our YSA group and stay until closing time. Considering how much time we spent there, I decided to apply for a job. I asked the manager if they were hiring, and he replied that they were short-staffed and needed someone to work their snack counter. I could start next week.

On my third day, the DJ came over to the snack bar to greet me. He was my age, maybe a few years older, with blonde hair and blue eyes, and much taller than me. We chatted for a while, and I found out his name was Phillip. He went to school at Western, played the sousaphone in the marching band, loved music, photography, and exploring the outdoors.

At the end of the night, he offered to give me a ride home, and I accepted. It had been raining a lot the last couple of days and we passed a muddy field. "Can you be a few minutes late?" he asked with a small smirk. He drove off the road hitting the first mud hole with a large splash. He drove the truck slipping and sliding through several more mudholes before getting back on the road. The truck was covered to the windows in thick red clay. He asked if he could take me home again the next day and I felt butterflies in my stomach as I agreed.

For the next few weeks, he continued to drive me home each night. We talked about his education, his fraternity, and his friends. We talked about my family, my goals, and where I wanted to go to school. We made plans to go hiking, visit waterfalls, and spend time by the many rivers around us. He took me to Gatlinburg, Tennessee, where we walked for hours through the small town. His friends became my friends as our two worlds began to blend into one.

∞

"Hey Steph, the mail came for you today?" Mom said handing me a large envelope. It was from Southern Virginia University. I was anticipating the letter but had tried to forget about it to calm my anxiety. It felt like my GED all over again, another place in life where I would either pass or fail based on my own effort.

I opened it, scanning the page and looking for my acceptance. Before I opened the envelope, I knew the results. I knew from the moment I sat in that church camp and became overwhelmed by the need to be here. It was as if my life had no other option.

"Dear Stephanie,

It is with great honor that we have accepted your application for the fall of 2001."

My heart was beating with excitement as I read through the rest of the information.

"I guess they are just letting anyone into college these days," dad said mockingly. I glared at him. I didn't need or want his approval.

133

Turning my back to him, I finished reading through the documents they would need and any deadlines. I was vibrating with positive energy and needed to share my news with someone who would be excited for me. I called my sister and had to hold the phone away from my ear as she squealed in delight for me. "I always knew you would make it!" she told me. "I know! I love you for that" I exclaimed, feeling the delight of being supported by her.

For the next few days, I involved myself in making sure everything was in place. I needed a computer and a car to get there. I talked to my parents about these things, and they agreed that they would help. Dad used to be a computer programmer and had built several computers. This was an easy ask of him, because he had most of the parts he needed.

One of my friends from YSA would be house-sitting her grandparents' house for the summer and asked if I would stay with her. She lived in Bryson City, which was closer to where we used to live in Sylva. After the summer, I would move from the house we were sitting to SVU.

I didn't have a car, but Kelli said that she could help me get my license and a job with her at Burger King, where she would be my manager. It was perfect, and I agreed to the deal. A few weeks before I was set to move in, Kelli came back and said that her grandparents had invited Betty to stay the summer as well and offered her one of the bedrooms. If I was planning to go, I would have to sleep on an air mattress in the office.

Betty was one of those people who would go out of her way to spew hate on anyone she thought was beneath her, which was almost everyone. When I was younger, she had been the worst of the older girls in the church who sought out my friends and me when we were away from the adults and drop comments meant to tear us down. She did it in a passive-aggressive way so that most people didn't see her ruthlessness. There were a few people who thought she walked on water, and she catered to these people in the same way that my dad acted when he wanted approval. She had some of the same characteristics as my father in how she treated people. The idea of living with her was awful, but if I had to choose between her and my dad, I could give her a chance, I guess.

Betty moved right into the master bedroom. This reflected the type of person she was, at least in my experiences. I felt like the room should have been given to Kelli as the house belonged to her grandparents and she was the reason we got to be here at all. But Betty's personality was simply an echo of my father's, and she only took herself into consideration.

I had packed my things in a trash bag because we didn't own suitcases and the boxes at home were useless or still packed from previous moves. The room was small, and there was no place to put my things. I folded my clothes and placed them on the floor by the edge of the air mattress.

In the house, the dislike between Betty and me was palpable. I kept to myself and tried to ignore her constant snide comments as she mocked my clothes, the way I talked, or what I ate. I focused on spending time with Kelli and her exuberance helped to block out Betty's negativity. Kellie taught me how to drive that summer using her car and then drove me to the DMV to get my license. Most of our time together was spent working the morning shift at Burger King.

Our coworkers were happy to be there, funny, and hard-working making the environment very uplifting. My favorite person there aside from Kellie, was Jose. He didn't speak any English, but that didn't stop him from communicating. Whenever a cute guy came to the counter, he would hide from the customers, but where we could see him, and make kissing faces while hugging himself like he was making out just to tease us. He occasionally used props like the mop or broom as his object of affection. It was nearly impossible to keep a straight face around him.

Kelli and I drew notes with pictures of stick figures, slipping them back and forth to each other between customers and work. They were filled with hilarious antics involving the people around us. These notes fluttered back and forth, occasionally being caught and altered by Jose to add a dose of comedy. I still have those notes tucked away in a photo album. This job was lighthearted, fun, and a place where I could relax and be myself. When I wasn't working, I spent my time on the phone with Phillip or hanging out with my YSA friends.

I was also trying to get my FASFA filled out for SVU and figuring out how to take out student loans. I was having trouble getting the needed tax information from my parents who were delaying their taxes. I would call them, and we would end up arguing about that or the car I was supposed to drive there and the computer that I had been promised. I felt the pressure to make SVU happen but was having trouble working through the logistics of getting there. Dad was still making comments about how it was a stupid idea to go to SVU and that I needed to finish up at the community college, resulting in more arguments. The fighting increased and between dad's words that I would never succeed, and Betty constantly throwing me disparaging remarks, my confidence began to drop, and my anxiety grew. It took a conscious effort to block out the hurtful words, and most of the time I was able to stay positive. Most of the time.

I didn't see the emotions I was burying so that I could stay positive. I didn't notice the resentment towards God that had been growing. I was desperate to be perfect, to make SVU work because that is what I thought God wanted, and to be a worthy woman in God's eyes so that my family would heal. None of these things seem to be working out and my prayers were starting to go unanswered. I felt abandoned by God. Why did he give me all these expectations and then just leave me? I didn't understand the distance and it left me feeling fearful that I would always be in a battle for my happiness and my sense of self-worth. I prayed more that summer than at any other time of my life just trying to get a connection back to him, back to my own intuition, but I was failing. My emotions felt like a ping pong game ranging from total elation that I had moved, that was going to SVU, and that I was going to live a happy life, to complete despair as I felt those things slipping away.

My air mattress must have gotten a hole in it because it was deflating. It represented my repressed emotions that were escaping as I questioned everything in my life. Maybe I wasn't over how dad talked to me, his words wearing my confidence down and shattering my heart. Perhaps Betty's constant teardowns were getting to me. Maybe it was the stress of not knowing if I was going to make it to SVU. The mattress deflated even more, and my back pushed against the hardwood floor. I wondered if I had been better off staying at home than on the floor, in this office, where there was nowhere to place my things. I didn't belong here, there was no place for me. Maybe I was never meant to go to SVU. Did I make the whole thing up? It's possible that God isn't answering because he isn't real. Had I made him up to survive the challenges of my childhood? Maybe the church is fake too and there would be no happy ending. I marinated in my own depression unsure how to stop the cycle of thoughts from spinning downward even further and so I just kept falling. This time my failure was my own, the stress was a creation of my own choices and I was feeling the weight of them. It just all seemed so impossible, so unreachable. The tears that had been slipping down my face became more like a fountain. I curled myself into a ball and hid my face in my pillow so no one could hear my anguish.

Out of pure desperation, I poured my heart out to God. I didn't know if he was real or not at this moment, but I just had to let go of all the pent-up emotions that were taking over my mind and my life. I was feeling like a failure and that I was becoming everything that dad said I would be. That I wasn't meant to make it to SVU. There were just too many obstacles, and they were blinding me from seeing anything positive.

"God, why did you put me on this path? Why did you lead me this far, just to leave me alone?" I asked him, or maybe I was just asking myself. It all seems so impossible. "Are you even real? Had I just been fooling myself? If I didn't make it to SVU, then I would have to move back in with my parents, as a failure. Then what would I do? Would that mean I could never make it on my own? "Why aren't you helping me, God? Why does it have to feel so hard?"

The air in the mattress had almost completely deflated and I was lying on the hard floor. Even the air mattress had given up on me. My thoughts were a self-defeating pattern.

"Why did I have to have the father that I did? Why must he always be so destructive? Why couldn't I have had parents who would have supported my dreams? All of dad's words from the past and those of other people who had torn me down over the years were colliding into my thoughts. What if the things they said were true? I was feeling sorry for myself, and I knew that but that just made me angrier because I was usually in control of my thoughts and emotions. This uncontrollable outburst of my own emotions made me feel like I was failing even more.

My entire body was reacting in rhythm to my crying. My muscles tensed up making breathing impossible only to release in earthquake-like shuddering. The lack of air was making me feel like I was going to hyperventilate. I had lost control of my emotions and now I couldn't even control my body.

I had tried to be the best Mormon girl I could be. However, I judged my father harshly, and I didn't like the temple ceremonies I had gone to in the past, and I had missed a few tithing payments here and there. What if I wasn't smart enough, funny enough, skinny enough, kind enough, or faithful enough? What if I just wasn't enough? Is that why God had stopped talking to me? I just wasn't enough in his eyes, or anyone else. What if I wasn't even enough for myself?

I don't know how long I had been lying on the floor, but exhaustion was settling in. Between the attacks from my thoughts, blissful silence would settle in for a few seconds at first. I reached for the silence and focused on it, stretching them into minutes. I turned my focus to my breathing until it was under control and that allowed my crying to stop; or maybe there just were no tears left in my body. As my muscles relaxed, I reached out one last time to God in a desperate plea , "Please God, if you are real, just let me know." I felt his calm peaceful presence pushing away the remaining negative thoughts. "You're going to make it," he said to me right before I fell into a deep sleep.

∞

That was all I needed to hear to pick myself back up. I called my parents the next day and finally got the tax information I needed. They said there was no way that they could get me a car right now. However, they offered to drive me to campus six hours away and assured me I would have my computer by then. Dad had a few more negative things to say but my heart was louder than his condescendence and I brushed it off.

The anxiety from the summer was clearing away as the path to SVU became clearer. I had to work to retrain my thoughts again and again to stay positive and focus on my goal. I contemplated what had led up to my breakdown to ensure I never let myself get that low again. I had constantly been questioning my own choices and if I was right, even though I already knew that I was on the right path. I had to relearn how to trust myself and my intuition and stop doubting myself.

I analyzed the living situation I was in, the kindness of Kelli, and the sour attitude of Betty. I watched how Kelli lifted people around her up, how she made people laugh, and how she paid attention to other people's emotions and showed them love when needed. Kellie's world revolves around making the people around her feel happy. Betty was always in her own world, and her life centered on her and her problems. She was unhappy and taking that unhappiness out on those around her. We all have a choice about who we want to be, I thought. I had experienced enough people like Betty, and the darkness she created. I was drawn to the light that Kelli so freely shared.

There is no grand moment in life in which we suddenly become either mean or nice, filled with darkness or light, hate or love. It's all about the countless small choices that we make every day that culminate in who we are.

I wanted to make a difference in this world. I guess we all make a difference. Some do it consciously and others, well, they just let whatever happens to fall out of their mouth define them. I felt responsible for understanding how my words and actions affected other people. I knew I wasn't perfect; I still struggle with the Bettys of this world and people like my dad. I struggle to contain the hate that boils to the surface from time to time. But, after watching these two extremes this past summer, I knew who I wanted to be. I made the choice to bring light and positivity into the world. To erase some of the damage caused by people like my dad and Betty, I'm choosing to let go of the hate and looking for ways to help others. Mostly, I just hope I can add some love to the world.

Chapter Fourteen
Buena Vista, Virginia

I woke up with every cell vibrating in anticipation and excitement. Today I was moving to Buena Vista, Virginia, into my dorm at Southern Virginia University. I packed some clothes and a few other belongings and loaded them into my parents' big blue van. I had worked so hard to get to this point and could hardly believe it was happening.

On the six-hour drive, I reflected on everything I accomplished to get to this point. The years of fighting with my dad over homework and the relentless messages from him that I would never make it. I figured out how to apply for school, sign up for classes, and then pay for school on my own. Dad still promised to get me an old car and a computer, but he had not followed through on it yet. Just getting my parents to take this trip with me had led to several fights. It had been years of accumulated stress, but I made it! I would miss my SGA crew from the community college and the church members of YSA, who had been my foundation of sanity over the past few years. We had created so many positive memories that they took over the unpleasant ones. It was like my childhood was a bad dream, cloudy and distant.

The drive itself was tense because we had been fighting that morning about the car and computer. I was still upset that I would be six hours away without transportation off campus, and I needed the computer to complete my schoolwork. In response to my concerns, dad told me, "You can do your work in the computer lab. You'll be fine," as if that made it better. "I'll mail it to you this week. I just need to order a part before I can fix it," he added, brushing off my concerns. Instead of arguing further, we just didn't talk. That sums up what was left of our relationship. I still got along with mom and loved to talk with her, just not when Dad was around to bring in his cynicism.

When we pulled into the campus, the main building came into view, stunning me with its beauty. It looked untouched from the original 1876 design. The campus had initially been a school for girls and passed through several organizational transfers until 1996, when it was taken over by a group of Mormons who turned it into a mini-BYU for the east coast. It wasn't owned by the church the same way BYU was. However, because it was owned by Mormons, they still implemented the same type of standards and an honor code to enforce them. The campus hosted about 400 students and continued to grow each semester. The dorms were separated by gender; the opposite gender was prohibited from entering the building except on moving days.

It only took the three of us two trips to unload everything I brought with me. Afterward, we stood there for a minute by the van, staring at each other silently. I figured they would take me out to lunch or walk around campus together before they drove off, and I was waiting to see what was next.

"Well, we will see you at Christmas I guess." my dad said, turning to get into the car.

That took me by surprise.

"What about Thanksgiving?" I asked him, confused. We had always spent the holidays together with my grandparents and I had simply assumed that wouldn't change.

"We have too much to do and it's too far for us to travel again just to take you back in a week. We will be back at the end of the semester to pick you up if you can't find a ride home."

It was insulting. We used to travel every weekend for years when we worked trade shows, and a six hour drive seemed nothing compared to that. I felt that this was a dismissal, a thrown dagger. He wanted me to know how much of an inconvenience it was to drive me here.

My parents got back into the van and drove away. It had been less than five minutes since we had taken my things to the dorm. I felt a profound sadness as they drove away. This was a big moment for me, and I wanted to share it with them. I wanted them to say congratulations on my accomplishments. I wanted them to be proud, to celebrate this moment with me. Instead, they just left me, with no car, no computer, and barely a goodbye or I love you.

I took a deep breath to keep my emotions in check. I walked back to my dorm room to make my bed and put my belongings away. My roommate bounced in. She had a face full of freckles and curly red hair. She seemed to have the fiery personality to match.

"Hey, did you see the hearts on the door?" she asked me. Her eyes sparkled with mischief.

I walked back outside to look. There were two hearts made from construction paper. One with an S for Stephanie and the other was an M for Maggie. I walked back in and looked at her, confused.

"S&M, get it," she laughed, smirking at me.

I really didn't understand.

"Sadism and masochism, you know, sex bondage stuff," she winked at me "It's going to be a fun semester"

"Oh…" I said, not sure what to think of her. At least this won't be a boring semester, I thought.

She ended up being a bit wild and ostentatious. She loved adventure and creating her own story. She would sit in the window wearing only a bra with some sleep shorts, just to cause a stir. I always knew where I stood with her, and I appreciated that. I was a bit taken aback by her large personality at times but loved the fresh perspectives she gave me.

The school honor code included some of the silliest rules, such as you can't wear pajamas or gym shorts to the cafeteria. All clothing had to be in line with the church standards so you could wear nothing that showed your shoulders or shorts above your knee. I didn't mind the rules that much; I lived by Mormon standards my entire life. What I didn't expect was how the honor code had been used to weaponize the students against each other. It created an environment where you were constantly policed by the other students who could report you for the smallest infraction. There was always someone interested in personal matters. For example, if you had drunk alcohol off campus, had sex with anyone, or if you were attracted to someone of the same gender. These were all punishable offenses, and someone was always eager to submit a report. Even if you had done nothing wrong, a person could still make a false accusation, and there was a chance you would have to go before the honor council to defend yourself. It made it hard to know who you could trust and who just wanted to know what you did wrong so they could report you. I appreciated my roommate because she didn't indulge in the culture shaming that the honor code brought out in people.

The girls in my hall were all good people. They were kind, funny, and engaging. They liked to play pranks on each other for fun, but then were supportive of each other when they saw a need. One girl let me borrow her computer when I needed to get work done or just to chat with friends on AOL messenger. It was the only time in my life where I hung out with a group of all Mormons and there was no mean girl, or mean group, at least not in my hall. They were friendly, open, and just all-around good people. I never fully clicked with them, though. I guess I've always stood apart from the Mormon mold. The more I watched them all interact, the more I realized I didn't want to be like them. I felt that they were just a little too sweet in a way that felt fake, and a little too caught up in finding Mr. Right and getting married. They were really great people; they just were not my people.

I only developed a deep friendship with one person that semester, a girl named Miwa. Sometimes in life, you meet the right person at just the right time for them to have a lasting impact on your life. That was Miwa. I don't know why she picked me to be friends with, but I am forever grateful that she did. If I was having a bad day, she would come to my room and drag me out for an adventure. She had her own car, and we would drive away from campus several times a day just to give us space to breathe. The honor council minions made the campus feel small and suffocating. She taught me how to parallel park and worked through my fear of getting her car, with a manual engine, in first gear on a steep hill. On the weekends, she would drive us to Cullowhee, North Carolina, where I was from. We spent time with Phillip and his friends and stayed the nights with friends from YSA. The long drives were spent listening to Miwa's playlists as she drove us through the mountains and sang at the top of our lungs. I didn't know most of the words, but I did the best I could. The Beastie Boys, Brass Monkey, is included on every playlist I make to this day. I can't hear the song without thinking of Miwa.

∞

It was halfway through the semester, and I had been calling my dad weekly to ask when he would ship my computer to me. He kept saying that he was working on it and would ship it soon and then gave some excuses to put me off. I had been grateful to my friends who let me use their computers, but it wasn't always reliable. I had several papers that I needed to write and was struggling to find a computer to write them. I used the library when I could, but the

143

library closed early and I didn't always have free time until after it closed. I also wanted to communicate with the new college students in the YSA back home.

I picked up the phone to dial my parents' phone number.

My dad answered the phone, "Rocks, can I help you?."

"Hey dad," I answered.

He responded in a rush of words, "We're fine, we're busy, and we don't have time to talk." This was his normal vibe when I called the house. Even when I just wanted to talk to my mom, he had to make it known how much of an inconvenience I was causing him. Even though mom was usually happy to talk with me. When I moved out, I had become the outsider just like Jason had been growing up.

"You mentioned you were going to ship the computer out last week, and I was checking on that. It's halfway through the semester." I tried to keep a non-biased tone, but it didn't work. The irritation he showed at my phone call had just intensified my own, and it was evident in my voice.

"You're so damn pushy and I'm getting sick of you calling and harassing me all the time." He said in a brusque tone.

"I only call once a week," I pointed out to him.

"I'm so tired of this, I'm putting an end to it. I'm not sending you the computer, so stop calling." He said the words as if it was my fault that he was breaking another promise.

"What? Why? I asked, shocked. He used to be a computer programmer. He built computers for fun and most of the parts were lying around the house. He said that all he needed was one $200 part, and he had everything else. He could have just said he wasn't planning to get me one and I would have found another way. Instead, he strung me a long, and I let him, once again putting my faith in a father who had done nothing but fail me.

"You keep calling me and wasting my time just so you can whine about not having a computer?" he kept on talking, but I tuned him out. I knew it was just a computer, so why did I feel so angry? A new kind of rage was building inside of me that I couldn't figure out. I could feel the anger through the increasing pressure in my forehead, taking away my ability to think straight. I was so disappointed in myself; I had trusted him. Why did I ever believe him? How did I let myself trust him again? Ugh, I knew better.

Dad was still ranting, "Do you even know how much work we have to do? I had to hire a couple more employees from church to keep up with the demands of all the orders we are getting." Does he ever think of anything but that business? I knew that the business was always more important to him than I was. I even pointed it out to him a few times. His response was that "The business pays for you to eat" confirming that it was more important. He never tried to smooth it over or explain it away. It was just a fact in our house that the business was always the most important thing to him.

Trust; that was the problem here. I had trusted him. I would not make that mistake again. My temper flared up again. I could feel my body heating up this time, forging a permanent separation. I felt as if I was disconnecting from the allegiance that connects a child, tethered in a subordinate type of obedience, to their parents.

Dad was in a full rant now, "I just can't stand how pushy you are all the time." "You always want to call and take your mother away from her work. We have so much wor…"

Click.

For the first time in my life, I hung up on him. I couldn't take his lies and destructive words any longer. I wished I was strong enough to block his words out, to block the hurt they caused. I threw the phone across the room, not caring if it broke. I wasn't going to be calling them anymore.

I always made it a point to treat everyone with respect. However, at this moment, I didn't have the words that would make this situation better. All I could feel was this rage that burned deeply through my body, and I didn't even know where it was coming from. This was surely an overreaction to not getting a computer. Why was I feeling this much anger? Where was it coming from? Why did I throw the phone? Why had I lost control?

I'm a mix of people in this moment, the one feeling the rage and the one who is trying to figure out why I'm acting this way. I'm a logical person, and this was an illogical response. The rage was overwhelming me as my logical side fought to understand what was going on inside me. Then it clicked, putting words to this rage. I wanted so badly to quit working for him and enroll in high school. The school was close, I could have ridden a bike to get there. I could have threatened to call DSS, they would have taken me and I could have been sent to high school. I know I could have found a way. I chose to stay and work because he had made so many promises to me about paying for college, helping me with getting a computer, and getting my first car. I had held on to those words like they were my lifeline, and he held onto them like they were my noose. They were the reason that I let all my other ideas go. He had used his mountain of lies to manipulate me for my entire life. This was just another broken promise, and it brought back all the emotions at once.

I should have learned my lesson when he didn't pay for college. He drove me to this school though. He had continued to promise me the computer. He gave me just enough hope to believe him each time, and I stupidly fell for his tactics. Now here I was, realizing all over again that every word out of his mouth was leading to exploitation or a transaction, a maneuver in his game. He never intended to do these things for me. They were just a play of words to him, a control method so that he could keep his little employee, his pawn, longer. When would I learn to stop being his pawn? The betrayal of his actions sank in. I would never trust him again.

I paced around in my room, trying to get my thoughts together, when Miwa walked in. She took in my red face, puffy from crying.

"You look like hell; you need to go for a ride," she said bluntly. I looked at her. I didn't want to be around people. I was so drained, and I wasn't sure I was up for any kind of conversation. She grabbed my arm, "You don't have a choice," she said, dragging me out of my dorm room.

It was dark outside, but the stars seemed to twinkle just a bit brighter than normal. I glared at them. The music was loud in her car, blocking out communication and my thoughts. Her windows were down, letting in the crisp mountain air. I could feel my mood lifting as she drove up the blue ridge parkway.

Thirty minutes later, she pulled over into a scenic overpass and we got out of the car. It was too dark to see anything. Miwa walked to the car and cranked her music up even louder, then she ran into the street and danced. I watched her wildness and felt her love for life at that moment. It was contagious and made me laugh. "Come join me!" she screamed over the music.

"I don't know how to dance" I screamed back. As she danced with total freedom to the music, I was self-conscious, having never danced like that before. My nerves were about to get the best of me before she hollered, "COME ON!" she said. "It's more fun when we both dance." I couldn't just leave her hanging; I ran to join her in the middle of the road, throwing my arms in the air and jumping chaotically to the music. I felt all my stress and anger melt away,

146

leaving every single negative thought on the asphalt as we danced in the crisp autumn air. After a few songs, we saw the headlights of a car and darted out of the road, laughing. We spent the drive back to campus talking about how crazy our lives felt and the plans we had that weekend to go to Cullowhee.

That night, my thoughts lingered with the residual anger. Maybe this was just another life lesson. God teaching me I need to forgive, right? But the anger was still there, pulsating in my conscience, a constant reminder that I had allowed myself to be used by him again. Each time, I would make a point to push the thought away, to push the anger down. I wanted to be a righteous Mormon, and righteous Mormons forgive and forget. It is preached so often that it's ingrained into me. They focus on the eternal plan, the idyllic family, and if I could just play my part, then everything would work out in the long run. I just needed to have faith.

I didn't know how to cope with all the anger, and the church provided a way for me to push it down. I was told by church members that I just needed to refocus on God, to let the past fade away. Whenever my anger flared, I quickly pushed it back down so that I would not have to deal with the damage that had been created. I was grateful; I needed the church to refocus on the things that brought me joy like spending time with Miwa, passing my classes, going on road trips, and meeting up with Phillip. I had too many other things in my life at that moment that were good, and I didn't want to face that anger. I just wasn't ready yet. I pushed it all away, giving it to that little girl. The one I locked away at fourteen-years-old when dad asked me to forgive him. She held that anger for me then; and throughout the years. She had the weight of the world on her, but she was silent so I could still find a way to thrive.

∞

I woke up the next morning, groggy from our late-night drive and the restlessness of my emotions. I walked outside of my dorm room, down the hallway, and headed to my 9 a.m. english class. As I passed the lobby, it was filled with almost every girl on my floor. They were piled on and around the couch, crying and hugging each other. I watched, confused about what would create such emotion. They were watching the TV which had a picture of the world trade center that had been hit by a plane. I heard something about terrorists but didn't stick around. I didn't want to be late for class.

I slid into my seat and listened to the students around me as they talked about the plane crash. The teacher came in to dismiss the class. I walked back to my dorm and heard that another plane had crashed and that both buildings had fallen. The surrounding people were devastated as they tried to connect with their loved ones but were unable to.

I think the heightened emotions around me sort of numbed my own. I knew I should feel something, that I should sense the danger they were talking about, but I just didn't. I was too worn down. The rest of the day, Miwa and I ventured out to a local trail and did some hiking to avoid the chaos around us.

∞

The following month, I made plans to spend the weekend in Cullowhee with my YSA friends and Phillip. One girl in my hall was driving to Waynesville, North Carolina, which was only twenty minutes away from Cullowhee. I reached out through instant messenger to my old YSA group and asked if anyone could offer me a ride. One of the YSA members that I had not met in person yet, Christopher, offered to pick me up and drive the additional distance.

The girl dropped me off at Taco Bell in Waynesville, North Carolina. Chris was sitting in a white, 81 Honda civic. He was slightly taller than me, with brown hair, and looked a little skinny. He was wearing green khakis with a white wonder bread t-shirt. He had bright blue eyes that seem to hold back a smirk.

"Hello" he greeted me with a crooked smile.

"Hey, thanks for the ride!" I was slightly nervous to be in the car with a guy I didn't know. He seemed nice enough. I mean, he did just drive twenty minutes out of his way to pick up a stranger, I reassured myself.

"What are your plans for this weekend?" he asked. I told him about my plans to visit with Phillip, and how I was staying the night with church friends who lived near campus. I asked him about where he was from and where he served his mission. Conversation flowed easily, and the drive passed quickly. As I was getting out of the car, he asked me if I wanted a ride to church that Sunday and I accepted it.

Saturday, I enjoyed hiking with Phillip through the trails of the Pisgah National Forest that led to several waterfalls. The path was well worn from all the tourists that visited over the summer, but now that school had started, there were not as many people, leaving us to enjoy the scenery in peaceful isolation. Fall was setting in, and the leaves were changing to form an array of colors that ranged from vibrant reds and oranges to dark green and browns. The sky was bright blue, interlaced with a few cirrus clouds that looked like the tips of ocean waves across the horizon.

We took our shoes and socks off so we could walk in the water and jump along the top of the rocks. The water was cool, contrasting with the still warm air. It was my favorite season in the mountains, and we were soaking in as much of the sunshine as we could.

Phillip and I walked back to the car, hand in hand, telling stories about our past and what we wanted to do in our futures. He constantly made me laugh with his relaxed ability to joke around. I was comfortable around him and felt like he brought out a more authentic version of who I was. The rest of the night, we spent time with his friends until he dropped me off at my friend's apartment for the night.

The next morning Christopher picked me up, and we rode over to church together, the one in Camden that I had spent my teenage years attending. I said hello to my old youth leaders, and to the others who had been kind to me in the past. We sat with the other YSA members, a few of which I had known before, but most were new to me. These new people seemed to glow with a vibrant type of energy. They welcomed me as if we were old friends. We talked more than we listened that day as we all worked to get to know each other. Betty, the one I had lived with last summer, even tried to shush us once. However, one of the new girls shushed her right back, making us all giggle. She gave an indignant look, making us laugh even harder. These were my people in the same way that SGA had been my people. They had the same humor as me, they stood up to bullying, they were outgoing, and best of all, they accepted me. I had only been around them for a day and I was already sad to be leaving them.

After church, Phillip gave me a ride over to Taco Bell. It was difficult to walk away from him again. Over the last year and a half, he had become my best friend, my first phone call when I wanted to talk and my last before bed. He knew everything about me, about my family. I had even told him about the abuse from my childhood and he still loved me. He promised to visit me in Virginia in a few weeks as we hugged goodbye.

∞

Tuesday morning, back on campus, I headed into my English class. I slipped into my chair and noticed the Diet Coke on the teacher's desk. My parents had each drank a 64oz Diet Coke every day for as long as I could remember, but it was unusual to see a caffeinated drink in this setting. They didn't even sell them in the campus store or in vending machines.

Once the rest of the class was seated, the teacher closed the classroom door. She seemed a little nervous about how she should properly respond to students' questions. I could tell this job was a sort of culture shock for her, which intrigued me. After class, I stayed behind to learn more about her story.

"Are you Mormon?" I asked her.

"No, I'm Catholic," she answered as she walked to the door to close it again before saying anything more. "Big Brother is always listening," she told me as she turned around to face me again. It may have seemed like a crazy thing to say, and anywhere else it might have been, but on this campus, I had seen it happen. Some students took it as their personal mission from God, literally, to ensure that everyone was living to their exact standards of how they interpreted the church commandments.

"How many times have you gotten set straight on your Diet Coke?" I asked with a smirk, joking with her.

She rolled her eyes "every single day. What is with that?" She asked me seriously.

"It originated through Joseph Smith and is a part of the word of wisdom which is found in the book Doctrine and Covenants that makes up part of the Mormon scriptures. There is a part that says we should abstain from addictive substances and some people interpret that as caffeine. It didn't start that way, though; it was first interpreted as coffee and tea. When we go to bishop interviews and they ask about the word of wisdom, they mean coffee and tea. I feel like it became a part of the culture when Mormons tried to out obedience each other."

"What do you mean?" she asked me

"Well, once everyone is following the same rules, it's like they have to make up additional rules to follow so they can tell who is the most obedient. They have to out Mormon each other," I said, making both of us laugh.

I continued, "Really, it is more of a cultural rule. You won't be kicked off campus for drinking your Diet Coke," I grinned at her "but watch out for the evils of coffee, that is the real deal breaker that will get you fired," I joked, laughing. She laughed too, but there was an edge of worry in her laugh because we both knew there was truth to my joke.

"Guess I better hide my chocolate then; it has caffeine in it too," she bantered. "I heard some students talking about how chocolate had caffeine in it, so they would not eat it."

"As long as it's loaded with sugar, the officials won't complain. Sugar doesn't seem to make it into the official Mormon definition of addicting." I mocked.

That night, as I tried to sleep, I reflected on the conversation. She was such a delightful person and an insightful teacher. It bothered me that she felt like she had to live in fear, for just being her authentic self in a place that was supposed to be of God. Was this really where I wanted to be? I had fought so hard to be here, and now I wasn't comfortable with the things I had been witnessing.

Just that morning, as I had been waiting in line for them to scan my card so that I could get into the cafeteria, a guy was denied entry because he was wearing gym shorts. They denied him entrance to the only food source on campus because of the material of his shorts. I had another friend who had gotten kicked out because she smoked a cigarette off campus and another student saw her and reported her to the honor council. The guys were not allowed to have any facial hair, the girls' shorts had to be below their knees, campus curfew was at 10 pm. It all felt so controlling and illogical. The rules didn't reflect the values of the God I believed in. They reflected an organization that wanted to see how far they could control people. It reminded me too much of when my dad used to force me to eat biscuits. It was never about the biscuit being good for me, or about a lack of food. It had all been about forcing obedience.

Like my teacher, how could I be true to myself here? I followed the rules because they were ingrained in me, but I couldn't support them when I saw how they tore people apart and created so much internal shame. I didn't want to support a community designed to turn students against each other as a way to enforce control. I couldn't support the guys not being able to have a beard and the girls constantly shaming each other in the name of modesty. I despised the idea of people inflicting arbitrary rules on each other in the name of God. It wasn't a place of love, it was a place of shaming, guilt, and control.

I didn't fit in here, and I didn't want to.

But after fighting so hard to be here, it seemed wrong to leave. There was a lot that I still wanted to do here. I wanted to go on innocent date nights where we got ice cream and went bowling as a group and explore more of the surrounding area. There was so much that I loved about this place, like the view out of my bedroom window that showed the goldfish pond silhouetted by the blue ridge parkway. I loved the old building that I lived in that was rich with history. I enjoyed being around people who understood my religion.

"God, am I supposed to stay here? The journey was so difficult and there is still so much I could learn here," I prayed.

"It's time to leave. Your time here is over." He replied to me. Silent tears slipped down my face. I didn't understand. I may not like all the things, but I felt like my journey here had just began.

"But why God?" I continued to pray. "Why did you send me here just for me to not fit in? This was supposed to be the pinnacle of my journey. Why direct me to a place where I couldn't grow? I had fought so hard to be here," I pleaded with him. I had overcome so much just to leave after one semester.

I heard his soft reply to my heart.

"You learned so much. It was always about the journey."

Chapter Fifteen
The Last Promise

I was both elated and mournful that I was leaving Southern Virginia University and returning to North Carolina. Cullowhee is a tiny town that is almost entirely populated by Western Carolina University and its students. I was moving in with a couple of Mormon friends who lived within walking distance of the campus, above a video rental store. My sister and her family lived less than a mile away, and I was thrilled at the prospect of having more time with her. I would be back in the Camden ward with the new YSA members who I already loved. I was most excited that I would get to spend more time with Phillip, as the late-night phone calls didn't feel like they were enough. There was just so much to be excited about!

However, I was giving up the future I had envisioned for myself. I had planned on staying at Southern Virginia University for the next four years, eventually finding an honorable LDS man who could take me to the temple and live out my life as a stay-at-home mom who was active in church and my kid's school. I would miss Miwa and our daily adventures together. There would never be a person who could replace her in my life.

Planning is a part of who I am; It saved me. Planning gave me the hope I needed to believe that my life was worth living. I knew that if I could just plan out the details of higher education, I could eventually move out of my parent's abusive home. I knew that with careful planning, I would be worthy in God's eyes and save my family. Planning had become my foundation and now I was throwing all of that out the window and moving into an unknown space. I was throwing all my plans out the window for a life that was unknown.

When it was time to leave Southern Virginia University, I rode with the same girl who had given me a ride to Waynesville once before. Everything I owned in this world fit into the backseat of her car, filling only half of it. I stared at the two trash bags filled with a quilt I had made in the Young Women's youth group at church, and the other held my clothes. Laying on top of the bags was a framed picture my mom had painted that never even made it onto my wall. I was surprised at how little I owned.

I moved in with two girls from church; the apartment was tiny. I slept on the couch, grateful that I had an affordable place to live. They both worked at Walmart, so I got a job there as a cashier while attending school at Southwestern Community College again. I wanted to finish my associate degree before attending Western Carolina.

I had slipped back into my life as if nothing had changed, and yet everything had changed. My friends and school were the same, but the place where I lived and worked was different. I saw my parents occasionally on the weekends and talked to my mom on the phone, but they were not a large part of my life right now.

My free time was spent with the YSA. Ariel was the one who had shushed Betty on my last visit, making her a bit of a hero in my eyes. She was easy to talk with, and always up for an adventure. Levi was quieter, but when he did talk, it was something funny. Chris, the one who had given me a ride before. He went out of his way to help people and always made me laugh. Johnathan and Felicia who had lived with us in the store in Sylva were both members as well. There were several other members who were very active.

For YSA, we would get together multiple times a week. On Mondays, we had Family Home evening in which we would get together with an activity, a lesson, and most importantly, snacks! These would sometimes be on campus or inside the homes of families we attended church with. On Thursday we had Institute, which was basically a religion class. Our professor was the same one who taught me in seminary years earlier. He was a genius when it came to teaching religion. He was open to talking about the challenging parts of the church without sidestepping the topics. He also brought in a lot of humor. He had a very distinctive laugh that was often heard throughout our lessons.

As a get-to-know-you activity early in the semester, the YSA got together for a game of volleyball on campus. Several members had already shown up. Ariel was the first to greet me and offered to let me play on her team. After a few more minutes Levi and Christopher walked over from their dorm. Chris played on my team and Levi played on the other. Levi served the ball and I jumped forward to hit it, at the same time Christopher tried to hit the ball and we crashed into each other. We were both laughing as he helped me stand up. I took his hand and pulled myself up, kicking sand at him for knocking me over. Behind us Ariel laughed as Chris kicked sand at her. "Ok, ok, enough of that, someone needs to serve," Levi said to stop an all-out sand war. We continued to play for the next hour.

After the game was over, a few of us walked to Chris and Levi's dorm to watch a movie. We popped popcorn and piled onto Levi's old neon green and yellow floral sofa. The conversation quickly shifted between people and movie ideas as we tried to decide what to watch. In the process of trying to agree, the conversation slipped away from movies and into other topics for the rest of the evening.

The following week we met at one of the church members' houses for Family Home Evening with the YSA group. We were sitting in the living room of the host family, eating dessert, and talking. I can't remember exactly what we were talking about. I just remember Betty coming in with a snarky remark that was made to put us in our place. I looked at her, shocked. My mind had blanked out completely as I was trying to register how rude she had just been. I chose to ignore her comment and turned my attention back to Ariel.

"Hissssssss" my eyes shot to Christopher who was the source of the sound. He was staring at Betty with his fist up in the air playfully bobbing about. "Wanna fight about it," he said mocking her. I swiveled my gaze back and forth between them. Chris, who was still bobbing about and hissing, and Betty, frozen in shock that someone had called her out so bluntly. Ariel and I burst out laughing. Chris stood his ground until Betty rolled her eyes, huffing, and turned her attention to someone else.

I studied Christopher, his eyes sparkling as he joked around with Levi. He was intriguing. How had he been able to defuse the situation so easily while stopping Betty in her tracks? He had a natural gravitational pull that I had not noticed before. There was no ego associated with his confidence. He kept the people around him laughing and helped others to be more relaxed. I turned back to talking with Ariel but continued to watch him out of the corner of my eye.

∞

Phillip and I had been dating for a year and a half. As we spent more time together, we talked about what our future would look like. That weekend, Phillip and I drove to Gatlinburg an hour and a half away. As we climbed in elevation, the snow became covered in a thick blanket of pristine snow. It allowed you to see further back into the forest than you can in the summer. It was a beautiful scenic drive through the twisted mountains, and I was thrilled to be there with Phillip. We drove past a few people who were climbing on the ice that formed from a mountain spring. It was rare to see anyone ice climbing in these mountains.

The main strip in Gatlinburg is covered in the small type of shops you see in any tourist destination. A fudge shop, an arcade, ice cream shops, and plenty of souvenirs. The main strip also included a Ripley's Aquarium and a Ripley's Believe or not museum that had a large 4ft, sphere suspended by water pressure, making it easy to turn and rotate.

It was cold as we walked around, and as I snuggled into his side for warmth, he looked at me and smiled. It was the perfect day where everything just felt right. I could imagine at that moment what it would have been like to be with him forever. It would have been easy. He was a good person and would have treated me like I was his queen. I loved him so much. However, it was like we could both feel that the end of the relationship was coming, and this was the last perfect day to say goodbye.

It was a week later when he broke up with me. He was Baptist, which conflicted with my Mormon beliefs. The pressure of different religions had become too much for both of us. My family was peppering me with questions about our future with a mixed-faith marriage. How would Phillip feel when our child turned eight and wanted to be baptized into the Mormon church? What about when one of our kids wanted a blessing? Blessings were performed by the head of the household who held the sacred church authority called the priesthood. This wasn't something Phillip would have access to and therefore, I would not have immediate access to. Would Phillip be willing to convert so that we could be married in the temple? It was a mandatory step to have an eternal family, and one I was not willing to negotiate. As I discussed the questions with Phillip, our relationship had gotten tense.

It has been my experience that most Mormons date less than a year before getting married, and often at a young age. As a nineteen-year-old, I felt pressure from my family and religion to get married. I don't think Phillip was ready to even consider the idea.

Even though I could feel it coming, I was still blind sighted by the break-up, and completely heartbroken. I had hope that we could work through it, that there was still a chance. I tried to see him one last time. A mutual friend drove three hours to pick me up for Easter weekend to visit him. On the way, a car ran a red light, and we t-boned them in the intersection. Luckily, we were not moving too fast, and all I had was a bruised cheek from the airbag. After the accident, standing by the cars unsure what to do, and waiting for the police to come, I saw my parents drive by. I waved to them, relieved; surprised that they were there at that exact moment. My dad made eye contact with me and then kept driving. I was on my own. When I asked him about it later, he said he didn't see me.

I took the car accident as a sign; Phillip was no longer someone I was supposed to be with. For a while, we tried to be friends, but the emotions were too raw, and the friendship dissolved in a matter of weeks.

There were so many memories, letters, e-mails, and online chats that showed the progression of our relationship from friendship into love, and then out of it. I searched through my apartment, gathering anything that reminded me of him. I threw the memories into a box. I didn't know what I wanted to do with it all. I just knew I didn't want the constant reminders of him.

A few nights later, I was hanging out with the Young Single Adults at a picnic area on campus by a small creek. There was a lot of shade, and the grass just seemed a shade greener in this area. It seemed to be an undiscovered part of campus because there were never many people here. We played Frisbee until we were worn out. Then we gathered around the campfire and roasted hotdogs and s'mores. I told the group that Phillip and I had broken up. Ariel put her arm around me smirking, "now look at your options" pointing at the surrounding group. I laughed with her knowing the joke. If you wanted to marry a Mormon and you lived in the south, options were very limited.

Even though I know she was joking, it made me think. I knew the main reason Phillip and I broke up was because of religion, and that wasn't something I wanted to put myself through again. It meant that my options to date someone were limited to the few Mormon guys in the area. The idea of enrolling somewhere else like BYU to have more options didn't appeal to me after having spent last semester at Southern Virginia University. I wasn't in a place to rush into a new relationship. Every semester brought in new people, and I was content with the freedom of being single. But life never works out the way I think it will.

Later that night, Christopher stopped by my apartment to check in on me. He saw my box of discarded memories and asked me about them. "What are you planning to do about them?" he asked me.

"I don't know yet. I'm still having trouble getting rid of it," I replied. I was tired from the cookout earlier and the homework I had. This was the first bit of downtime I had that day and looking at the box brought an onslaught of emotions that I didn't want to   . I was too tired to be strong, too emotionally exhausted to hold back the tears. They spilled out, I tried to hide them, but it was impossible. Christopher walked over and put his arms around me. He stroked my hair and rubbed my back for over an hour before I could gain my composure back.

I got up without looking at him and walked into the bathroom to clean myself up. When I returned to the couch, we talked for a few hours. I told him about the skating rink when we met, the trips to Gatlinburg, and the time he had his whole fraternity sing to me. Christopher listened as I mentioned how Phillip drove to SVU just to take me to a dance, and all the things I would miss about him. I told Christopher why I loved Phillip, and then why we broke up. For one of the first times in my life, I took the time to process everything. I didn't shove the hurt down; I didn't give it to that part of me that kept all my secrets. With Christopher, I was able to work through them.

After a while, Chris asked me, "Want to burn that box?"

Did I? It was so final. I looked into Christopher's eyes; they pierced through the pain I felt. He was trying to help me let go, wasn't he? Was I ready to relinquish so many fond memories? I didn't hate Phillip; I still loved him. This felt like throwing away the last two years of my life. He had been my strength and those letters were like a journal of the past two years. I was making an excuse, and I knew it. I needed to let the past go.

"Ok," I whispered.

Chris picked up the box and carried it to the car. We drove back to the place we had a picnic earlier that day and built a small fire. I shared my memories with Christopher as I threw them in the fire. I shed a few more tears through the process. Chris listened and empathized with me as I let them go one by one.

It was past midnight by the time he dropped me off at my apartment. I waved goodbye to him, knowing that I would see him again in a few days at the next YSA activity.

For the next three weeks, I spent all my free time with Christopher. We would get a bite to eat at the University Center on campus and then head back to his room to watch movies. We walked around campus and spent a lot of time with the other YSA members. I accompanied him and his family to the Mountain Heritage Festival that the campus hosts every year. We walked through the booths of homemade pottery, crafts, and food. I brought him to my sister's house and introduced him to her family and then brought him over to my parents' house. We drove to church together and held hands during the meetings. The attraction was unlike anything I had had with Phillip. This was a stronger, more vibrant energy. He captured my attention entirely and I could tell he felt the same about me.

He was the perfect Mormon man. He had served his mission in Tacoma, Washington. He had a close relationship with his family. He was active in church and carried a temple recommend which meant he could take me to the temple. He was quick to help those around him, the kind of guy who stayed after church to put away the chairs and help clean up.

∞

I was cleaning my apartment one afternoon when the phone rang.

"Hello" I answered it.

"Hey Stephanie, are you busy?" my dad's voice came through the line, he sounded excited.

"What's up?" I asked him, confused. I can't even remember the last time he called me, if he ever did.

"I bought you a car, come down and get it," he said.

"Uh, ok. I'll see if I can get a ride," I said shocked.

I had given up the idea of him following through on this last promise. What was the purpose of this? Was it a trick? A prank? There must be a catch, there is always a catch with dad. He didn't do things unless it benefited him, but it was a free car and I desperately needed one.

I called Christopher to see if he could give me a ride down to my parents' house. He agreed and pulled into my driveway a few minutes later.

"What kind of car do you think it is? Chris asked me.

I replied, "Dad wouldn't say, he wanted to surprise me. But, it's my parents, so I don't think it will be anything new. Maybe like an older Ford of some kind, that seems to be their favorite brand."

I knew to keep my expectations low. At least, I should have known. I was hoping for an older car that would be reliable with a paint job that wasn't completely rusted. I was unprepared for the car that was sitting in their yard. It was an 81 Peugeot station wagon. It looked like it had been sitting in a junkyard for the last thirty years. The paint that was left was a matte gray that blended in and out of the rust. I opened the car door and was blasted with the stale musty air. The fabric on the roof was falling down and the sunshades were tattered. At least the seats were still in reasonable condition, I thought to myself.

"Is this it?" Chris asked, dismayed.

It was the only car in the yard that I didn't recognize. I was hesitant to accept the fact. "I guess," I replied. "But it's free, right? So, I'll make the best of it until I can afford something better."

"Maybe it will run better than it looks," Chris stated as we walked inside the house to greet my parents.

Dad was excited, he looked like he had just won the lottery.

"I got the car from the same guy I buy my gemstones from down the road. It had been sitting in his yard for years and he doesn't need it anymore. It works just fine, although it takes a while to crank up because it's a diesel" dad was telling us about the car as he grabbed the key and walked outside with us.

Was this just a business deal? Stay positive, stay positive, stay positive. I repeated my mantra over and over in my head. He was doing a nice thing; he didn't have to get you the car. I tried to pep talk myself into being excited.

I took the key and tried to start the engine. It rolled over a few more times before I gave up. I looked at dad expectantly. He replied to my silent question "It's a diesel, you just gotta let it warm up, keep trying."

It took me another five minutes before the engine roared to life. We drove it down to the church and back. The air conditioner kept spitting out bits of what looked like an old liner. The brakes were a little squishy, but the windows worked and so did the radio.

It's a gift, I reminded myself. If I was honest with myself, it was a lousy gift. However, I felt pressured to take it because it was the only time he had followed through on a promise. The brakes didn't really work that well, and it felt like it was about to fall apart as it vibrated down the road. I didn't know if I was getting a car, or a death trap. Despite that, it was a car, and it was a gift, so I needed to be grateful I reminded myself.

We walked back into the house to talk about the car.

"This car was part of a business deal," dad explained.

Here it comes, I thought, the attached strings.

"The car cost $1000. You can pay me $100 a month for the next ten months," he said it so matter-of-factly.

There it is, I thought. That is the father that I know. For just a minute, I had believed that he had at least tried to do something good. I had given up on the idea of him getting me a car. In fact, I had not thought of it in months. He gave me hope all over again, I dared to believe him because he said he had the car in his possession. Instead, this is the situation he drops on me. A deal he made so that he could make a profit. At least he is consistent, I thought to myself.

I sat stone-faced as I was trying to decide what my next move would be. On the one hand, I felt pressured to accept the car and show gratitude, on the other, I was disgusted by this show of false promises. I didn't want to take the death trap that sat in his front yard. I detested the pressure I felt to take it, but I really needed a car. It didn't matter what I chose, I lost. If I took the car, then I would have to put on a face and show that I was grateful. In addition, I would have to make payments to dad every month as a reminder of this situation. If I didn't take the car, I would continue to be without transportation. I didn't know how to pick a car out, or how to buy a car on my own.

"We can't take the car back. It's your car now and the money will be due on the first." He said it like I had no choice. I should have run out and left him with the car or yelled at him to pay his own debts to his gem dealer. I should have told him what a horrible person I thought he was; that I saw through his charade. I know him, the person he hides away in the shadows of his character. I know his shame and I understand his selfishness. I lived with his manipulations and his abuse. I should have done something that would have gotten me out of this deal, but I didn't know how. I still believed in respecting my elders, and I didn't have the words or the knowledge to get out of this respectfully. I took the key he held and walked out the door into my brand-new rust bucket that my sister quickly named the puke-go.

Over the next few months, the car brakes gave out on me multiple times. The first time I tapped into a building, and the second time I tapped into a car. Luckily, no damage was caused in these two instances. At this point, dad offered to have the car looked at and he replaced the master cylinder for me, but that did not fix the brake problem. The last time I was just inches away from sliding down a steep embankment into the Tuckasegee river. After that, I gave dad the car back. I didn't care if he had a deal or not, it wasn't going to be life, or my responsibility any longer.

I could feel the anger and resentment building up again as I walked out of my parents' house. "Forgive him," I heard the voices of past church leaders dominating my thoughts and elevating my stress. I didn't want to forgive him. He kept hurting me over and over. Why do I have to be the one to forgive all the time? Why can't he be accountable for his own actions? Why do his burdens always fall on me in the form of forgiveness? Why do I have to constantly Rockville myself and my thoughts in reaction to his? I always must forgive but he never changes, I thought angrily.

I heard the reply in my head from a scripture I often heard, found in the Mormon scripture, Doctrine and Covenants chapter 64 verse 9.

"Wherefore, I say unto you, that ye ought to forgive one another; for he that forgiveth not his brother his trespasses standeth condemned before the Lord; For there remaineth in him the greater sin."

My heart was reminded again of how those who don't forgive commit a greater sin. I could never let myself be worse than him. I wasn't sure I believed it, but the pressure I felt from the lessons of past church leaders weighed on my heart. I worked again to let go of the anger. We were still an eternal family after all. I needed to do my part so that at the very least, when it all fell apart, it wasn't my fault. I didn't really see someone like him making it to the highest kingdom of heaven. Maybe the second kingdom if he straightened up, but not the highest kingdom. Surely God would know that he didn't have a pure heart. Maybe that would mean I wasn't tied to him for eternity? I could almost feel the relief of this eternal burden being lifted when again, I could hear the church speaking to me "wrong thinking Stephanie, you need to do your part." I took a deep breath and worked even harder to let go of the anger, pushing it down. I knew the anger stopped me from forgiving, and I knew I had to forgive so that I would not be worse than him. Forgive and forget, these words plagued me.

I had been working to save as much money as I could so that I could buy a car. I found a Volkswagen Golf in an advertisement for $500. Chris came with me to look over the car and take it for a test drive. Everything looked okay, so I handed over my money. On the way home, the engine blew up, leaving us stranded on the side of the highway. We called my brother for help to tow the car back to my apartment.

Chris's dad had the same model of car that I had just bought sitting unused in his driveway. He towed his car the three-hour distance from Winston Salem over to my apartment and spent the weekend swapping parts out on the two cars until I had one working car. Before giving me the car, he made sure it was safe to drive and that everything worked correctly. He had no expectations, no strings attached to it. It was the kind of generosity that I had wished to see in my own dad. I was left speechless as I realized there was no way that I could properly thank him for the gift of his time and the car. I understood now where Christopher got his unusual sense of compassion. His dad just made the world a better place when he was around. He showed everyone, without judgment, a pure style of love. He was funny and used humor to make those around him feel lighter. It was like he could see the most ideal version of each person, and in his presence, it was easier to be that. He wasn't an overwhelming presence, but more like a backdrop of serenity where if you were in his bubble, you just felt better about yourself; about everything, really.

I was again presented with the same type of duality from when I was living with Kelli and Betty. One person who exuded kindness and love, the other filled with self-centeredness and arrogance. I was grateful for this dichotomy, the obvious slap-in-the-face differences so that I could learn from both types of people. From my dad, I can see what happens when you treat others with such malicious disregard. I understood on a cellular level how that made me feel. I could see how his actions affected everyone around him. In contrast, I could also feel how Chris's dad made me feel with his acts of goodwill and overall embodiment of altruism.

Chapter Sixteen
Flames of Commitment

After dating for only three weeks, Chris asked me to meet him at the volleyball court where we played earlier in the semester. He met me on the path, and we walked there together hand in hand. He pulled me into the middle of the court and dropped to one knee.

"Will you marry me?"

This should be the moment I freak out, right? I mean, it's only been three weeks. This is ridiculous. I barely knew him, really. Even though all logic was telling me that this was crazy, I couldn't deny the soul connection that I could feel, even if I was still trying to understand it.

"Say yes," I heard God whisper to me.

"This is crazy!" my head was screaming.

"Just do it," I heard my heart say.

God spoke to me again, "This was meant to be."

These thoughts flew by in a second because I knew the answer before he even asked.

"Yes, of course!" I told him.

He stood up and gave me an enormous hug, picking me off the ground and spinning me around.

I looked at him with a mischievous grin. "You know this is insane, right?" I asked him.

"Pretty much," he said with a smirk.

That night, as I lay in bed, I reflected on the recent events. I couldn't believe the turn my life had taken. Did I really just get engaged? Phillip and I broke up only a month ago after a two-year relationship; could this just be a rebound? It was too fast. Could we even make this work? Did I want to make this work? My parents had met and married in three weeks, and they were still together. That was unfortunate though. they stayed together out of religious obligation and fear of the unknown more than love. It didn't matter, I guess; I couldn't deny the strong guttural instinct that Chris was who I was supposed to marry. Did that make him my soul mate?

Was that why this force pulled us together, despite the fact we had just met? Did I even believe in the idea of a soul mate? Mormons didn't really believe in soul mates, at least not the ones I grew up around.

To really know, I needed to fall back on God. He had led me through so much already and I knew to trust the intuitions that I received from him.

"God," I prayed, "Is this for real? Is it right to marry him when we are both so young and just getting to know each other?

"You could be happy with other people, but you will be happiest with him." was the whispered response.

My path was clear.

∞

We chose to get married on August 8th, 2003, due to practical reasons. It was one of the few days left that the temple had an opening. We also wanted to live on campus and needed to provide a marriage certificate to apply for a married dorm. August was only a few months away I felt stressed out from everything that needed to be planned.

My parents offered to pay for a budget-friendly dress and make food for the reception. The actual ceremony would take place in the temple and therefore would not add any extra cost. Chris and I would need to cover everything else, like the decorations, a venue, and photographer at the reception. We didn't have any extra money and so we found a public park with a gazebo we would rent. Our friends took pictures, and our decorations were a few vases I bought at the dollar store. But it didn't matter, I was getting married to my soul mate.

To get married in the temple, you have to take through a series of classes that explain the covenants we would make in the temple. I was assigned a teacher who would meet with me one on one, once a week, to go over the lessons. There are seven lessons in total. The first lesson was about the plan of salvation. This is the idea that we are on an eternal plan that starts before we are born and continues until we reach one of God's kingdoms in the next life. In the Plan of Salvation, we start in the premortal world as spirits. Those who chose to follow Christ would come down to earth. Life on earth is one big test. At death, we proceed through a judgment that

166

determines how worthy our lives on earth were and which kingdom, or heaven, we will be placed in. The highest kingdom is the one everyone wants to ascend to. It's the one where we get to live with God and make our own planets, although I'm not sure if they teach the part about planets anymore. At the second level are the people who tried but were not faithful enough, or maybe chose a different religion. The lowest kingdom is where all the murderers and rapists will live. Well, unless you ask God for forgiveness in this life, then somehow that makes it all better and you have a chance to level up.

The second lesson is about being morally clean. This included topics like, if I had paid a full ten percent of my income, known as tithing, to the church. Did I followed the word of wisdom by staying away from coffee and tea? Did I abstain from masturbating and any kind of sex before marriage? Did I keep Sunday, the day of rest, holy by not working or shopping on that day? This question always confused me as Sunday was the most stressful day of the week for many families due their duties at church, or the pressure to make their family look perfect even though church is right in the middle of their child's nap time. There were supposed to be more lessons, but they were canceled. The person who was assigned to teach me was friends with Betty. The lessons came with an undercurrent of resentment from my teacher that made the entire situation awkward. It was a relief when she cancelled them. I flipped through the handbook on my own time and made sure that I understood all the information. It was stuff I had been taught over the years, nothing was new in the booklet.

Before a Mormon temple wedding, I would have to take out my endowments. Before the endowment session, I had to go through a ritual called the initiatories. In this session, I will be washed and anointed, much like I imagined Jesus washing the feet of his disciples at the last supper. At least, that was my understanding of how the ceremony would be. Afterward, we are to put on the Lord's underwear, known as garments. Garments are a layer of underwear that endowed members wear as a constant reminder of the promises we made with God. In the second part of the ceremony, known as the endowments, we are making covenants to and with God. I understood these commandments to be much like the ones we have already committed to, and that was laid out in the temple prep booklet I had studied. Things like pay your tithing, don't consort with those who are against the church, follow the word of wisdom and to stay faithful to the church and my husband.

The wedding dress requirements for the temple had to have sleeves and a high neckline to cover the garments I would wear after the endowment ceremony. I know the groom is not supposed to see his bride in her wedding dress, but I've never been one for following the rules. Chris and I searched in several local stores, but it was summertime in the south and finding a wedding dress appropriate for the temple seemed impossible. Each time there was something that would stop it from being temple worthy. It had to be pure white with no color. One of the dresses I found had an almost Renaissance style and fit my frame perfectly, but it was off white, so we had to walk away from it.

Mom and Dad brought home several dresses from one of the other vendors at the flea market. They wanted me to try them on. Chris and I drove over to their house, feeling hesitant on what my parents would offer. The dresses were tinged with yellow from age and had huge fluffy sleeves of 80's style dresses, which is the era they were from. I looked at them sceptically, I didn't even want to try them on.

"I don't think I want any of these," I told my parents.

"You can at least try them on. We already brought them all home," my dad said. It wasn't worth the argument, so I picked one up and carried it to the guest room, leaving behind a trail scented with mothballs. I tried on the dresses each one more ridiculous than the last. I checked out the price tag on each dress and they were all around fifty dollars. Seemed a lot for dresses that should have been recycled a decade ago.

"We are trying to help you out here," my dad said, irritated that I didn't want any of the dresses.

"I appreciate it," I said, "but they are not the style I'm looking for.

"It gets the job done," he said with irritation.

We walked out without a dress.

My parents offered to buy me a dress if we traveled to Clarksville, Tennessee with them to help work at a show. We drove five hours to Clarksville and my mom met me at a bridal store. I tried on several dresses that were beautiful and flowed elegantly, but they were all over $500 which was just too much for my parents. I wandered over to the clearance rack.

Running my hands over the different fabrics, I searched for my size. There were only a couple on the shelf. There was one that had long belled sleeves that were sheer, but the chest was high enough to be considered modest and the sequins were well placed. We would have to modify the sleeves by adding additional cap sleeves under the sheer fabric, but it would work. I was thrilled that we finally found a dress that would meet all the specifications that the church dictated, and fit me well enough.

It was $300, but that was still a bit high for my parents. My mom bought it for me anyway, and I was grateful. However, there was still a nuance of irritation from my parents that showed in my dad's eye roll when he found out the price. It's like he wanted me to know that this was problematic but didn't feel like he could say too much about it either.

∞

The phone rang one morning. I opened my eyes in the darkness to look at the clock. 6 a.m. Who was calling me this early? I let the phone go to voicemail. I could check it later. Before I could fall back asleep, it rang again. A double phone call, the unofficial signal in my family that it was critical. A chill ran down my spine, alerting me to the idea that this phone call was bad news. I crawled out of the waterbed that I had picked up from my parents' house after I returned from Southern Virginia University and answered the phone.

"Hello" I said, still groggy from sleeping.

"Hey Steph, it's mom. We are ok, even the dog made it out. However, I just wanted to let you know we had a fire this morning and most of the house was destroyed."

I was suddenly wide awake.

"What happened?" I asked.

"A space heater was left on the night before and it ignited the fire, they think. It's chaotic over here and we are still processing everything. I still need to call your sister. I just wanted to let you know." She sounded disconnected from the conversation.

"Ok mom, I'll pick up a few things for you and I'll be down there as soon as I can to help you out. Love you," I said, concerned.

"Love you too," she said as she hung up.

I called my job and let them know I could not go to work today because my parents' house had burned down. I drove to Walmart and picked up some clothes and toiletries for them to last a few days until they could develop a plan. While in the checkout line, my manager walked up to me.

"What are you doing here?" He asked with a raised eyebrow. "You called out today."

"I told you my parents' house burned down; I am just picking up a few supplies for them," I responded, pointing to my purchases. He surveyed them. "I thought you were joking," he said. "We will see you next time you work."

"Bye, thanks for the day off." I waved goodbye to him. Confused about why he thought I lie about something so serious? De people do that?

Chris picked me up, and we drove to my parents' house. When we pulled into the driveway, we could see into the charred blackness of their living room from the car. We stepped over the threshold and noticed that the boxed tube TV that once belonged to my great-grandparents had melted. I walked downstairs and saw that several jewelry work stations had burned where the fire originated. The fire moved up into the house instead of burning the entire downstairs. The rooms left untouched by the fire were still destroyed by smoke damage, making the contents of the house unsalvageable. We walked through and helped organize as much as we could that day. The Red Cross came and provided my parents with clothes and a place to stay until they moved into a temporary rental.

The fire reminded me of what I could have lost. What would it be like not to have my parents?

My parents had failed me in many ways. There was abuse, broken promises, and selfishness, but I still loved them. I could see the good in them. I could see my mom's potential for unconditional love, and my father's knack for strategic planning. I could imagine a version of them without the abuse and I still had hope that if I could just love them enough, or if they became involved in the church enough, that maybe they could become the most ideal version of themselves.

In the lifetime of memories we had created, there were plenty of enjoyable moments. We celebrated holidays together, and we always went out to eat for our birthdays. When we worked the flea markets, I felt safe because I knew no one would mess with me once they knew who my dad was. He just wouldn't tolerate that, I had assumed. We bantered and joked with each other and acted silly at times. Mom would always pick something up for us when we went shopping together, her way of showing love. The situations that we had to work through made each day a choice to love them. They were the people I grew up with, my family. Each time I made the choice to love them, the bond became more resilient.

It was difficult, though, to live with this duality of loving them for the good they have done, or could potentially become, and understanding who they were now, and who they had been in the past. I knew that in their own way, they loved us and wanted us to succeed, even if it was only their version of success.

From the church perspective, I had to love my father. I had to find a way in which he would play a healthy role in my life, despite all the negative things. At times the love was forced, and at others it flowed naturally. Once I had moved out of the house and gained some distance, it became even easier to focus on only the positive things. Chris and I started having family dinners on Sunday at their house, along with my brother, sister, and her family. It had taken a long time, but I could sense that healing was happening. Maybe the church had been right all along. Maybe by forgiving and forgetting I could forge through the terrible memories into a happy eternity.

Chapter Seventeen
Is This What Heaven is Like?

Over the summer, I worked on Western's campus as a counselor for Upward Bound, a youth program designed to help kids further their education. Chris stayed with my parents over several weekends, working for them so that we could spend time together. To prepare for living together, I packed up the belongings in my apartment and put them into storage and then closed out my lease.

Planning the wedding and temple endowment dates proved to be exhausting. There was a temple in Georgia which was closer to my parents, and a temple in Raleigh which was closer to Christopher's family. Each set of parents was adamant that we plan the wedding in a way that made it easier for them. This stuck us in the middle of a growing feud. They both wanted a reception that was in their separate locations. Chris and I wanted our friends to attend as well. After weeks of feeling the strain of being pulled in different directions, we split up the ceremonies. We would have the endowments in the Atlanta, Georgia temple and the actual wedding ceremony in the Raleigh Temple two weeks later. Because most of the people in our lives were considered unworthy by Mormon standards to be at our wedding, it made sense to have the receptions later in a central location. We would have a reception in Camden near the church we both attended and another one in Winston Salem for Christopher's family a month later. It was hard for me to not resent that our decisions were being made for the practical needs of everyone else, with little consideration for what we wanted.

I was completely unprepared for the pressure that a temple ceremony created. I had literally been preparing for this moment from the time I was born; actually, before birth. A temple marriage is the precipice from which all our choices are made. It is the foundation of every righteous family, and the standard by which we are measured.

There is also parental pressure. They have been waiting for this moment to know if their parenting was a success or not. If your child is married in the temple, then you were successful in your parenting and can level up in your righteousness.

To ensure that we are worthy, we are interviewed before being allowed into the temple. The questions are the same as any other interview. Do you pay tithing, believe in God, stay away from coffee, tea, masturbation, and sex? Do you believe in and support the prophet and local authorities? Do you respect and obey their authority? Do you associate with people or groups who are against the church? If you fail the questions, then you can't get married in the temple and the rumors fly.

Maybe you failed because you drank coffee or smoked a cigarette, drank alcohol, or didn't pay the church enough tithing. The other ward members would figure out the reason and judge you for not being obedient enough.

Did you have sex? That seems to be everyone's first assumption. It had been taught to me repeatedly that if I had sex before marriage, I was as good as a chewed piece of gum, used and unwanted. You could repent I guess, but there is no way to reclaim virginity and that was shown through the condescending looks that were given.

Church members watched to see if you are still taking the sacrament. If you fail your interview and have something that you need to repent for, you may not take the weekly sacrament. A form of public shaming that you are no longer in the good graces of the church or God.

Everyone else in the church knew, or assumed they knew, that you were just chewed gum or disobedient and suddenly no one wants to be associated with you. You become a missionary effort or a charity case for those who want to feel better about themselves by taking you on. You have the potential to remain single for the rest of your life, and even though no one would outright say it, you could hear how problematic it was in the hallways of church. In the same hallway conversations, I heard that if you are not married, you have the "opportunity" to be sealed to a man in a possible polygamous union. Without that sealing, your progress is stopped for eternity.

I would not be that girl. I loved my God, and I was determined to show him how much by doing all the things I was supposed to do. I had lived all the standards set before me as if my life depended on them. Because it did, at least for my eternal life. So were the lives of my future children through the eternities, and their children. We were a spider web; each person was to play their part to ensure a blissful eternity.

I could feel the people watching us. My family, Chris's family, the church we currently attend, and the ones we had visited previously. There was so much pressure to get it right. I was ok with it though, I had already done the most difficult part, I had already lived in real devotion to all the principles I had been taught. I had already taken to heart that the church was true. Too much depended on this moment for me to fail.

Nobody talks about what happened in the temple. Members are specifically instructed not to discuss this subject. It was sacred, not secret. That is the mantra that was chanted when I asked for more information. We go to the temple prep classes where they talk about covenants made and talk about the philosophies of the church. However, no one talks about what actually happens in the ceremony. I had heard rumors of secret handshakes. When I asked why it was kept a secret, I was told that it was sacred, not secret and that to casually talk about sacred covenants would be the same as casting pearls before swine. Regular people, uncovenanted people, unworthy people, simply could not grasp how valuable the information was, and therefore it was not to be shared with them. In response to my questions about blood atonement, the veil, prayer circles, or the symbolism people whisper about, I was told that these things are sacred, not secret.

I heard rumors of receiving a new name that I could not share with anyone aside from my husband. Sacred, not secret. The only bits I could piece together was that this was the process in which we could become like God, or a God, depending on who taught the lesson. But I knew the temple was how we were sealed together as a family for eternity and that this was the only way to have true and everlasting happiness.

Despite all the pressure, I wanted this. I wanted to be married in the temple with Christopher for time and all eternity. I longed to have the eternal family I had been promised and to marry a person who was worthy in the Lord's sight. With those promises came the unspoken promises that he would be a good person. He would be honest, kind, hardworking, and a family man. That he would lead our home with honest and sincere intentions as he prayed each night to Heavenly Father to make sure he always made the best decisions for our family. Now was my moment to receive all the blessings I had ever been promised. The temple was supposed to be a small snapshot of what the highest kingdom of heaven would be like. I couldn't wait!

∞

The day of the endowment in Atlanta, Georgia, I stopped by the church clothing store to buy my new underwear, the garments. They would be my daily reminder of the promises we were going to make this day. I knew beforehand that I would have to wear them. I had seen my dad walk around in them naked half my life and I knew my mom wore them as well.

Chris's grandma bought me my first temple package. It contained a temple dress, shoes, and a slip. Things I had seen in the temple by the workers when I had performed baptisms for the dead as a youth. The package also included a bright green half apron with a fig leaf pattern embroidered onto it, a sash that went over one shoulder and hung past my waist, a piece of ribbon to tie the sash on, and a veil. I had never seen these clothes before; she told me to tuck them away for the ceremony and that I would understand later.

As we walked up to the temple entrance, I observed the perfectly manicured lawns and the picture-perfect people as they wandered about. There was a family taking pictures of their little girl in a white dress; I assumed she was eight years old taking photos for her baptism announcement. There was another family dressed all in white that looked like they were about to get sealed together, probably an adoption. A group of youth had just arrived to do baptisms and were hustling about to get their Sunday dresses on and in a line to enter the temple.

My nerves were on edge as we walked inside the temple, and I handed my recommend to the two people at the front desk. While they looked over my recommend, an image created by fear flashed through my mind of them rejecting it. If you don't have a recommend or they choose to stop you, you can't go into the temple, there are no compromises. We would have had to make another three-hour drive on another day. It felt a like the security gate at the airport as they smiled at you, but also watched your every move. I let out a sigh of relief when they handed it back to me

"First time?" the gatekeeper asked me

"Yes." Chris's Grandma beamed with pride as she walked with me through the door. An older lady, the matron, showed me where the endowment room was, the locker room, and the initiatories room. She gave me a key to my locker and let me know which room I was to go to once I was dressed. I took off my dress and put on my temple slip, dress, and shoes. The clothing felt weird, they just had an eerie energy about them that I could not process. This was God's place, I reminded myself. I was in the holiest of holy places. There was no evil here, there was no devil tampering with my clothes. I ignored the hairs on my arms as they tried to warn me of impending danger. My stomach was in knots and my throat was tight. I stayed conscious of my breathing to stop myself from hyper ventilating. I didn't understand why. My instinct has never failed me, so why did I suddenly feel like I wanted to run?

Chris and his family were waiting for me in the endowment room. They had been through this before, so it must be ok. Almost every adult I knew from church had been through this before, I reassured myself. If I wanted to get married to Christopher, if I wanted that eternal family that I had dreamed about for so long, then I needed to doubt my doubts, as the prophet once said. I pushed aside the warning signs my body gave me and walked into the initiatories room.

When I walked in, the matron was waiting for me.

"Please take off all of your clothes, including your bra and underwear, and put this on." She said, while handing me a gown. "You can lay your clothes over there", she said, pointing to a chair. "I'll be back in just a minute after you changed." She walked out of the room, softly closing the door behind her. I stood there, shocked. I didn't know I was going to be taking my clothes off. I guess it isn't any different than a doctor's visit, right? I held my head up high trying to hold back the vomit, I don't particular like those visits either though.

I slipped off my shoes and socks, my dress, and my slip. I hesitated as I took off my bra. Did I really have to be naked? My mind flashed back to the game of war when I was a kid and dad made me take off my clothes when I didn't want to. I didn't see how to get out of this though, not if I wanted to marry Chris. I didn't want the church rumor mill to be focused on me. I didn't want to disappoint my family that was waiting for me. But these feelings were the same as in the moment of dad's card game. I felt out of control, forced into a situation I didn't know how to get out of. I took off my underwear for the last time. After this, I would only be allowed to wear the church garments.

I stacked my clothes up neatly on the chair and put on the thin sheet. It had a deep V neckline and had slits on the side that went as high as my torso. The church had always been strict on what was considered modest. This gown was showing more skin than I was used to showing, which made me very uncomfortable. I felt more exposed than when I was wearing a hospital gown.

I sat in the only other chair placed in the middle of the small room, feeling my nakedness under the gown. The matron walked in. "Hello sister" she sounded distant and cloudy to me. The words echoed in my head as I tried to clear it. I could feel the blackness from my youth coming back, sitting on the edge of my awareness. I tried to sit as motionless as I could, trying to hide the fear that showed in my trembling body. It had been years since I had felt the darkness. I thought I had overcome it. Why was it back? We were in God's house, the safest place I could be. However, I was overwhelmed by the nightmare of my past, that felt like the present, in this moment. The room dipped in and out of focus. Breathe. I could always count on my breathing to steady me; you just have to suck it up and get through this, I thought, trying to steel up my resolve. I had too much on the line to bolt now.

The matron towered over me as she started the ceremony. There were words about covenants and how to wear the garments, but I couldn't hold on to them. She mentioned blessing my body as she reached under the sheet to touch me right above the knee with consecrated oil. I knew it was just my knee, but that didn't stop it from feeling so violating. I wasn't consenting to this. I wanted to scream, but we were not allowed to make any noises above a whisper. I wanted to whisper that this wasn't ok, I wanted to run out and demand why no one had told me about this. More incomprehensible words were said about washing and anointing as she grabbed the cloth and pulled it away so that she could reach down the gown and touch my chest. She didn't touch my breast, but my mind was already in panic mode. I could still feel her breath across them as she looked to make sure she touched me in the right area.

There was a moment in which she whispered my new name to me. This was supposed to my true name, the name that I would go by in the next life. She whispered my new name to me and told me I wasn't allowed to tell anyone, ever, except my husband in the next ceremony through a hanging sheet called the veil. "Will I get to know his?" I asked? "No", she said. "He only gets to know your name as he will be the one to pull you through the veil and into heaven." That's why we needed to be married to get into the celestial kingdom. We needed a man with the priesthood authority to pull us through.

She handed me the new garments. "Put these on, you should wear them day and night from now on. The only exception is when you're having sex or taking a shower. When you shower, be careful not to drop them on the floor as these are sacred garments from the Lord and represent the promises you will make today." She stepped out of the room while I put the garments on, The shorts were extra long on me and went below my knee, even when I pulled them up to my belly button. The shirt was baggy, and the lace neckline refuse to line up with my outer clothing. I was told to wear the bra on top of the garment, which made the bra slip around and not stay in place. There were symbols embroidered on the garments to symbolize the places that had been washed and anointed. A small backward L on one side of the chest, a V on the other and a dash over my belly and another over my knee.

There were more unprocessed words, but I couldn't hold on to them. It was too much. I was too nervous. I was never able to stop shaking, and I was doing everything I could to just sit in place. This was only the first part. Now it was time for the two hour endowment ceremony to start. Christopher and his grandparents were waiting for me. They had driven over five hours to be here today. I didn't want to disappoint them. I didn't want to disappoint God. I put on my white temple dress and shoes. I held my head high as I walked out, more to assure myself that I had survived than for any other reason.

I clutched my white bag of ritual clothing to be used in the next ceremony and walked down the hallway where Christopher's grandma led me into another room. That had to be the worst of it, I thought.

When I walked into the low-lit room, all the men were seated on the left side of the aisle and the women on the right. I had been looking forward to sitting next to Christopher and feeling his reassurance. Why did we have to be separated? He gave me an apologetic look as I sat down next to his grandma, feeling like I was drowning.

The authority figure, called the priesthood leader, began talking.

"You are about to make sacred obligations and covenants with God. If you violate these things or share them with others, you will bring upon yourself the wrath of God, for God shall not be mocked. You are making these promises and covenants with God of your own free will and choice. If you are not in agreement with this, now is the time to leave."

I had to suppress the snide snicker that threated to escape. They had orchestrated the pressure so well that there was no way a person could just walk out with their dignity, their future, or their marriage intact. That was why they would only allow us to go through the temple before a big event such as a mission or before we were married. It increased the pressure; it made it a public event. Did he realize how shallow and deprecating his words were?

"You are under solemn obligation to not discuss these sacred matters outside of the temple,"

I was ok with this. I had heard that we were under oath not to discuss these things. Sacred, not secret. Why did it all feel like an unpleasant secret then?

The speaker went to explain how, today, we were being anointed to be literal Gods, Kings, Queens, Priests, and Priestesses in the future based on the decisions and choices we made.

The lights turned off and a movie theater size projection came on, starting with a story of Adam and Eve. During each part of the ceremony, we would have to stop and add a piece of the strange outfit I had been given. First, we had to put on the floor length sash and tie it on. It was made of shifty material, and I had trouble keeping it on. Chris's Grandma helped me pin it the best she could. Then we had to add the apron and veil. I could not get the clothes to stay in place in the darkened room and every attempt I made created waves of sound that brought more attention toward me. I was hot in these layers of clothing and on the edge of a panic attack. I felt like these clothes were suffocating me and could feel my heartbeat picking up its pace, but if I walked out now, the eyes of 100 people, including Chris and his family, would be watching me. It would cause a scene. There was no way out of here without causing a spectacle, making me the problem.

My mind flashed back to when I was a child at my Granny and Pappy's house. Pappy had set up a large wooden box trap lined with chicken wire propped up by a single stick. He placed bird seed underneath it and we waited around the corner until a hungry squirrel crawled under and took the bait. Then we would pull the string attached to the stick, collapsing the box and trapping the squirrel. We raced over to the box and watched the squirrel panic as he tried to escape. He was only in there for a few minutes before we raised the box and let him go back to his friends.

I felt like that squirrel, trapped. No one was letting me out.

I tried to listen to the words the priesthood leader was saying, but found the words to be long winded and convoluted. We were making sacred oaths, but I was so lost in trying to understand his words. I did not know what or who I was making an oath to. There were sections that stood out to me like when he explained the law of consecration. If we were ever asked, we had to give up all our earthly belongings to the church. I thought it was so strange that I was giving these things to the church and not to God. It didn't feel right.

The patriarch proceeded to teach us the three secret handshakes that represented the different priesthoods. These were the handshakes we would have to know to get past the guards at the gate of heaven. Did they really think that God would ask for a handshake like in a secret society? I could feel my anxiety peaking again, by gut telling me this was wrong, this wasn't the way of God. What kind of ceremony was this? What kind of organization is the church? I didn't understand any of this. I looked around at the people around me, waiting to see if anyone else could recognize the level of crazy that I was witnessing. I was looking for an advocate, someone to help me out of this situation.

Those in charge walked around shaking hands with each of us to make sure we understood the specific hand hold we had just been taught.

Somewhere in the middle of putting on all the clothing, sitting and standing, and learning new handshakes, I looked over to Christopher and I must have looked terrified because he reflected my concern. They asked for volunteers and about twn couples came up, still dressed in their ritual clothing, and made a closed circle around the altar. They chanted in unison "O God, hear the words of my mouth. O God, hear the words of my mouth. O God, hear the words of my mouth"." It was at that moment that a lightning strike of terror raced down my spine as realization dawned on me, this is a cult.

Stop it, Stephanie. You can't think like that. I tried to push the thought away. There was no room for thoughts like that. They couldn't coexist with the life I had lived so far and I was in too deep now. The church had to be true. If it wasn't, I would have to redefine every aspect of my life, I wouldn't even know where to start. Just thinking about the church being a cult was shutting my thoughts and body down. The blackness threatened to engulf everything. This was why they didn't want us to talk about it outside of the temple, why they didn't want the truth to be known. My thoughts were turned to stone. I had to take control of this situation. Focus on the good, only the good, I thought fiercely. I was rigid as I worked to control my thoughts, my shaking body, my facial expressions. Every slight movement was exaggerated like the way sound is when you have a migraine. I wanted an eternal family, and this ceremony was the only way I knew how to get it.

Christopher used my new name to pull through the hanging sheet that symbolized the veil between heaven and earth, and we were allowed to walk together to the celestial room. This room was a lavishly decorated room with white walls, white furniture, white carpet, and a massive crystal chandelier hanging in the middle of the room. It was supposed to represent what the highest kingdom in heaven would look like. I wondered at the cost of the chandelier. It had to be well over two hundred grand. Would God really approve of his money being spent on such ostentatious decorations? Shouldn't that money be used to help those less fortunate? That one chandelier would have built many, many homes in other countries. It would have fed thousands of people. It seemed to be a mockery of how I imagine God would choose to spend his money. I thought of the mormon scripture about big and spacious buildings that represented those who mocked God, and this felt like what the scripture was referring to.

I leaned over to whisper to Christopher, "That was weird." He looked at me with an expression I couldn't understand, like he was putting me off. "What oaths did I just make?" I asked him, pressing for a response.

"We can't talk in here," he whispered back to me as a matron came over and asked us to be silent.

But we are not allowed to talk about these things outside of the temple. This is the only place I CAN talk about these things. Christopher picked up a bible and leafed through it. I sat with just my thoughts, unable to share them. Why did you want me here, God? Why was my hair standing on edge, urging me to run when I was being told to stay? I looked around for a trash can in case my stomach followed through on its threat to release its contents.

"There is a reason that will present itself in time," was God's reply.

After about fifteen minutes, the matron came over again and asked us to leave to make room for people. So much for God's divine space, I thought darkly.

After we walked out of the temple, I packed up the entire experience and put it away on my shelf. A new place in my mind where I put all the information about the church that I couldn't process. It was starting to get heavy.

Chapter Eighteen
For Time and All Eternity

The night before my wedding, I slept on the living room floor of Christopher's parents' house. The day I dreamed of since I was a little girl would come true tomorrow. I had done my part; I had stayed true to the path, held to the iron rod, and chosen the right. I had done what God asked of me and now I was finally getting married for all time and eternity in the Raleigh, North Carolina Temple.

It was nearly impossible for me to fall asleep through the excitement. Instead, I stared at the bag hanging on the TV armoire which held my dress and visualized what it would feel like to wear it. I imagined how beautiful I would feel as we took photographs in the flower gardens with the temple as the backdrop. We were planning to create the same pictures I had looked at in all the church manuals and inside my friends' homes of the perfect family. I pictured myself sitting across from Christopher inside the temple and looking into his eyes as we exchanged vows that endured into eternity. I didn't fully know what to expect because I had never been to a temple wedding before. However, I knew there was a part in which we kneeled across an altar. There was an oversized mirror behind each of us reflecting our images in a pattern that repeated into eternity, representing our ancestry both in the past and the future.

This was God's plan for me, and I was ready to take the next step to my eternal salvation, to our own eternal family.

The next morning, I put on a simple dress and makeup while Christopher's sister helped style my hair. We packed the car in preparation for our weeklong honeymoon at the beach, a gift from my sister. We double checked to make sure that we had the right documents for the ceremony.

Christopher's grandparents would be able to come inside with us. However, his parents could not be a part of our marriage ceremony as they had not paid the church enough money, tithing, to pass the interview questions. His siblings could not attend the ceremony because they were too young and had not gone through the endowment ceremony yet. Despite those reasons, they drove the two-hour distance just to show their support.

My sister and her family did not make the trip. Her husband was a non-member, and therefore she had never been through the temple. Even though she was my best friend, she would not have been allowed to attend my wedding either. I think it was to much for her to drive five hours just to sit outside, knowing that she wasn't allowed to see her sister get married. It would have been too much for me too.

My parents had driven five hours from their house. My mom could go inside with me, but my dad would have to stay outside. Honestly, I was grateful that I would not have to deal with him inside the temple. How do you cope with the person who abused you sitting in the most sacred place on earth with you? I was grateful that I didn't have to find out.

Once we arrived at the temple a few hours later, we realized we had left the marriage certificate. It was only a slight moment of panic before Chris's dad offered to drive the four hours round trip so that we could proceed with the ceremony. I'm not sure how fast he drove that day, but he was back in less than three hours. He had come through for us yet again.

I said goodbye to my dad before turning to enter the temple with mom. I handed the temple gatekeepers my temple recommend, and they let me through. I watched as my mom gave them her recommend and walked inside. My dad then pulled a recommend out of his pockets and handed it to the gatekeeper. I held my breath, watching closely as he returned it back to my dad. The gatekeeper told him to have a nice day as my father walked past them into the temple.

That was not supposed to happen.

You can only be allowed in if you are worthy. You can only get in if you've been a virtuous person. This was God's place, and I had taken comfort in that. I stared at him, shocked into silence, as I looked back and forth between the gatekeepers and him. Dad looked at me with the biggest grin on his face, like he had just won the Olympic gold medal. He was waiting for my reaction.

Am I supposed to be happy? Because I just feel infuriated. This wasn't supposed to happen. I had trusted that he wouldn't be at the ceremony. Why is he here when my sister was banned? Why is he allowed inside when my in-laws must sit outside? They had just missed a few tithing payments, nothing compared to the atrocities of this man. Why had no one warned me? Shouldn't I have known he was going to be allowed inside for my wedding?'

"How?" I managed to get out, keeping my face neutral so it wouldn't betray my thoughts before I decided how to handle this situation.

"We flew out to Salt Lake City and set up a meeting with one of the seventy" he said. The seventy refers to a council of seventy men who are the authority leaders that local leadership can contact when they need help in a situation. They are assigned different regions to rule over and they help the quorum of the twelve, who rule under the prophet. To meet with one of the seventy was a big deal, especially if it was just for a temple recommend.

An image flashed through my head of dad sitting in the office of a seventy. His face contorted as he cried, his body slumped in a show portraying how he just wanted to go to his baby daughter's wedding. Realization dawned on me; he used my wedding as an excuse to play on the emotions of the seventy. But weren't they supposed to see through this? Wouldn't God know I didn't want him here and let his seventy know that? Where was the power of discernment that we were told every leader had? My dad had been excommunicated for being a pedophile. He had been re-baptized since then, but that means the church absolutely knows about him and yet they allowed this.

He hadn't changed. We had just gotten old enough to stop the abuse ourselves. He had never apologized in a way that felt genuine. Instead, he apologized only when he wanted us to make him feel better, or if the church told him he had to do it. He never tried to make amends. His abuse still manifested in the way he treated his family, employees, and church leaders. It showed in the strategies he used daily, as if he were still playing chess with the lives around him. This move wasn't about being there for his little girl's wedding, it was a blatant show that he was still manipulating and winning at his game. He was a walking charlatan, and he had made it into the Lord's Temple?

"I wanted it to be a surprise," he said to fill the silence.

This wasn't a surprise; this was an ambush. He knew I would have asked him not to come. He didn't make his move until we were inside the temple. If I talked above a whisper, the workers would be

185

asked to leave and then the wedding couldn't happen. He waited until I could show no other reaction except what was expected of me if I was going to get married today.

I gave him a tight smile. "Glad to see you made it," I told him as I spun around to hide my reddening face. I walked into the dressing room and gripped the counter, trying to keep my composure. I looked at mom through the mirror and she gave me a big smile. She did not know that this felt like a betrayal to me. How could she not see him for what he was? I guess that was her way of protecting herself. How was I supposed to react? How was I supposed to be reverent in the temple when that contrasted so starkly with how I felt right now?

I tried to remain calm, I tried to breathe, but it kept catching in my throat. I have to get through this I thought as I raised my head and squared my shoulders. I pushed out the negative thoughts. I had no control over him and his choices. I needed to do what was right for me, and in this moment, that was getting my wedding dress on.

I felt the silky satin run over my skin as I put the dress on. I focused on how the sequins shimmered and how the waist made me appear thinner. I noticed my hair and appreciated how it looked picture perfect. I looked into my eyes to make sure I had the strength to follow through with this. I had no doubts about Christopher, but I did not know how to handle being in the temple with its weirdness and now dealing with my father at the same time.

The matron came in and said it was time for me to sit in the waiting room. I followed her out of the bathroom foyer and into a simple room with a few benches and a large mirror in it. She brought over a long sleeve bolero top and told me I had to pull it on because my dress was not modest enough. Even though we had put in sleeves to cover the garments and made sure that absolutely no cleavage showed, it wasn't enough. I sympathized with my dress; I knew what it felt like to never be enough in the context of the church. I held back my tears as I put on, so that I was covered up to my neck. This small thing was pushing me over the edge. I sat there looking in the mirror at my beautiful dress, covered by a plain, slightly yellowed, cover up that screamed I had not tried hard enough. I could see the sadness in my own eyes. This isn't what I wanted at all. They covered my dress up in the same way I had to conceal my authentic self, so that I could fit into my religion. I wish I had the freedom to choose my own wedding. This just didn't seem in line with how the God I knew would treat people. This didn't feel like a place of God. Maybe dad wasn't the only fraud here today.

"Get yourself together," I reprimanded myself.

I was guided to another room where they asked me to put on my ceremonial temple clothes. I held back my sorrow as I added yet more layers of ritualistic clothing, hiding the elegance of my dress. I could feel my soul being buried and lost under the layers of misfitted and uncomfortable clothing that was supposed to be of God. At least with the veil, my sadness would be hidden. Maybe they do that on purpose. I can't imagine how any bride would want this on her wedding day.

I was brought into the room where they performed the sealing ceremony, which is the name of the wedding ceremony. The chairs were filled with a few people, of which I only knew four, Christopher's grandparents and my parents. Looking at the reality of just four people was staggering, and I felt a deep sadness for those that should have been here. The people I loved made the effort to be here, and it was the church that was keeping them outside. I couldn't understand how this was Christlike, or of God. These were good people, people who deserved to have a place at my wedding. They had done nothing wrong and yet my father sat here as a mockery of the entire situation.

As Mormons, we are strongly advised against having a civil wedding ceremony, as it is believed to take away from the sacred nature of the temple. If for any reason you decide to have a civil ceremony, you must wait a year before you are allowed to be sealed in the temple. It is the sealing ceremony that makes it possible to have an eternal family and to live with God again. I regret that now. I wish I had bucked against the teachings and just had a civil ceremony. Then my friends would be with me, and not outside in a public display of who is unworthy. My stomach churned with these thoughts.

"Please kneel here," the matron told me, bringing me back to the present moment. She pointed to a padded bench along the altar.

I kneeled next to Christopher as the temple president talked about our futures. My eyes slid past him and stared at my dad. He didn't belong here. This was the person who abused me from birth, that fired me every time I didn't work one of his twelve-hour days, the person who tore me down at every opportunity. Who tried to stop me from gaining an education. He was selfish and self-absorbed. He berates and manipulates anyone who doesn't play his game, by his rules. My first memories are infused with sexual abuse. It had been six years since he asked me to forgive him in a mock display of meekness for the previous fourteen years of abuse. Those six years were filled with relentless emotional and spiritual abuse. He used the church's idea of forgive and forget to keep me silent for years, and even though I did my part, he still carried the weight of all those sins.

"Please join hands in the patriarchal grip," the temple president said. My focus shifted back to the ceremony. I pushed back the too long sleeve of the backward bolero and let Christopher grab my hand in one of the sacred handshakes we had learned previously in the endowment ceremony. I didn't like the handshakes. They still made the entire thing feel like a secret society, or a cult, but we were not allowed to say that word without getting shut down immediately. I didn't want it to be a part of my wedding. If I was honest with myself, I didn't want any of this anymore. My view of the temple was tarnished. I just couldn't see it as God's holy temple anymore. This was never what I imagined for my wedding. I was devastated.

We took a moment to exchange rings. It wasn't part of the ceremony, more like an afterthought that was allowed to appease common culture. Afterwards, the few people that the church permitted at our ceremony came up and gave us hugs and congratulated us. It was easy to hug my mom. I was so grateful for her presence. However, it took every ounce of strength I had to give my dad a hug. I was being forced into playing a part that betrayed my emotions. It left me feeling resentful and disgusted, and yet I dutifully acted the part.

I hurried back to the dressing room and quickly changed into the dress I had originally worn that morning. While I was inside the temple, I could hear thundering rain outside. What were my friends and family doing right now? Anger flashed as I thought of them in the storm. I hope that they had found a place to stay dry. I pushed the anger away, I had just gotten married, I wanted it to be a happy day.

It was dark by the time we were outside. We tried to take pictures under the small awning right outside the temple doors, however, the wind was fierce, blowing the rain in sideways, leaving us soaking wet. We managed a few pictures as we huddled together in the lamplight lighting. I was relieved to be outside with my friends, out of the temple clothing and in the fresh air. My parents gave us each a hug and said goodbye. Christopher's family took us out for a celebratory dinner before we checked into our hotel for the evening. We spent the next week in Myrtle Beach on our honeymoon.

∞

I never returned to the temple. I was told by many people that if I just kept going back that eventually I would understand what was being taught. This did not sit well with me though. It felt like I was being told to go against my intuition so that eventually I would be desensitized to the ceremony. I tried one last time as a good faith effort. Christopher and I drove three hours down to the Atlanta temple, but once we arrived, I realized my recommend was left at home. We tried to call our bishop and get approval over the phone; however, we could not reach him. I spent the day outside with the others who had been kept out and enjoyed the warm spring sunshine. It was a relief really, to have made the attempt but not have to follow through with it.

I understand the ceremony now. Christopher explained the parts that I had missed. I just didn't agree with the very foundation of what the temple teachings brought into the religion. I loved the idea that we would be a family forever, but I didn't think it was only for the elite. I didn't believe that we needed a new name or a handshake, and I did not feel that the ritual clothing came from God.

I still had to wear the garments in lieu of underwear every day and night as a reminder of the promises I had made. They made me feel claustrophobic and uncomfortable in my own skin, they gave me yeast infections and skin rashes. At first, I thought I was along in this, but as the internet became more mainstream, I learned that it was a common problem. I tried to get special permission to not wear them, but was advised to try different fabrics, but that didn't help. I was told to wear regular underwear underneath them which compounded the problem. I was talking with men who had no idea how the garments and layers affected my body. I was told over and over that I had to wear them to be considered worthy to attend the temple, and worthy in the sight of God, and so I did.

I kept my temple recommend active, and went to the bishop interviews every two years. There was a part of me that still wanted to believe. This religion was such a large part of my identity that without it, I didn't know who I would be.

Chapter Nineteen
Happily Ever After

Christopher and I moved into the married dorms on campus. It was a place of new beginnings. The space in the kitchen was small, as were the stove, sink, and counter space. The compact hallway doubled as a walkthrough closet that led to the bathroom. The living room came furnished with a full-size Murphy bed in the living room that we had to pull down from the wall each night. After we unpacked the small number of dishes and household goods from my apartment, we still had room to spare. Even though it was tiny, it was the best place I had ever lived because I shared it with Christopher. It was the place where we began our lives together and the moment in time that marked when my dreams came true. It felt like magic seeped into everything we did together.

Our friends from YSA came over to visit us often, and we quickly formed a community with the other newly married couples around us. We played cards, ate dinner together, and dreamed about what we wanted to do after graduating. It was the kind of place where you could walk next door and borrow a cup of sugar, then spend the next twenty minutes talking and learning about each other. Everyone was looking for friendship, and it was easy to find.

We stayed active in church and taught the primary kids their lessons on Sunday. We were back at the church in Camden with the same people I had grown up with since I was twelve. It felt like I had gone back in time because it was the same building, filled with the same furniture and artwork, inhabited by the same people. It felt strange that I had changed so much since that twelve-year-old girl who lived a life in a state of survival. Moving six times in eight years gave me experiences that morphed my life from chaos to building a life I had dreamed of. I had overcome the odds that my childhood had set against me by trusting God, sheer willpower, and maybe a bit of luck. Yet this place seemed content to stay the same.

Josh and Deborah lived on campus, and we spent an occasional evening at their house and played with our niece and nephew. They were both still working for mom and dad, but they were also focusing on building their own jewelry business. Both of them worked on Western's campus in the budget office. Their lives were full, but they always made time for us.

Since the wedding, I could take the time and space that I needed to heal, both from the abuse of childhood and from my experiences in the temple. Maybe healing isn't the right word, but I was able to create enough distance so that I could keep those things packed away in a place where they no longer impacted my daily routine and thoughts. I still saw flaws in the church, but I had a place to put those thoughts that allowed me to focus on more positive aspects. Dad hadn't changed, but I didn't work for him or live with him anymore, so his words and actions held little meaning for me. The overwhelming number of good things that I had brought into my life created a buffer between his actions and my thoughts.

I was no longer in a place where I had to always monitor my thoughts to keep them positive. My past was just that, in the past. I felt lighter, and healthier, without all the stress that came from depending on my parents. I had successfully forgiven and forgotten and received the happy ending that I had strived for. It was mostly peaceful with my parents now. Humor became my way of dealing with everything. It gave me a slightly sardonic sense of humor that reminded me of my first English professor who loved to make fun of all taboo topics. It just made things easier to talk about, which allowed for the healing I desperately wanted.

I called my mom almost every day just to check-in. Dad still gave me grief about taking too much of mom's time, but I just ignored him and talked with mom anyway. I talked about my day, the plans we had that weekend, and about that one professor who taught sociology that always got on my nerves. She talked about the business and how many orders they had and how the new employees were doing. It was all small talk that had nothing to do with what we said and everything to do with building a relationship.

A couple of times a month we drove down to my parents' house with my sister and her family for Sunday dinners. We celebrated all the big holidays together with only the occasional disagreement. Their food was still inconsistent and a portion was past its expiration date. They were still using cans of food that had been through the fire over a year ago, the labels burned off. We worked around these things by eating before we arrived.

I still had struggles, but they weren't as heavy. They were more typical and easier for me to handle. Christopher was by my side now and I was no longer alone. Not that I was ever alone. I had always had Deborah and my friends. But Christopher brought a new calm and strength into my world. He made it feel that now that we were together, we could accomplish anything that we wanted.

I was still working towards my degree. I decided to major in Parks and Recreation Management because the outdoors had always brought me joy. While I was considering which classes I should sign up for, I realized that with a couple of extra classes, I could have a second degree in Sociology. It was not that much extra work to improve my chances of getting a job after college.

I loved being in school. I loved the teachers, the diversity of people, and the experiences outside the classroom. I really enjoyed listening to the WCU drum line practice by the bell tower while I ate my chicken sandwich. I loved watching other students skateboard to and from classes, watching the sororities move in clusters and different organizations petition for their causes. There were opportunities and new beginnings in every direction.

When I walked around campus, I could see mountains in every direction and the sky was often a bright blue. The sunsets were varying shades of cotton candy pink to light purple backdropped with a gradient of blue. When there were clouds, their patterns rippled across the expanse of the sky as they showed off their bright white to thundering gray colors. There were plenty of green spaces for picnics and throwing a frisbee. There were several creeks and rivers close by to campus where we could go tubing or rafting.

I loved the parks and rec teachers. They were supportive, friendly, and literally always had their doors open to us (or at least a schedule to know when they would be there). I thrived with my schoolwork under their care. We set out on a ten-day backpacking trip with our professor, Maurice, as a part of our coursework. He told us stories and sang us songs around the campfire each night. At the start of every year, he would invite the seniors to his house for brunch. He marked his house by hanging a towel printed with the British flag on a bush at the end of his driveway. When I was a senior, we stole the flag and each took turns taking it on adventures. At the end of the school year, we presented a slideshow of all the adventures that his towel had endured.

In my experiences on three different campuses over six years, Debbie Singleton was my favorite teacher of all time. She used her time and words carefully to lift everyone around her. Her classes included several senior-level courses and were much more intense, but the love that she put into her class and her students made me willing to work hard. She had an open-door policy that allowed me or the other student to sit on the couch in her office and just have a place to be. She listened and advised us on schoolwork, but also on the things that were going on in our life like family, religion, and school issues. Every time I left her office, I felt a little more confident about the problem I had brought to her. She is the true definition of everything a teacher should be and more. I love her for those memories of feeling seen and appreciated for who I was in that moment, while also allowing room for growth.

In contrast, the sociology department was a total mess. I remember sitting in a statistics class in the sociology department where the teacher made math even more complicated. I had to tune out his teaching until I could teach myself at home. This class was taught in a computer lab, so we were each sitting in front of a computer. Several students, including me, would play games when the teacher wasn't looking. I was probably the worst one in the class for this. Another student was caught playing games. I looked up when the professor screamed at the student and then slapped his back. The unexpected sound seemed to bounce off the walls while we tried to process what had just happened. After class, I walked with several other students to the department head who refused to do anything about it. I called the news to involve them, and hopefully incite change, but my nerves were too high, my voice too shaky. I couldn't tell the story in a compelling way that could catch attention. But did I have to? Do I have to make the story interesting before anyone will listen? I was disappointed that no one would stand up against a teacher. This was a person in authority who had just gotten away with abuse in a classroom full of kids, and the school did nothing. I understood how my dad could get away with the things he did for so long.

The sociology professor with whom I had the most classes was very good at presenting information in a way that was easy to learn. He was a storyteller and could inspire his students with his words. Instead, he used those words to systematically tear students down based on his biased opinion of what and how they thought and how he viewed them. He was my academic advisor but failed to do his job, becoming a hindrance to my education. I didn't trust him enough to help me.

Before the semester started, I met with him, and within ten minutes he said I was a brown noser and that he would never give me an "A." I was shocked. Of all the things I have been labeled, this was new to me. And within ten minutes of meeting me? I wish an older version of me could have stopped by just then and let me know that this judgment was more about who he was than who I was. But I didn't know that and so his words got into my head and swirled around as I tried to deconstruct them.

I did not take my education for granted. I had fought hard for it, and I took it seriously. If there was a way to get extra credit, I would gladly accept it. If I had a paper to write, I brought it to the student writing center to edit out the finer points. If I had homework, it was always turned in. I strived for A's, and although I didn't get them every time, I knew I had given my best effort. Did that make me a brown noser? I honestly wasn't sure what he meant, especially because he had labeled me so quickly.

I was kind to everyone I met whether I liked them or not. People would tell me that I had a bubbly personality. I had to be that way; it was how I survived. Being positive was engrained in me. I worked in retail my entire life at that point and knew how to behave in a way that avoided conflict. Did that make me a brown noser?

At first, I worked harder in his classes, thinking I could prove him wrong and get an "A" in his class. I put twice as much effort into his classes. Then I heard rumors of how he had treated other students, and how he had messed with their grades, too. He graded homework with words like "you should never be a sociologist, you just don't understand anything" and other words that had nothing to do with the assignment. On multiple occasions, I stood outside the classroom and listened as he mocked both me and my religion to the other students, quickly changing the subject as I walked in.

We had to write opinion pieces in a journal once a week, and because it was based on opinion, it gave me the freedom to experiment with my homework. To prove a point to myself, I would write his opinion even though I disagreed with him, and other times I would write my opinion backed by my experiences. My grades were handed back to me based on how closely they related to his opinions and not on the quality of my work or even the accuracy.

We filled out a teacher survey every semester. I wrote an honest review about how he was a good lecturer, but inconsistent with grading and treatment of students. My grades would always tank after these reviews. We both knew he was grading me according to the reviews and not my homework.

There was a part of me that desperately wanted to prove him wrong about me. I wanted him to know how hard I had worked to be in class, and how much it meant to me to sit in a classroom each day. I wanted him to know my history and why education was important to me. That I was not some spoiled little girl who had the world handed to her. Why did he think that anyway? Was just being happy offensive to him? I didn't understand, which made me believe I was the problem. I felt like I had to be polite to him despite his mocking judgments. I said hello to him in the hallway one day, but he ignored me and walked past. Rude, I thought. Maybe he didn't hear me. I turned around and said hello again. He looked at me annoyed, "the world doesn't revolve around you Stephanie" he said angrily and then huffed off. It had taken me a few years of processing that moment to realize that the problem wasn't me.

He stayed true to his original word and despite my "A" in most other classes, he refused to give me an "A." It infuriated me because I knew the grades he assigned me had nothing to do with my work and everything to do with his biases. I talked to the department head about this at one point. However, just like when the other professor slapped his student, it was all ignored and swept under the rug.

I was in the Parks and Recreation department and the sociology department for three years. During this time, I spent a lot of time reflecting on how each department interacted. The parks and recreation department had a tougher course load that demanded more time and thought than sociology. The sociology department was fairly easy and predictable in what each class would require, a few tests and a research paper or two. The classes were straightforward in that you just regurgitate what you learn. In Parks and Recreation, we often had to come up with ideas and plans and then implement them in most cases. We also had to do extensive research to write a paper we worked on the entire semester.

I noticed how each department, each teacher, treated their students. In a lot of ways, my sociology professor reminded me of my father and the abuse he handed out to people in the form of microaggressions. Just enough so that you feel the impact of his words, but not so much that you realize it's abusive. I watched the students in Parks and Rec thrive and excel in their fields. In sociology, it just wasn't the same.

∞

My feelings toward the church shifted even more during this time period. Chris and I were co-teaching the eleven-year-olds on Sundays, and then I taught the same girls once a month on Wednesday for activity night. We loved our kids. They were smart, fast thinkers, and funny. We had a few who had been labeled as wild, but those kids became our favorites and showed the most growth while in our class. We had been teaching for over a year and loved our church kids. It was then that we started having trouble with the new primary president. She was the same lady who refused to teach me the temple lessons and who I knew indulged in gossip about me and my family for years.

I was planning a special activity for the kids in which they would cook dinner for themselves. My budget was tiny, and this event took half of it. That was ok, I had carefully planned around it. I had talked with my kids about it for the last few months and I knew they were excited too. On the Wednesday we had scheduled the event, I bought all the food and supplies I needed and drove the thirty minutes to church. When I showed up, none of my kids were there. Another mom let me know she had received a call from the primary president that my meeting had been canceled. I was furious. I was upset for myself, and for my kids who had been looking forward to this. It was the third time she canceled the activities I planned without my knowledge.

When I confronted her on the matter, she just sat there like she had done nothing wrong. When I pressed harder, she gave an answer that felt like a lie. I could tell she was being spiteful and petty, but I didn't understand why. I talked to the bishop and pursued the correct avenues to get help, and all they did was throw their hands up and said they didn't know what to do. There were several other acts of aggression and vindictiveness, and the results were always the same. As the situation became more toxic, Christopher and I decided to leave the situation and that congregation. We had to get special permission from the church area leaders, and the stake president above them to change churches and attend with my sister and parents. A part of me resented the fact that we could not choose the church that we wanted to go to.

I could see a pattern emerging in my life. Each time I tried to speak up about any kind of abuse, I was told, in a variety of words, to be silent.

I saw the pattern in how the church leaders told me that I needed to put the past in the past, forgive my father, forget his sins, stop causing more drama, and let my father heal.

I saw it again in church when I tried to speak out about several church leaders who had been verbally abusive and vindictive for years to more people than just me. I was told that I needed to turn the other cheek and give them grace because I didn't understand her situation. I needed to stop being the problem.

I saw the pattern in the professors when they used their position of authority to intimidate and tear down students. I saw the pattern in the department head as he minimized my words and then ignored the problem signaling that I had simply created more work for him.

That is why people stay silent.

It takes courage and bravery to stand up against someone who has abused you. There is a fear that you will not be believed or taken seriously, and those fears are real, based on experiences like these. When I stood up, I was told to shut up.

How can we know how to stand up to the more dangerous types of abuse when in these smaller instances, the moments we are testing the waters of speaking up, our words are devalued and casually brushed off as if we were just "causing drama?"

I get it, I guess. It is easier to ignore the problem just as my mother, church leaders, and the department head had done. To acknowledge the abuse means that you have to face the problem or knowingly ignore it. It is much easier to blame the informant assuming they are the problem. It's ok to ignore someone who is viewed as a troublemaker, but it isn't as easy to disregard the abuse once it has been brought into view of society and believed. Just because it is easier, doesn't make it right.

The abuse was allowed to continue in different aspects of my life. When I spoke up, I was cast as the troublemaker. The ones in authority minimized the abuse, and the ones who abused continued, protected by a higher authority.

It is very difficult to continue fighting when I am standing alone. Where is everyone else? I see those in authority keeping their eyes on me, seeing how much trouble I will cause. The people who should have stood up with me, I know they know what is happening. Why will they not take a stand with me? We could be stronger together if they would just be courageous enough to cause some drama themselves.

What I know, is that I had the responsibility to change myself. I could choose to be more like Debbie from my parks and rec classes and less like the sociology teachers. I could choose to be more like my old roommate Kelli and less like Betty. I could choose to not be like the primary president who displaced her anger on everyone around her and more like my seminary teacher who accepted us the way we were. I know that I am responsible for being aware of abuse, in all its forms, and making sure it stops with me.

Chapter Twenty
The Calm

I finished my time at Western Carolina University. My parents, grandparents, and sister were sitting in the audience at the graduation ceremony. Mom and dad had taken the day off work for me. It was another sign that our family had healed from the past. I was excited that they were a part of the crowd sitting in the stands, and that they had come just to celebrate with me.

I stood backstage with the other Parks and Recreation majors. We were waiting in line to walk in a procession to our seats under the bright lights in front of the stage. I had my two gold cords hanging down on each side, symbolizing that I had graduated with honors. I stood outside with my Parks and Rec graduating class laughing and joking and trying to pretend that we knew what was next, but few of us really did.

I spotted my Parks and Rec teachers on stage and smiled at them; they were beaming back at all of us. They felt the same level of success for us that we felt in that moment for ourselves. I looked for my family in the crowd and waved up at them. The announcer called our names as my classmates moved forward in front of me.

"Stephanie Taylor."

I walked across the stage. I could hear my family cheering me on across the large stadium. My friends, who were graduating with me, cheered in line as well. They handed me a presentation binder holding my diploma. I shook hands with the Chancellor, paused to smile for the camera, and then walked off. It took less than a minute to walk across the stage, less than a minute for my graduation to become official. My body vibrated from the positive feelings of accomplishment and success that I felt in that minute.

Afterwards we all gathered around for a photo, my parents, grandparents, sister, and my husband. This was the first time in my memory that my family joined around me in celebration, here for no other reason than to support me. There were no side comments, no undercurrent of annoyance, no negativity at all.

I wish I could go back to seventeen-year-old me living in Bryson City that summer struggling to go to SVU, the fifteen-year-old me who didn't know the state capitals but desperately wanted to, and the fourteen-year-old me who had had enough of this life and wanted to be done; I wanted to show them the picture we had just taken. It showed genuine smiles and a happy family with arms around each other. It rivaled the pictures I looked at as a kid in church magazines. Through my own grit, independence, and determination, I achieved everything I ever wanted at that point, and there were no limits to my future. I was proud of myself. The picture showed my accomplishments academically, but more significant to me, it showed that we had healed as a family. I had worked so hard to forgive and forget, like I had been taught. We all survived and recovered from the past that I locked up. I had followed the church and earned my eternal marriage to my best friend. I was on top of the world. My heart was exploding for myself, my family, and pure gratitude for the God that held my hand through all the dark nights.

After graduation, we moved to a little two-story townhouse style home in the center of Waynesville. Chris started a job at Haywood Regional Medical Center, and I was now working at a small mom and pop shop down the road. The church taught that it was best for the mother to stay at home. Now that we were considering children, a career job would have been a distraction from that plan.

God had followed through on all his promises, and I owed it to him to continue following his plan the way it had been laid out for me. This career choice was not based on practical matters such as finances or other worldly matters. We saw it as a sacrifice that we had to make to ensure our family's eternal salvation. A show of faith that we were still on the right track, except now I was fighting for my future family instead of saving my past.

I remembered a few years ago, the day my niece was born. Deborah let me change her outfit and I remember being in awe of her little hands and feet and her fluffy blonde wisps of hair. She looked at me with the brightest, blue eyes that spoke of unlimited potential, and I knew she had me and Christopher wrapped around her tiny pinky for life. I handed her to Christopher and the look in his eyes reflected what I felt. As we held this little girl, we adored her. We knew it was time to start our own small family. We wanted our children to be close to their cousins, to have a close bond that would bind them together through this life.

It took me almost a year to get pregnant with our first child. It was a rough year of doubt and wondering if something was wrong. I wasn't sure we could get pregnant, or if we needed to meet with a specialist. I had told myself after a year of trying, that we would start to see a specialist to make sure that nothing was wrong. Just a few months shy of that deadline, the pregnancy test finally came back positive! We were flooded with joy and excitement at the idea of this tiny new baby.

Other than some exhaustion and a little morning sickness my pregnancy was fairly easy. In preparation for the new baby, we wanted to own our home. We found a foreclosure on a three-bedroom, one bath 1100 square foot house. It came with a half an acre of yard with an oversized garden, a shed out back. The property bordered a creek that was stocked with trout each year. At 58k, it was an amazing deal for the great condition that house was in. It was older, and it did need some fixing up, but it was a solid house with no underlying conditions.

We were a few dollars shy of the closing cost. Mom and dad, with the help of grandmother, helped us with the remaining amount. It was made clear that it was a loan, but that was ok. There were no other strings or motives attached. I was grateful that they were helping us. I took it as another sign that he had changed.

Our baby boy was comfortable in my womb and was in no hurry to leave. We scheduled his eviction a week after my due date. They tried to speed up his delivery through medications, but the labor dragged on for almost twenty-four hours before he made his debut into the world. At seven pounds and eleven ounces, Stephen entered our family with a fierce cry. He was perfect. He had my nose, but everything else was a copy of his father.

The nurses came in and out in a flurry of information for new moms. I watched the pile of paperwork grow to an intimidating size. They offered us lactation information, a group for first-time moms, how to register for his social security number and official birth certificate among other information. I could hear in the background of my mind the people as they came and went, but my focus was on discovering this tiny piece of our hearts. Memorizing his face, his sounds, and his new baby smell. He captured us entirely with each new sound and movement that he made.

While I was still in the hospital, a phone call caught my attention. It was my realtor. I didn't have the energy to answer but felt that it was important.

"Hello" I answered

"Hey Stephanie, I'm just calling to let you know that you have been cleared to close on your new home!"

A new house and a new baby in less than a month created a lot of change for our lives. I was grateful that Stephen was a happy baby, only crying when he was hungry or sleepy. He was a good sleeper, waking up a few times during the night and going back to sleep quickly after filling his belly.

The church youth came out and helped me pack up the townhouse, and the women made meals for me while I learned to take care of the new baby. Two weeks later, we moved into our first home.

Chris's dad spent many weekends with us helping with projects like a new water heater, adding an attic ladder, or helping Chris work on the cars. We loved the weekends that he came to visit. His mom came on some visits as well to see the baby and she allowed me some time to recover.

My parents stopped by for an occasional visit. They usually only stayed for an hour at most and I was happy for that. Even though I had left our past in the past, my father would always make me nervous around our children. He had told us on numerous occasions that he knew he 'had screwed up as a father' and wanted to make it up to us by being the best grandparent he could be. I would have thought he was grooming the situation, but thoughts like that mean I had not forgiven and forgotten. There was no room for thoughts that, I had to prove to God that I had followed his path.

My mother was genuine in her abundant love for her grandbabies, and I felt nothing but admiration as I watched her with them. I hoped that they could have a healthy bond with both my parents, free from the struggles that we had gone through. This was the second chance dad had always wanted. It had been almost ten years since any sexual abuse had occurred. With the church's guidance, I was willing to allow, even encourage, their relationship as I kept a close eye on his every move.

Chris worked the night shift at the hospital. He would come home at 7 a.m. in the morning, right as the baby woke up for the day. Chris would take care of him while I slept a few more hours after being up with Stephen for several nighttime feedings. It was lonely to be a stay-at-home mom of a newborn. There was a group for first-time mothers that the hospital offered, but I didn't really click with the other moms and the relationships were all short lived.

When Stephen was about a year old, I took him to the library once a week for reading time. After a few weeks of regular attendance, I made friends with several of the other moms. The friendships grew, and we soon began meeting outside the library at the local kids' bounce house, lunches out, and anywhere that was friendly to kids. Eventually we got together at least once a week and our mom group expanded to include the dads who also got along as well as the moms did. Another year passed by in this routine when we all became pregnant with our second child. Our bond grew deeper as we talked about all things baby, being pregnant again, our daily struggles, and all the funny stories we had to share. If I ever needed anything, I knew with no doubts that someone would be available, and they never failed me. I did my best to offer them the same support.

The Church was still important and integrated into our daily life. We met new, friendly people in the Waynesville ward, but there was never a group like YSA again. Church felt like I was going more to help other people than for my own needs and I was ok with that. I loved helping people and lifting them up. I had seen hard days and knew how much a kind face could mean on a bad day. I relied on the community in church less and less though, and found my village within my mom's group.

Since I had gone to the temple, my relationship with the church was slowly shifting. I found myself disagreeing with some of the smaller things. I just couldn't believe that God cared if we drank coffee, or what clothes we wore. I struggled daily with wearing the under garments that the church required. Even after years of experimenting with different styles and fabric types, they just never fit me right. They shifted weirdly under my clothes, always sticking out the back of my pants or along the collar line. I had to readjust and fidget with them constantly, making it difficult to relax. This caused a lot of social anxiety. They made me feel claustrophobic in my own clothing. I followed the rules despite my personal feelings because I trusted in God, and I wanted to live up to his expectations.

Deborah had developed her own group of friends through work in Cullowhee and had dinner with them often. Deborah and I intertwined our friends groups. For the next two years it was a magical time of love and support from an entire community of caring and giving souls. Anyone was welcome to join us. That's another thing I loved about them, they were inclusive of everyone and looked to bring people into our group. They were so different from the people at church who built cliques and walls that kept people out.

It was a mostly stress-free time in our life. It was a time to rest and restore from all the years before. A time to thank God for all he had done and to simply be, to enjoy life and soak in the love that we were surrounded by. We had dinner with Josh and Deborah at least two or three times a week. We would drive to their house or they to us and make healthy dinners together. We would have campfires in the back yard and watch the kids as they grew up together creating a lifelong bond. Jake would build the most amazing Lego creations for my kids, and this spoke to Stephen's more technical mind. From a young age, Jake would capture Stephen's imagination through his own. Kaylee loved to dance, and she would dance all over my house showing us her new moves. Liam, my second child, was always on someone's hip handing out huge smiles to anyone who looked at him. Deborah and I would talk and laugh for hours about anything and everything much like we did those many nights ago when we shared a room together, but now we bonded even more through the journey of motherhood.

∞

I sat on the couch with Christopher, watching the kids play on the carpet. Outside, the sun was shining over a bright blue sky. The tree leaves wiggled gently with the soft wind. It was the time of day in the late afternoon when our day slowed down for an hour or so and allowed us to just enjoy our time together.

The phone rang. I picked it up to see who was calling and if I wanted to answer it. It was my sister. Whenever my sister called, no matter when it was or what was going on, I always took a few minutes for her, and those minutes often turned into an hour or more.

"Hey sis!" I answered the phone

"Hey, I have some news" she responded in a voice that was devoid of emotion. It sounded like she had been crying. My muscles tensed sensing that something was very wrong.

"What is it?" I asked her, concerned.

"I have breast cancer."

This has to be a joke. She was thirty. It's not a very funny joke. Her voice said it wasn't a joke. Oh no, this is real. This can't be real. She has two young kids, a husband, a full-time job. She is happy and vibrant. She makes everyone around her smile. Is she going to die? She can't die. What would I do if she died? What about her kids? What would they do? Could her husband raise them without her? She isn't going to die because she can't die, she just can't. The thoughts came faster than I could even recognize them.

"How serious is it?" I asked in a neutral tone. Keeping my voice neutral was critical, because otherwise the fears would overpower my words.

"Stage three" she responded, still in a flat tone.

Shit, that was serious.

I wanted to crumble, but I couldn't, I had to be strong. She needed me to be strong. She needed to have the room to crumble and that meant I needed to be strong. I can't think about her dying. She isn't meant to die. I really felt that on a cellular level. I was scared for her, for me, for everyone in our worlds, but a part of me knew, or maybe I just hoped, that she would not die. This wasn't the end, just something we had to get through, and we would get through it together. I slowed down my thoughts to get through the rest of the conversation, trying to learn as much as I could about her situation. I wanted to take away some of her fear, but I didn't know how, so I just let her talk.

Over the next few months, she was subjected to chemo and radiation. Her hair fell out, but she rocked a scarf like no one else. I thought I would have to be strong for her, but she remained a steady source of strength for everyone who was concerned for her. She eased our fears with her vibrancy even in the middle of chemo and radiation. She continued working and living her life to an unbelievable level. She had hard days for sure, there were days when she cried and days when the clutter on the counters grew a few inches higher. But she never failed in giving love to all those around her. With a scarf covering her bald head, and a smile that encompassed the room, she became an inspiration to everyone around her as she radiantly worked to overcome cancer.

Toward the end of her cancer treatment, when she was struggling to think through the fog of radiation, another turn of events would change our lives forever.

Another phone call.

I can hear the dread in my sister's voice as it cracked. She was crying. Did the cancer come back? What else would cause the agony was hearing in my sister's voice?

"I have news that is going to destroy the whole family."

Chapter Twenty-One
The Storm

My heart sank as I felt the truth of her words numb my thoughts. Was she going to die from cancer?

Her voice came across as dead, emotionless.

"Dad is up to his old tricks."

My racing thoughts didn't want to understand this truth she was trying to tell me. We had moved forward, we moved on, we overcame, we forgave and forgot, just like we had been instructed.

"What do you mean? I asked cautiously, not wanting to jump to conclusions or believe my fears as they processed through my mind in a quick succession of memories and darkness.

"Dad has been caught trying to molest another little girl here in Rockville. He followed her into the bathroom and unbuttoned her dress." My sister provided more details about the situation. We had gone to church with this family. They were friends. It has been over a decade since he had abused us. I thought he had healed or recovered, or whatever it is pedophiles do to stop being pedophiles.

An image popped into my mind of my father, like cancer, turning everyone he touches into darkness as he ruthlessly and selfishly ripped away their innocence and purity, leaving only destruction behind. A small smirk on his face exposed his sociopathic tendencies as he triumphed in a fresh round of the same old game of chess. I could see the girl, once bright and vivacious, left abandoned, broken, tears in her eyes as she tried to make sense of her world. I wasn't sure if I was looking at the newest girl or a reflection of my past. It could have reflected the girls we knew about and the ones we didn't.

In my attempt to forgive and forget, I had lost my ability to protect those who needed protection. I could feel the teardrops slide down my face as I recognized my own failures. I should have known, I should have been more vocal, and there should have been a way that we could have stopped this. How was I supposed to defeat this thing that was so much bigger than me?

I could feel my shoulders sagging with the weight of this news. It was just too much. I thought about all the people who had been in my situation. My mom, grandmother, and church leaders had felt the weight and chose to pretend it wasn't real. Was I like them? Would I crumble under this pressure? I saw the choice I needed to make: be like them and hide, or stand and fight.

Unanswerable questions rolled through my mind. Why would you do this, dad? What is your motivation? What part of molesting children brings you joy? We gave you a second chance. Do you not understand how difficult that was? I told you in the past that if I even heard a rumor of your vileness being repeated, I would be gone, and the family destroyed. You would never see your grandchildren again. This was more than a rumor.

Why were you willing to risk your family again? How could you so deeply scar another person? Do you not realize how your actions have destroyed everything? Do you even care? Without speaking a word to you, I can already hear your justifications and how you manipulate your words to downplay your actions. How can you take advantage of another little girl and look at yourself in the mirror? How does the mirror not shatter under the gaze of your soulless eyes? Are you really soulless? I don't understand how you can have a soul and do the things that you do.

We did our part, and you were supposed to hold up your part. Is it really that hard to not molest children? Can you not keep your thoughts and your hands to yourself? Do you have to create such traumatizing damage to everyone who crosses your path? Do you know how far the ripples of trauma extend? It's not just one person, but their family, their children, their community, and an entire society that is harmed by you. You have caused toxic, generational, damage.

All the things that I forgave and forgot came flooding through my mind in a barrage of memories that had been hidden in the darkness but now filled my mind until there was no more room. The intense anger seethed under my skin, just waiting for when it could erupt like a volcano to cleanse away the damage you created.

I remembered everything. I remember who you are, and how you made me feel small, fearful, insignificant, and out of control. I remembered the years and years of an agonizing journey to rid myself of all that trauma. You had a second chance; we gave you that. You didn't deserve it, but we gave it to you anyway, and this is what you did with it? It was like you had been waiting for us to let our guard down, just so you could strike again.

You took advantage of the trust and innocence of a little girl who just wanted to be a little girl. You tore that away from her, from us. You took the light out of her eyes, out of her soul, and you filled her up with that intense darkness that no one should ever have to go through. You failed as a parent, a grandparent, a person in the community, and a human.

This time, I will hold on to my anger, because hatred is the fuel that will ensure you finally face the consequences of your actions. There will be no getting out of it this time. You and the church have given me an unending source of bitterness and hatred, stored away just for this moment. All that you gave out will to come back to you.

Forgive and forget was my downfall, and I will never make the mistake of forgetting again. Those words will not save you anymore. My own regrets are adding to the foundation of my will to fight. I will be the advocate that I so desperately wanted when I was a child. It is time to fight.

The bishop in his ward called the local authorities only because the state has mandated reporting. You will not get away with it this time. We are old enough to fight for this little girl and to finally fight for ourselves in a way we could never do before.

This time, dad, your mommy can't save you as she has in the past when you were caught. No expunged records and no letting the church hide your sins away as they did in Utah and Florida. This book started with my first memories, but the abuse began long before I was even alive. For over thirty years, you have been abusing, hurting, taking, and destroying life after life after life.

This anger has created a distance between me and you, dad. It allowed me to see you from a different perspective. I have spent my life trying to view you through the light of the church. I tried to respect you, to find the good in you. Now the church lens that protected you is shattered, and I will not fix it. Now, I just see you as a lying, conniving, pedophile trying to escape your own prison. Your shadows have been exposed and I can see more clearly than ever before. Up until this point, I had always tried to allow a place for you both in my heart and in my home, despite your actions in the past. There is no more place for you. It is time for your eviction from my heart, my home, and my life.

At least, my logical side wanted to evict you. I was angry, but in my heart, there was still a part of me that wanted to hold on to the eternal family I had always pictured. I thought we had made it. I had relaxed into the idea that we had succeeded, which made the pain of these events even more poignant. I know that to fight against this battle would mean I had to choose between my family and the truth. I hated that. Why did I have to make that choice? Why can't I find a way to keep them both? Why can't mom leave dad so I could at least keep her? I still had hope that there was some way I could keep both. I wanted my father to be a good person. I wanted to have that story of an eternal family when good, conquered evil. I desperately wish you were not a pedophile.

∞

At first, my father admitted that something minor had happened, but never the full story. Then, once we talked with the local authorities, his story changed, getting smaller and smaller until all he would admit to was helping her undo a button on the back of her dress. That was all, "just a few buttons" you repeated over and over with your head hung low so that everyone would see you as a victim and feel your pain. But that was a lie, and I knew it.

I had seen a few things recently that put me on edge, stages of grooming. "Forgive and forget," I told myself as I overruled my own intuition. The signs were so subtle. Am I just being paranoid? Why were you suddenly spending money on her? Why is your hand on her leg? Are you grooming her? Are you just being nice to her? But why? Why can't you keep your distance? I noticed these things, but each incident was weeks apart and there was nothing so overt that I could call attention to it without destroying my family. I wasn't even allowed to use the word molest in front of my parents without them getting mad. There was no way to share my concerns, no one to tell. Besides, I needed to forgive and forget, right? I was frustrated with myself for not speaking up when I noticed these things. I was angry at the church for protecting him for so many years and creating a belief system that made it impossible to speak up. I was also angry at my parents because even if I had spoken up, they would have shut me down in anger.

When the girl told her parents, they listened and recorded the story. They worked with the proper authorities. In their own shock, they could still advocate for their child. I wish my mom could have been like that; I wish she would have believed me and fought for me. Maybe this time she would. I still hoped would fight with us.

As angry as I was, it was still hard to fight. My heart still wanted to keep my family together. Dad called and asked if he and mom could come over, and I agreed. I cleaned the house with furious anxiety and paced the kitchen while I cooked dinner. My emotions ranged from fear, anxiety, sadness, and calm as I vented to Christopher about each new thought that came to mind. I was preparing myself for what I would say. My thoughts just confused me more. I wanted to both punish my dad and save our family.

Dinner was awkward, just a shallow conversation about menial things. After dinner, Mom and I went into the back room to watch the kids and fold laundry while Christopher and dad talked in the living room.

"Why did you stay with him?" I asked my mom tentatively.

She let out a sigh of regret as she replied, "I didn't know how to leave. I had four small children, and I didn't have a job. Besides, the church frowns upon divorce. We are married for eternity...." Her voice drifted off at the end, lost in her own thoughts.

"What about now?" I asked, "You could stay with Deborah, or me, until you get on your feet. We would love to have you." An image flashed through my head of my mom. Her shoulders were back, her head held high, and her confidence was shining through as she had the time and space away from dad to figure out who she really was. I saw her gaining self-esteem through making a living at a job she loved, probably by helping other people. I saw a huge smile on her face. She was thriving in this image. I felt this image could be real, and I wanted that for my mother. I believed in her. We lived in a small town where the easiest place to get a job was at Wal-Mart, and I enjoyed my time as a cashier.

"You could get a job at Wal-Mart until you figure out what you want to do next." I encouraged her.

"I don't know what else I would do." the words she spoke were heavy with self-defeat.

"But you would have the time to figure it out, and it's ok if it takes a while. You could just work the Wal-Mart job until you figure out what you would like to do," I said to encourage her. I knew it would take time, but I wanted that image for her to come true. I wanted her to have time to find herself so that she could find a career and a life that she loved. I saw a spark of hope in her eyes as she allowed herself to imagine the possibilities.

"I'll think about it," she said. I could tell that she was torn about what to do. We walked into the living room to see what dad and Christopher were talking about.

Dad was sitting on the floor, his head hung low. He was portraying meekness and sadness. I could feel his deceit, it was an act. With a soft voice resembling humility he stated, "I'm planning to join the addiction and recovery program that the church offers, and I want you to attend with me," he told Christopher.

The addiction recovery program? For a pedophile? What a joke. The program is a cheap knock-off version of AA ,but by people who are following a basic church manual and with no professional training on how to deal with serious problems. Sure, it's helpful for some people, like those wanting to get off caffeine or sugar. This wasn't the type of help he needed. I felt the flare of anger, but didn't say anything. I observed his body language. My dad NEVER sat on the floor; this was a power move for him. He wanted us to see him as the victim.

"I don't think that is going to be what you need," Christopher responded.

"It was just one moment of weakness. I just need help," he said, looking at us, his face contorting as he conjured up his tears. "I was just the target of an unfortunate circumstance."

My mouth fell opened in shock as my throat locked up preventing sound. One moment of weakness? I knew he saw this as his truth. He wanted to believe his story so badly that he could no longer understand what the factual truth was. This was much bigger than one moment of weakness. It took me a moment to transform my thoughts into a coherent sentence.

"You need a lot more help than the church programs can offer you" I was careful with my tone, keeping it as neutral as possible. Even though my words were calm, I could still detect the vibrations of anger in my voice.

He looked up at me, his tears disappearing in an instant as anger flashed across his face. The change happened fast, too fast. It demonstrated again that his tears were fake. Dad started screaming, "You have no idea of the damage you are causing to your mother. Can't you see how this is breaking her? Can't you just let me be? I'm trying to heal. I am trying to get better through the church, and you're the one who is blocking me." He raged on, trying to turn the conversation in such a way that he was the victim, and I was the aggressor.

A memory floated up, one that my mind had been unwilling to accept until this moment. Mom and Dad had come over one evening for dinner. After they left, Chris was pale, like he was going to throw up. "What's wrong?" I asked with concern. In a voice filled with disgust, he responded, "I think your dad was grooming me to be like him." I heard his words, but I couldn't comprehend them.

"What do you mean?"

"Your dad told me... he said..." Chris was struggling to get the words out. I waited without interrupting his flow of thought. "Your dad said..." he started again and then paused "...It isn't as if they don't enjoy it, their bodies have the same reaction as an adult." He finished in a rush of words that were so vile that he couldn't stand to hold on to them any longer. My stomach lurched as I felt how his words crushed my entire body, the air rushing out of my lungs as I bent over, bracing myself by putting my hands on my knees, trying to keep the panic attack at bay.

The memory stayed with me as I continued to observe my dad's every move. Fight or flight was bubbling up, and my nerves were on fire, making me hyper-aware of every tiny movement or facial expression my dad made.

Dad must have realized that he had stepped out of character, he stopped screaming and let his head drop again as he spoke in a soft voice "I said I was sorry, I don't know what else I can do to prove to you how extremely sorry I am for that one moment of weakness. It will never happen again. I just need you to forgive me."

I could see right through his act, this charade he was putting on. It was a pretense of being wounded and having humility so he could weasel out of any consequences. It reminded me of when he faked his way into my wedding. I heard his words, but his body language screamed at me that this was all fake. Al manipulations. I heard words being spoken to me, maybe my own thoughts, maybe a higher power. "You have to remember this is an act."

"I understand that you are sorry, Dad." I matched his tone and demeanor at first, but then I lifted my chin up and squared my shoulders, preparing for battle. I looked him straight in the eye and said, "I have no doubts that you are very sorry that you were caught and that we plan to hold you accountable."

His face instantly turned red, his nostrils flared, and his eyes burned into me as he tried to break my composure. I could feel every ounce of his anger directed at me; I could see the different thoughts flicker across his face as he chose his response.

I spoke again, "You need to stop playing the victim and take ownership of your own actions and their consequences. You should try some honesty for a change because that is the only thing that has the power to keep this family together."

There had been a time in our life when my dad was furious with another person and for weeks, he stomped around the house, talking of all the ways he could torture or kill this person. His face reflected that kind of rage with those kinds of thoughts. I stood my ground, staring at him defiantly.

"We need to go," he said, looking at my mom.

∞

Over the next few weeks, we worked with local law enforcement. It was past the statute of limitations for my sisters and me to come forward. However, our testimony would be what the court needed to prove his history and send him to jail. The detectives had mentioned that there were probably more girls that we didn't know about. That a person like my dad, a sociopathic pedophile, doesn't just stop. They mentioned you were one of the scariest people that they had come across. They pointed out behaviors and actions that terrified them. These thoughts haunted my dreams.

Dad called to ask if he could come over and have a chat with us. Deborah and Josh were already at our house when mom and dad showed up thirty minutes later.

"Can we go for a walk?" dad asked us. We left mom and Deborah at my house while Josh, Chris, dad, and I went for a brief walk. We walked in silence for a few moments. No one wanted to start the conversation because we all knew what it would be about. Facing truth is hard, fighting the anger and rage that rioted through our minds to create a constructive conversation is harder. Josh was the first one to start the conversation.

"I want to know your 'why'? Tell me how you can justify yourself."

Dad gave a few reasons he thought would pass as acceptable. None of them were logical or acceptable. Josh pushed harder for an answer, and I watched as dad became more frustrated as each excuse was knocked down. Dad's face was turning red. He was losing his composure. After several more back-and-forth interactions between Josh and Dad, dad flippantly blurted out, "Well, my wife won't have sex with me, and I have needs!"

The world paused. Josh, Chris, and I stared at Dad in silence.

I'm amazed that you're still alive sometimes. Honestly, I think if a gun had been in range at that moment, you might not be. I'm not even sure if you know how absolutely terrifyingly wrong those words were, and they were your truth. A moment where you slipped up with your carefully placed plan and a bit of your core thoughts escaped.

"I have needs."

These words were left ringing in our heads. Memories of a broken past were now wrapped in these words. Images of my sisters and me as little girls ripped apart in the depths of your carnal world. That image ignited my courage to advocate for us, and for the unknown girls the police suspected you of abusing. The once broken girls of your past are coming together to be the army of your own destruction, and you just gave us all the ammo we would ever need in our moments of doubt.

"I have needs."

∞

We were only beginning to understand the way your brain works, catching on to how you play your games. Yet, I was always stunned when I saw other people fall for your made-up storylines. As we continued to work with law enforcement and time dragged on, I observed how you manipulated everyone around you, but specifically the people in the church. I watched as you used your words and tears to manipulate the bishop and other church leaders and how they rallied around you in support. It made me sick to my stomach.

I had heard rumors about our past from when we lived in Utah. Rumors like the church leaders allowed my dad to stay in their homes so that he could hide from authorities. I didn't want to believe those stories, but how could I not when I watched the bishop advocating for you? During this time, my sister was talking to the bishop about the legal case we were preparing, and the bishop's response was, "Our highest priority is to protect the image of the church." I guess his way of protecting the church was to believe your words and try to avoid a legal case altogether by encouraging a "higher" spiritual path. There was an undercurrent of pressure from the church to keep things quiet.

I knew the church was aware of your past. The church keeps a record of everyone who is a member filled, with important dates and notes. When a person moves, the records are transferred to the new bishop. We lived in Utah in the eighties when you were caught the first time. I was informed that during or before that legal case, the church hid my dad from authorities. When we lived in Georgia, the church was again made aware of your actions by several people. It was the reason we moved to Antelope so quickly. Again, in Camden, the church knew because you had to take part in interviews, an intervention of sorts, to regain membership in the church. More notes were taken and stored in the church vaults. Yet, I watched as the church put you in charge of teaching the youth on Sundays. Then, they placed you as the church activity coordinator, which put you in place to work with children again. The church didn't just support my father; they knowingly placed him, a pedophile, into positions of authority over children who had no way to protect themselves.

It's no wonder that the church wanted to protect themselves from both your decisions and their own reckless choices.

Chapter Twenty-Two
Threats do come true

I often thought about my mom during the months leading up to my dad's trial. At the trade shows when we were too busy to eat and when we went shopping, mom would pick up little things for us; her love language, it seemed. She drove me to church on Wednesday nights and to my college classes in the first few semesters. Even as an adult, I would snuggle up to her on the couch when we came for a visit. I never had to doubt if she loved us.

I know she did not save us when we were younger, but maybe, I could save her. I wanted to take her away from this person who had caused her so much misery. From the person who constantly held her back and took away all her dreams in favor of his own. She should have the chance to experience her best life. She could choose her own path and find her own passions. At times, she had a light that drew people in. I wanted that light to have the chance to grow. I saw this most often when she was the librarian at church helping others. I wanted to be there to support my mom through what I had hoped would be a separation from dad. It would be a silver lining as dad's crimes were brought to light.

I asked my mom to move in with us. If she wanted out, now was the time. We weren't young kids anymore, and she didn't have to worry about taking care of us. We had homes of our own and we would have loved for her to stay with us as she tried to figure out what her life looked like post-divorce.

She could find a job that she loved and then come home to her grandkids. She was so loved, and fully accepted by her children. I desperately wanted to keep her in our lives. I know there is so much blame to go around, and I'm not blind to the fact that mom could have prevented the abuse. However, she was not the threat. She genuinely loved us and her grandkids the way any mom/grandma would and should love their children.

If she moved in, I didn't think she would stay with us for more than six months or a year. She would have been too independent to stay longer. If she had wanted though, we would have kept her for as long as we could. I imagined her wanting to find herself, to make it on her own, to prove to herself that she could do this. If she moved in with us, she would be in a home that loved and supported her, and she would have thrived. I have no doubt that she would have made her own way and been stronger for it. She would have been better off unshackled by a man who mistreated everyone around him. She would have been free.

I did my best to share this dream with my mother. At first, there was this brief glimmer when she could see it, and my hope soared. Then she would go home with my dad, and it was extinguished. Her light was dim the next time we saw her. When I talked to her about getting a job, Dad took my comment about her working at Wal-Mart and twisted it in her head. He told her, "The best job Stephanie thinks you can get, is just a cashier." I loved being a cashier, and never looked down on that type of job, but he twisted it in her head so that it was an insult. I think she could be anything that she wanted to be. What I wanted for her was the time and space to find herself and her own passions.

Each time I saw my parents, I saw the effect of dad's words on my mother's grim face as she was receding into herself. It was getting harder and harder to reach her. Dad had been telling my mother how she was just going to be a burden on us if she moved in. My heart hurts just thinking that my mother believed the lies that my father spewed. They were never our words or our thoughts. They belonged solely in the mouth of my father.

Then, dad stepped up his manipulative aggression when he by calling my mom collateral damage. The first time I heard him use those words, I was so shocked that I couldn't even respond. I thought I knew what my lowest point was, but the emotional blows just kept hitting harder and harder. I felt my heart plunged to new unknown depths when I looked at my mom, and she had believed my father's words.

Collateral damage. He said it over and over, drilling the words into my mom's head, convincing her that this was how we saw her. He made her believe that she was just the trash we were willing to throw away in our attempts to seek an unrighteous justice; at least, in my dad's opinion. The closer to his trial we got, the more he pushed these words. It was my father's way of staying true to the promise he made us when we were kids. If we ever told anyone, we would lose our entire family.

Collateral damage. I hated those words. I hated that my mom believed them. Those words changed her. She chose to stay with my father, and she pushed us away. Each visit she became colder, more distant, and profoundly more despondent as she slipped into a deep depression, refusing to say much to us, look us in the eye, or hear anything we tried to say. I can't imagine the war she had going on inside her head, stuck with the words he used to drain her life force away. He said that we saw her as collateral damage, but I saw the pain he was willing to put my mother through just to escape punishment. It was clear to me that he was the one who used my mother as collateral damage. I thought I knew what hatred felt like before, I thought I knew what pain was from my own experiences, but watching my mother be systematically destroyed by my father brought an entirely new depth to these feelings.

I think Dad was terrified that my mom would leave him. I don't think he ever loved her. He loved not being alone, and he loved being able to control and manipulate my mother. But, to actually love another person, I'm not sure he has that ability. He lied to her over and over so he could keep her locked away in a prison of his words. Dad turned my mom against us.

We gave him a chance he should never have been allowed to have, and now we were paying the price.

∞

Dad called, he asked if Christopher and I would come down and talk to him and my mother alone. I knew what my parents wanted. We were set to give our testimonies to the investigators the following day. This was an intervention. But maybe, I thought to myself, we could get dad to understand that we were serious. Maybe, to save his family, dad would own the truth. If he would just stop playing the victim, if he could truly own his part and stop making his daughters the delinquents in his storyline, if he stopped turning my mother away from us with his lies, then maybe, just maybe there would be a space to heal. I desperately wanted him to own the truth. I should have said no. I wish I had.

You know those moments in life that as they are happening, you can feel your universe changing, your view shifting, and your world crumbling away into a thousand pieces? This was the day my family truly shattered, the day I knew we could no longer be a family. It was the day I broke. It was the day I had to become stronger than ever.

Chris and I walked into my parents' house, hand in hand. It would be the last time we ever walked into their house. The furniture had been arranged so that we would sit in a circle. Grandmother and Granddaddy Roy were seated on the couch by the front window. The same window where they used to watch us catch fireflies when we were children. To the left of my grandparents, dad sat in an overstuffed chair with mom in a separate chair next to him. Two kitchen chairs had been placed for us that completed the circle.

Dad, mom, grandmother, and granddaddy Roy; my lineage. My roots. They had all been participants in the perpetuation of sexual abuse. My grandparents had assisted in continuing the cycle of abuse by continually protecting my father with their wealth of money spent on ensuring Dad's freedom. Grandmother was the reason that he could continue abusing us, acting as if she was just a victim to his needs. My mother by her neglect and refusal to face the truth.

I had a discussion with grandmother in the weeks before the trial in which I called dad out for being a pedophile. I was looking for an advocate. She responded, "Can you imagine being his mother?." It took me off guard; I had never considered her perspective before. I imagine myself in her place. What would I have done? She continued to talk; her words faded out while I imagined all the ways I would have protected the children. Only on reflection did I realize that she had effectively silenced me by claiming the victim's status for herself. She was not a victim in my eyes, she was the perpetrator for always telling him he was right, always there to clean up his messes, always there so he never had to face his own consequences. Here she was again, cleaning up his mess. An advocate for the pedophile.

I realized dad had learned to be a victim as his get-out-of-jail-free card from his mother. I decided to go all in on Dad's game of chess as I took the chair placed out for me on his board game. Mom had always been a pawn for my dad, but Grandmother had been his true love, his queen. She had always been there to keep him safe as he sat on his imaginary throne as the protected king. The game ends when the king falls.

The air was extremely tense with the stress of the situation, like right before a war begins. There was no room for pleasantries, as nothing that was about to happen was pleasant.

The discussion started with grandmother talking about why Dad is the way he is. Grandmother told a few of her memories that offered the idea that Dad was abused as a child. I had heard these stories before, but only when strategically needed to invoke sympathy or when dad was trying to get out of trouble. I had been abused; I knew that pain. I would never allow that abuse to reach further generations. It is invalid, as there is never an excuse that could justify sexual abuse.

Dad spoke again. "I'm so sorry for my actions. I wished I had never followed her into the bathroom. It was just a few buttons. I promise nothing else happened. What will it take for you to forgive me?" he pleaded with us.

Chris and I looked at each other with an understanding. We knew he was only sorry that he had been caught. We already had this conversation with my father. His words were meaningless because he was still denying pieces of our history. He was endlessly trying to minimize his actions.

"You are only sorry you were caught," I said again. It invoked the same type of rage from my father as last time. His face flipped from being remorseful to one of controlled rage.

My grandfather spoke in a cool tone. "You're being rude Stephanie; you need to treat your father with more respect."

Christopher spoke firmly in my defense, "I think she is being extremely respectful considering this," he waved his hands in the air for emphasis, "intervention you guys have set up."

When dad and grandmother didn't get the reaction out of us they wanted, they changed tactics.

Grandmother spoke again, "Do you know what they do to a pedophile in jail? They will rape him, beat him to death, or both. Your dad is not a spring chicken anymore."

Dad chimed in, "With my health, I could die before they ever let me out of prison. There would never be a chance for me to truly repent and heal my soul. Is that what you want? Do you want me to die?"

I looked over at Christopher, looking for support. Were they really trying to make me believe that testifying against my dad would be the same as killing him? What if he died in there? How would I feel about that? Would it be my fault? I don't have to testify against him. Christopher squeezed my hand, communicating that we had already decided to stand firm. We had talked about this scenario on the way over. It was my job to share my truth, and I was ready to accept the consequences of my own actions. We turned back to dad who was still talking.

"If I go to prison, I won't be able to get the therapy I need to overcome this sickness. I want to go through the church's twelve-step program. I want to be a better person. Are you willing to stop my eternal progression based on one small act that I am so ashamed and remorseful for?" he pleaded with us.

Grandmother added to the conversation. "You have an opportunity to help your father out. You can save his life. Your family needs your support right now."

I took a breath to steady myself. I was trying to be strong. I wanted to keep my family together. Isn't that what I had fought for my entire life?

Grandmother continues, "You have the opportunity right now to save your family by not testifying."

I felt like I had just been sucked into a vortex that ripped the air from my lungs. I felt shocked and disgusted at how everyone was blatantly trying to push everything under the carpet, to pretend nothing happened. I stared at my grandmother as her role from the past was repeating itself at this moment. She was the same as my father.

I was getting lightheaded, it felt like my blood was being drained as my pulse picked up, the rage made me feel out of control, but I had to keep it in check. I didn't want to say or do anything that would permanently separate our family. I did not want to be responsible for our family falling apart. I didn't have enough control to let any words out, so I sat there in silence. How could I save my family when it had been shattered before I was even born?

Dad's mood shifted when I tried to stand up to him. If things were going his way, if he was the victim, he looked remorseful. But, if the conversation shifted toward him being wrong, his anger would flare. I wanted to keep the peace. There was enough pain, and I didn't want to add to it. Grandmother was there to give me a disappointed look whenever I said anything about dad that was not positive. Mom stared at me with an angry glare, letting me know how wrong I was to testify against my father. There was too much

223

emotion all at once, and so I felt nothing. The words came and went but held no meaning.

I wanted to keep the peace, but that was when I had hope that dad had called me and Chris over so that he could truly acknowledge and take ownership of his role in this. To really say he was sorry in such a genuine way that my soul could feel the truth of his words. That didn't happen though. He had asked us here to stop us from testifying. He wanted nothing but to protect himself and he would say anything to get what he wanted.

The conversation switched to the upcoming trial. We sat there, three generations of a family together. When Grandmother spoke next, there were four sets of eyes pleading with me, from the people I loved most. "Please tell the investigators that nothing happened. We will handle this as a family matter."

Could I lie for them? Would I lie to save my dad's life? Would I protect the pedophile? I sat there silently processing what they were asking me to do. My mind was screaming, all the words I wanted to say. I could feel the frustration and anger rolling through me. With a forced calm I stated, "No, I don't feel good about lying."

Grandmother's tone was casual, like she was asking what I wanted for dinner. "Then say you forgot."

"That would still be lying." My voice held an icy edge to it this time as it was harder to control the rage.

Grandmother's eyes narrowed, but her words came out casually. "It doesn't matter; they can't prove your memories." Her voice picked up an edge to it, and I felt the effects of them slicing through my conscience. "It's only a moment of your time, but it could save your dad's life."

I felt like I had been left abandoned in a fallen mine shaft as I felt the pressure crush me. Christopher squeezed my hand once again, reminding me that I was not alone.

These people, my family, were asking me to put aside all the years of abuse because they didn't want to deal with the consequences. The years of abuse that my siblings and I endured could have been avoided if they had just been proactive the first time they found out about his abuse. But they hid everything so that my dad could live a corrupt life while we were left to deal with the consequences. We were so little that my earliest memories are infused with images and emotions of incestual abuse.

These are the people that let it happen again and again and again. What were they so afraid of? Were they afraid the neighbors might find out we weren't a perfect family? Were they more afraid of the judgments of other people than the five little kids who were depending on you guys to save us? Now they were doing it AGAIN. They were trying to cover his horrendous actions up so they wouldn't have to face them.

Why can't they stand up to him? Why can't they acknowledge his actions? Why can't they see him for who he is? My father abuses and manipulates everyone around him for his own personal gain. Can't they see that? Can't they see how he is using his words and his fake tears and his woe-as-me attitude to get them to do what he wants?

He doesn't really care about you, mom, or he would never have called you collateral damage. Grandmother, he is just using you for protection. Then again, I don't think grandmother cares. Her manipulative actions tonight show me that she is just another puppeteer, and Dad is the star of her show.

Do they even know what they were asking me to forgive and forget? We never talked about any of the abuse. The conversations were forbidden. Maybe they don't understand, maybe they need to have the pictures in their head so they can comprehend their request.

I wanted them to see the confusion on my six-year-old face when I walk in on my sister and dad lying in bed together, naked. I wanted them to see me as the little girl who is being made to play strip poker when she was eight. I want you to see me as the little girl that is terrified as her daddy puts his mouth on her private parts. I wanted them to know the powerlessness of the ten-year-old little girl who had to endure long car rides with my dad's hand down my pants. I wanted them to know the fear and desperation of the twelve-year-old who had to sit in the car, trapped, while her dad groped her. I want them to know that my experiences were benign compared with what my sisters went through. I wanted them to feel the hopelessness that comes from trying to stand up for yourself against a 6'2" 400-pound father who knows he can get away with whatever he wants. A man that knows no one will stand against him. A man who is protected. I wish they understood what it felt like to look into the faces of my elders and be told to keep silent to protect my abuser.

Maybe they were right, maybe I should forget all that. I wish I could.

This is not a man who needs protecting. This is a man who needs to experience the consequences of his actions. He needs to look into the faces of each person he has hurt and feel their pain. He needs to understand how his selfish actions reach from person to person. His abuse has resulted in the type of generational trauma that destroys everything. This man needs to know that my sisters and I will not allow him to hide from the consequences any longer. We absolutely have not and will not forget his actions so that the elders in my family tree can continue on with their lives as if what happened to us does not matter.

Now it was my choice. Was I able to stand up for that little girl hidden deep in my heart, the one who held my pain so I could survive? So, I could live? Was I brave enough to stand up for my sisters who needed me, for that little girl in the community, for my own children, for the other young girls that the police suspected may be out there? Was I prepared to fight? Was I strong enough? Could I make it through even if it meant breaking the bonds of the eternal family I desperately fought for? Dad always told me that if I said anything, I would lose my family. Was I prepared for that ending? Would his threat come true?

I looked at each of their faces, trying to find a single person who would be brave enough to stand up for what is right. I looked at my mom with the sliver of hope I had, thinking that at least she could understand. I hoped she could look at Dad with the same knowledge I had. Hoped that she understood that this was the moment that she could make a change. I wanted with all my heart to look at her face and be reassured that everything would be all right. I had always had faith in my mom. I always believed that if she really knew what was going on, she would have saved me. I knew she loved me. I knew she tried to make up for things in her own way. I needed her to be my mom.

I was determined to know that I had done my best. That I stayed true to the facts, that I didn't yell, cuss, or name-call. I refused to lose control of my emotions. My entire body was shaking uncontrollably as I looked at dad. With the internal turmoil that raged, I was a mess on the inside, but my voice came out calm, controlled, and firm.

"Dad, it's time that you face the consequences of your actions. I am testifying, and I am telling them everything."

I looked at my mom again for any show of the support that I desperately wanted. She glared at me with such fierce anger that it felt like pure hate. It seemed that in her eyes, in her truth, I was the one who was destroying their lives. The look that she gave me broke my entire being, my heart, soul, and mind into a million pieces. I wanted to fall apart, I wanted to fall on the floor and sob until she came to tell me everything would be ok. Instead, I held my head high as I searched my mom's eyes for help, for love.

I felt her abandonment.

The silent screams of my seven-year-old self haunted this moment.

Mom, save me.

Mom…

The tears formed in my eyes and my chest was so tight that I saw black dots appearing in my vision and felt the chair wobble underneath me. I could feel a different sort of blackness trying to creep in. For just a second I felt my mind shatter as I struggled to remember why I was here and who I was. My world was shifting too fast, and I just couldn't keep up. I was losing my grip on reality as I just stared at my mom. Waiting…

She had made a comment leading up to the trial, referring to the abuse that "If you didn't like it, you would have tried to run away." She had reduced us to nothing more than the other woman in a grown-up affair. It felt to me, that in her truth, we were her enemy.

There was no time to fall apart. I had to make it through this moment. I knew my world was shattering around me, but I also knew that I had to be the change. I forced in a large breath and squared my shoulders.

Collateral damage. I never believed those words. There was a part of me that understood that mom knew about the abuse. However, that confrontation had never played out in my awareness and so my imagination was free to dream and to believe that she would choose us. Now she knows. I never imagined that my mom would choose a child molester over her children.

For the rest of the conversation, I heard nothing. My attention was only on my mother. She was either staring at the floor or glaring at me. She never stood up for me. She never once told my dad he was wrong. She never once tried to protect her children. My years of belief that she would protect me if she knew were shattered. All the moments when she left me behind with my dad, she knew. The endless nights, she knew. The car rides where he wanted just one of us in the car, she knew. She knew and she did nothing.

I couldn't process that I had lost my mom. I couldn't process anything. So, after the conversation, I tried to give my mom a hug, just one moment to say we could still be a family. I wanted to say, I love you mom, I want you in my life. But Her arms stayed stiff at her sides. She refused to hug me back.

I felt her blaming me. I know that her world was falling apart too, and I wanted to be there for my mom. I wanted her to know that I saw her strength and her courage. I know it was inside her, at least, I thought they were. I wanted to bring those elements out and show her she was strong enough to overcome her own fears. But it is impossible to see the truth when my father is in your head distorting it. It is impossible to see the truth when you are hiding from your own accountability in the story.

I never thought I would lose my mother. I didn't think it was even a possibility. I didn't believe that she could let that happen. I watched her change from my mom to this person who… hated me.

That look, the refusal to hug me, that was the moment that I knew my world was forever changed.

This was the moment that I lost all respect for the adults in my family. I knew that none of these people would ever protect us, protect me, protect the lives of the children around them. I knew that if I let fate play its hand around these people, my own children would be in danger. They would rather look away while a child was being molested in their home than take action. I know because I lived it.

I can't handle that. I can't be that person. This would not be the fate of my children. They might not be strong enough to stand up to this horrible evil man, but I was going to be strong enough to stand up to my father, and all of them.

From the start, I was threatened with losing my family if I ever spoke the truth. The threat kept me silent, but I had always hoped that if mom, grandmother, or grandad knew the truth, that they would have stood up for what was right. My youthful optimism and survival instinct permitted me to see my family in the best light. This allowed me to hide from the truth despite the quiet whispers that reminded me of our dark past.

I wanted to have faith in my elders. But how could I when I was staring at the truth reflected in the cold steely eyes of those around me, asking me to lie to the courts, cover up the abuse, and allow the pedophile to get away with it, again? They wanted me to follow in their footsteps, to act in the same manner they have for generations.

They were still giving him the message that it was all going to be ok, they would save him, that what he did was allowable.

I stood up for myself that night. I guess that was the greatest sin I could have committed, much worse than anything my dad has ever done. At least that is the story their eyes and their body language told me. That's ok, I was changing, I was realizing my own boundaries. I was finding out how strong I could be for myself, and my children. I was learning just how important that inner voice is that guided me through my life, through this moment, and I knew I could rely on it in the future. It was time to relearn who I was and who I was choosing to be.

I wish that this was the end of the night, but it continued in a mockery of what our family could have been.

I jumped in surprise when I heard a knock on the door. Unknown to Chris and me, the bishop and been asked to come over and give each of us a blessing using the sacred priesthood power of our church and to give us spiritual guidance on how to best handle this situation.

My body tensed up as the bishop walked through the door. This was wrong, a warning bell was going off in my head. Does he know they had been trying to get me to lie to the investigators for the past few hours?

Looking back and forth between Christopher and me, the bishop asked us, "Do you know your dad wants to go through the church's addiction and recovery program, and that the church will sponsor a church-approved therapist?"

This, again. I let out an exaggerated sigh of frustration. He wasn't here to save an abused child, he wasn't here to further the agenda of God, he wasn't here to mourn with those that mourn, he was here to protect the pedophile.

The bishop continued. "You know that if your dad gets sent to jail, his eternal progress will be halted, right?"

My emotions were already in such a heightened state that there was no more room for additional anger. The thought crossed my mind that this person had no right to use his church-given authority to ask us not to testify. The implications of his statements were clear. We would be responsible for halting his eternal progression and we would hold the bigger sin.

The church has a hotline that is a bishop's first resource when they suspect legal trouble. That information was consistent with a comment this bishop made in the last few weeks. His first priority was to make sure that the image of the church was protected. He wasn't here to protect the children; he wasn't here to understand the truth. He was only here to make sure that the church wasn't held responsible. He was a puppet for my father and for the church. The church knew about the abuse in each new state and church that we attended. They knew he was a pedophile when they placed him in authority over the Sunday School class of youth, mostly young girls.

The church teaches that girls are supposed to be submissive to their husbands and fathers and not to question the patriarchs of the community. One of the temple questions is, "do we support and sustain our local leadership and our prophet?" You cannot be supportive if you are questioning their decisions. You can't be a worthy temple attending Mormon if you question too much or question the wrong thing. I recalled the many times I had tried to push back over a variety of subjects in our church's history, like why did the founder Joseph Smith marry a fourteen-year-old girl. I was told I was looking for trouble. I was told to stay away from anti-Mormon material. I was told not to question the prophet's words. I was to listen and obey. If you are not obedient, you do not get to live with God, and your family in the eternities. The understanding that I construed was that God only loves obedience.

I numbly listened to the bishop as he pleaded with us to save my father's soul, never once asking what the truth was. I could see how impossible my situation was as a child of a pedophile in the Mormon church that through its theology, patriarchy, and culture, protected him. It was wrong for this man to be here as a representative of the church.

He asked if he could give us each a blessing. To say no would cause questions I was too exhausted to answer. I sat there emotionless, as he put his hands on my head and made promises that my family would be together in the eternities. He blessed my father, saying that our family will be reunited if dad speaks the truth. He then blessed Christopher by putting the burden on him that he would be the person to speak reason to my family and have the power to heal us all. A cynical thought flickered through the numbness; they just wanted him to control his wayward wife.

As he passed out his blessings, I felt the shreds of my belief in the church tear apart. I lost my family, and I knew my faith was next.

∞

We spoke to the investigators the next day and gave them our testimony. I listened to Deborah as she shared her truth, and she listened to mine. Although we shared the bond of this experience, we had never talked about what had happened. The power of my father and the church to keep us silent lasted over thirty years before we were finally old enough and mature enough to process and then stand against the abuse that started before we were even old enough to talk.

My chest was tight, and a tear slipped down my face as I listened to her words. There was strength and solidarity. My heart filled with love, as I knew I was not alone in this fight. My oldest sister, Rachael, who had fallen out of our lives so long ago, reconnected with us to share her story as well. The investigators believed our story and, as the truth came out, we found advocates in them. My dad was given a prison sentence. I could finally take a breath that wasn't based on the need to survive.

We shared our stories with advocates who believed us.

My sisters and I were united in our determination to set the truth free.

My father was forced to face the consequences.

Checkmate.

Epilogue

The problem is that life isn't a simple game with clear winners and losers. My sisters and I came together, and we shared our stories. We were able to withstand the intense pressure from church and family. We stood for what was right and held our father accountable.

We had lost our family.

Just like my father promised.

The outcome left several gaps in my heart that would never be filled, Dreams that would never come true. We were broken despite the win.

My father was sentenced to eighteen months of jail time under the verdict of indecent liberties with a minor.

18 months.

He abused children for over thirty years. His sentence was not even one month for each year. We could only convict him of the most recent event because of the statutes of limitations. "Indecent liberties with a minor," the courts said. That's like calling a gaping wound a mere paper cut. Like looking at the Grand Canyon and calling it a ditch. It was a mockery to the lives of each person he hurt. Dad should have been in jail for the rest of his life. At least for the first time in his life, he was being held accountable by the court system, even if it was only eighteen months. Dad should have been in jail the rest of his life. In some ways he will. A prison made from the memories of the destruction he caused, the family he lost, and the grandchildren he will never know again.

The following months were spent mulling over what had just happened. I still can't understand why mom chose misery over the chance of happiness. Why did she choose the pedophile over her children? I'll never understand why she couldn't stand up for us. She acts from a place of hurt, fear, depression, and anxiety. I want to give her grace, but in writing this book, I realized just how many times she refused the truth, how many times she knowingly left us with him, how many times she had failed to save us.

We took the time to talk with Grandmother and mom to smooth out what family matters we could. But it was too much for them; they were too angry. When you can't blame the perpetrator, when you can't see your own role in a situation, you lash out and place blame on everyone else. We were the target of their anger and hatred. They treated us like we were the source of all their problems. We had blown up what they had tried to keep hidden.

One day, mom stopped by my house to drop off an enormous stack of church talks from the prophets and other church leaders high in the organization and the book "Miracle of Forgiveness." The talks were about how we should not talk about the sins of the past. That if a person is forgiven, then we are to forgive and forget. To bring up the past stops the person from healing.

My teardrops fell, a trickle at first, turning into a waterfall that seemed to drain my body of every ounce of water. I realized again, or maybe for the first time, that it was my mother who wanted to silence us. It was my mother who had knowingly allowed us to be abused; then blamed us. The miracle of forgiveness is full of the theories of out-of-touch old men who collectively want us to forgive and forget.

I tried to call mom a few times, I sent e-mails to her, but she had frozen me out. She had all this anger built up, and she chose to aim it at me. I was an outsider now.

We were never your enemy mom, we were your children, and we loved you.

∞

We moved away from North Carolina to Boise, Idaho, a few months after dad was sent to jail. A few weeks before we moved, my sister planned a surprise going away party for us. My house was full of all the people I had loved over the past few years. Many of us had a baby on the hip while the older kids ran around in my backyard, blowing bubbles and splashing in and out of the baby pool. There were two tables overflowing with the food each family brought to share. We sat around in a circle laughing and sharing stories of

233

bounce houses, backyard cookouts, and parents' nights out. We relished the community we had created and the love that we shared.

I sifted through the streams of my memories that led to this moment, to these people that I loved, and that loved me. Captured moments of joy and sadness, excitement and fear, satisfaction, and pain. A pattern emerged, highlighting specific events that created who I was. The memories that stood out, that molded me, challenged me, and enlightened me, didn't come from events, places, or things; they came from the individual people who had shown up in my life. Each person brought me new life experiences, various ways of thinking, and excitement. They showed me acceptance, joy, compassion, laughter, and love.

My parents were each abusive in their own way, one purposeful in his actions and the other neglectful in hers. They created the foundation of who I am. It was from them that I learned resilience, hard work, and the ability to thrive in the harshest conditions. Dad's words about how I would never make it became the source of my determination. These words fueled my journey out of the house, through school, and eventually across the country. I had to lean on my own intuition and that gave me the strength to withstand the end of our relationship.

Then came friends who gave me support and showed that I was lovable, just as I was. They walked into the basement of the store in Sylva and saw the deplorable conditions of where we lived. They could feel the negative energy vibrating off my father and they looked past that just to love me. These people are invaluable in my life journey. There have been so many good people in my life that they do not all fit in one book.

Even the mean girls or groups at church who tear at insecurities and create depression, doubt, and anxiety have given me the chance to overcome obstacles. They taught me that I had the ability to choose whose words I let define me. Where their words once stung, there is now confidence that evolved through healing. The professor who used his narrow views to tear me and others down was an example of what I didn't want to be. There is value in that type of lesson as well.

The lady in our store who made an offhand comment about my lack of education shifted my world. This created an unbreakable will to get an education that carried me through the next several years. The random people at the flea markets who took the time to chat with me, so many of them brightened my bad day. They took me out of my thoughts of despair with their idle chit-chat and their random jokes. They saw me as worthy, and worth talking to. Because of them, I felt a bit more worthy of being considered a whole person

The Young Single Adults from church and the Student Government from SCC replaced my terrible memories with memories infused with joy and acceptance. Miwa brought a ferocity to life I had never experienced. She burned bright in my eyes as she lived free of the rules the world wanted to put on her. She taught me to live a little more boldly.

My sister, who was always by my side from the very beginning provided me with stability, safety, friendship, and love. She was there with me through everything, creating a bond that surpasses words. Our shared experiences will be something that few people will understand. I'm not even sure that I do. She was there in every moment to process my life with me, even when the conversation lasted hours. Then, once we had gotten through the hard part, she was there to laugh with me, to make light of things, and with that came healing. She has always been, and will always be, my best friend.

I miss each person. They are all a part of who I am now. I can only hope that I have left a part of me with them as well. I will always be grateful for their influence on my life. I will always love them.

The kindness of the other people helped me survive over a decade of abuse. I want to remember that. That each brief comment I make could potentially change their whole life. I want to honor it. I want to make sure that the words I give are carefully chosen words that uplift each person. That shows them they are worthy, just as they are. I want them to know that they matter in this world. The things we do and say, our own everyday moments of words and actions, are speaking volumes to those around us.

∞

When I moved to Boise, I had just lost my family and left behind my friends. I was excited to move, and it was the right thing for my family to do, but I did not like leaving my community. I was in a vulnerable place in my life, terrified my father would show up unannounced on my doorstep. I hid my physical address and locked down my social media. I would go to sleep at night and dream about what I would do if he showed up. There were so many things that I was still processing. My dreams were filled with racing thoughts, reliving each moment of the past few months and years.

I started to tell my story, just small parts at first. Someone would ask about my parents in casual conversation, and I had to say that we don't talk anymore. The conversation would get awkward as they contemplated changing the topic or asking more questions. The silence was deafening to me, and the words would slip out "My dad is a pedophile." My body would shake as I looked at their face for a reaction. Most of the time it was shock, and some of it was understanding. The worst reaction was pity. I didn't need or want their pity or sorrow. I just wanted acceptance. I wanted to normalize the words "my dad is a pedophile" so I could talk about it without my entire body visibly shaking. Sharing my story was the release that I needed. I was working on building up my courage.

What I didn't expect was the reactions to things in my life that had just been normal. When I talked about the places I used to live, I knew it was bad, but I had never viewed them through the eyes of someone else. I joked about the food we ate growing up, but the reaction wasn't laughter, it was shock. I mentioned I didn't go to school, and again, the same shocked look. I realized how different my life was from the mainstream when I saw it through the mirror of other people.

Each time I told my story, a little more detail came out. It took me years to talk without shaking, and sometimes I still do, I guess. It was like the story had to be told and the words kept spilling out in awkward moments of over-sharing. I knew I had been silenced by the church and my family, but as I watched the reactions of general society, I realized that they too, through their discomfort, silenced my words. Words that needed to be spoken.

The idea that it was taboo to talk about sexual abuse, incest abuse, and other uncomfortable topics wore away at me. How are we supposed to make societal changes when it is society itself that shuts down the conversation? Things needed to change, and so I shared my story anyway, pushing the boundaries of what was acceptable. I'm sure I made several people uncomfortable, but as my confidence grew, a shift happened, my words were less shaky and the awkwardness I felt went away. A few people listened, and then a few more confided in me. I was making a change for the people who were in my world. I saw how I could make a difference, simply by continuing to tell my truth and allowing space for others to share theirs.

∞

Over time, I lost myself. Before we moved, I always had to be strong, focused on the future, and how I was going to survive. I was forced to think three steps ahead so that I could find relief in the exit plan. Once I achieved that goal, I didn't know how to relax. I needed that escape plan, but there was nothing to escape from anymore. My life was going great and yet the unescapable feeling of flight or flight was still there, causing there to be a chasm in my soul that grew, filling up with anxiety, doubt, and diminishing self-esteem. It took me years to even understand why I had these feelings. I had no words to explain the loss that I felt. The loss of who I was, the loss of my family, and the loss of my religion. How can you fix something when you've done everything that you know how to do, and somehow you are still left a little broken?

I think about my dad sometimes. I'm sure he is still playing his game, manipulating people around him. He has been doing it so long that I'm not sure he even knows how to be different. We haven't talked in ten years. I imagine him on Christmas morning, an intense sadness as he looks around the tree, his children and grandchildren absent. He looks at my mom, who glares at him, her anger still unprocessed. He reaches out for comfort, but there is no comfort to be found. He is left to commiserate in the ashes of his decisions.

I don't know if my image is true or not. It makes me sad for them and I consider the idea of reuniting with them, but there is no trust there. My father is a toxic person. To be around him is to question everything he says and does. It is exhausting. I am angry with my mother. I did not figure that out until just a few months ago and I am still processing this. An encounter with her would put me right back into the night of the intervention when she refused to hug me. I do not think it would be different. It is not a relationship that I know how to salvage.

My Dad once called my mom collateral damage. It took me years to figure out that it was us, the children, who had been allowed to become collateral damage by both my parents because they were too scared to face their own inner demons.

There will always be a part of me that sees them as the parents I love, or at least loved. I have found peace in the idea that our time together wasn't meant to last a lifetime. They played their part in my life and mine in theirs. I hope this book reaches them. I want them to see the pain that they caused, the ripples of abuse that spanned generations. I want them to see this, not because I am angry, but because I think it is healthy to face the demons in your head with the true intent of healing. I hope my parents are willing to look inside themselves, to do the grueling work of healing and processing their own traumas. I recognize that it is not my job to heal them or a family that was shattered from the start.

I have been asked if I hate my dad. The truth is, I don't; not anymore. There was a time when I was filled with hate and rage for him, and it was the fuel that propelled me out of that critical situation. It had a purpose in my life. I am always working to let those emotions go; they no longer serve me.

The idea of forgiveness is still something I struggle with. I think it's because I was forced into forgiveness. Since that moment when I was fourteen, I have been told that I HAVE to forgive him over and over. But do I really? I do not hold on to the anger, hate, or negativity; those things that tear people down after a while. To me, saying I forgive you means, "it's ok, I have trust that you have learned your lesson and we can both move on." I don't feel that way. He was forced into accountability, fighting us the entire way, but he never accepted accountability in a way that felt genuine. So, do I forgive him? Not really, and I probably won't. I don't agree with many of the principles that go along with the idea of forgiveness.

I wrote letters to my dad, the rage filling up the pages as it released my heart from the pain. I wrote letters to my mom and grandmother too. For a long time, I was still trying to save my mom through letters I never sent. I had to let her go as she had already let me go. The pile of letters grew until they turned into this book.

I had lost myself, but I was determined to find myself again. I needed to work on my own inner demons. I needed to unpack all unprocessed emotions from my past. I learned and grew in any direction I could. I read a variety of books on self-help, memoirs mostly focused on leaving high demand religions, and biographies of others who had alternative childhoods. I felt connected with the book Educated by Tara Westover. I listened to podcasts including my favorite for a time, Mormon Stories Podcast which showed me I wasn't alone in my experiences. That podcast gave me permission to accept that the church was no longer a good fit for me.

∞

I am no longer a Mormon. I left the church on June 10th, 2018. It was the day that my youngest turned eight, and I knew he would feel the pressure of church leaders to be baptized into an organization I could no longer support. He did show a little remorse at missing out on the birthday candy they would have given him. I talk with my children often about the belief system I came from, and then I offer other ideas as well and let them choose what feels right for them. They are free from the confines of a predetermined belief system.

While the Mormon church may not fit me now, I cannot understate the good things that the church did for me. The church provided me with a path, guidance, community, and hope. It gave me a relationship with the divine that is the backbone of who I am. I am still friends with many of the people from my youth and college days. It gave me a place to feel comfortable in uncomfortable times. The church is filled with some amazing human beings.

The hope that the church gave pulled me through every hard day. Hope in leaving home, hope in a better family, hope in a better life. It gave me hope that all the bad in the world would eventually go away and everyone would be happy, and I needed that. I needed something to hold on to.

This is why I can never judge an individual who is of any type of religion. I don't know where they are in their life's journey. I don't know their struggles, the support they need, or what they are gaining from being in their religion. Maybe their church is sustaining them. Maybe they have a mission to fulfill inside the church that will not be discovered for years. Maybe the church is giving them support, or they are supporting the church; either way, I don't get to judge their situation. It is my opinion that the Mormon church has made a lot of surface changes, changes created to make the members feel comfortable, but not changes that make a solid difference in how they act. Their priority is to present a perfect image, their view of a godly image, I suppose. So long as they are caught up in hiding away things like sexual abuse and supporting bullying behaviors by "turning the other cheek" instead of confronting the problem. I still see the exclusion of anyone not in the clique and the harm that does to the excluded person. The church is still dividing people and families with their ideas of rules and obedience that create so much judgment and criticism. Just as my parents need to look inside to their very cores and face the demons that hide there, the church needs to do the same thing.

The Mormon church first teaches that we can have families forever, and then they use those teachings to control every aspect of our lives. From the things that we eat and drink to the clothes we wear, the friends we choose, and how we spend our money and time. They choose what is acceptable to read in their history, and what is considered anti-Mormon and therefore untouchable. I was taught that the prophets are infallible, even when their teachings hurt societies, and we cannot question them. It gives these men too much power over the lives of individuals. Choices are influenced by the need to have a temple recommend.

I used to believe in the Mormon idea of an eternal family until I realized they were holding my eternal family hostage to their demands. It is a church of control, manipulation, and division living under a façade of love and righteousness. Their God is power and greed, and he wants obedience. If you don't live by their man-made rules, they threaten you with the loss of your eternal family and salvation. I also can't believe in a church that uses God to demands literal cash payments to get into heaven, or to go to your son's wedding.

∞

"You've changed" is a statement I have heard throughout my life. You know what? I hope I have. I hope I am still changing. I hope that who I am next year is better than the person I am today. Or maybe I'm a worse person in the view of some people because there was an experience I needed to grow. Either way, I am a better person because my experience has expanded the way I think. It's ok if today I am a Mormon and tomorrow, I am an atheist, and the next day I just believe in a ubiquitous higher power. I may want to live at the beach one day, and then realize I prefer the solitude of the mountains. I can only understand what I want when I have experienced both. The danger lies in complacency, in the avoidance of change. It is the ability to transform that empowers us to be the best version of ourselves.

We were never meant to be the same person, to be stagnant our entire lives. We are each like our own version of a butterfly except that we are lucky in that we can undergo as many chrysalises as we want. We get to decide every day who we are and whom we want to be in the future. It is in the journey that we discover who we are and who we are meant to be. We must allow ourselves the freedom to explore different paths, to explore ourselves in different situations. I hope while reading this book, that it has left you changed in a positive way. Thank you for coming on this journey with me.

A request from the Author

Thank you for reading my book. I hope it has helped you know you are not alone in the struggles we all face.

Would you like to help me spread this message to more people?

By leaving a me a five-star review on amazon, you can help me reach more people, and together we can spread the message that we are not alone.

Together, we are stronger.

Thank you
Stephanie Taylor

Made in the USA
Coppell, TX
20 November 2022